michael f. jimenez

The *Crossroads* of
Class *&* Gender

Women in Culture and Society
A Series Edited by Catharine R. Stimpson

The *Crossroads* of Class *&* Gender

*Industrial Homework,
Subcontracting, and Household Dynamics
in Mexico City*

Lourdes Benería
Martha Roldán

*The University of Chicago Press
Chicago and London*

Lourdes Benería is professor of city and regional planning and women's studies at Cornell University.

Martha Roldán is professor in the department of sociology at the University of Buenos Aires and associate researcher at Facultad Latinoamericana de Ciencias Sociales, Programa Buenos Aires.

The University of Chicago Press, Chicago 60637
The University of Chicago Press, Ltd., London
© 1987 by The University of Chicago
All rights reserved. Published 1987
Printed in the United States of America
96 95 94 93 92 91 90 89 88 87   54321

Library of Congress Cataloging-in-Publication Data

Benería, Lourdes.
   The crossroads of class and gender.

   Bibliography: p.
   Includes index.
   1. Women—Mexico City (Mexico)—Economic conditions.
2. Home labor—Mexico—Mexico City.   3. Piece-work—
Mexico—Mexico City.   4. Households—Mexico—Mexico City.
I. Roldán, Martha.   II. Title.   III. Title: Crossroads
of class and gender.
HQ1465.M6B46   1987   305.4'2'097253   86-24901
ISBN 0-226-04231-6
      0-226-04232-4 (pbk.)

Contents

Foreword

Some intellectual mutations, crucial to any fresh apprehension of the world, first articulate themselves in muted ways. The changes in our thinking about the subject of women and development certainly did. In 1970, Ester Boserup, a Danish economist, began a new book with this sober paragraph:

"In the vast and ever-growing literature on economic development, reflections on the particular problems of women are few and far between. This book will show, I hope, that this is a serious omission."[1]

Nearly two decades later, our reflections on these particular problems are extensive. They are also serious and sobering.

The most significant ideas include those of a special generation of international scholars that followed Boserup. Fortunately, Lourdes Benería and Martha Roldán are a part of that generation. Like Boserup, that generation wants to show what happens to women during the processes of development. Like Boserup, it believes that such processes have changed men and women in different ways. However, because of Boserup, the new generation has a set of theories to refine, deepen, and alter. Many of its members also explicitly criticize socioeconomic and psychological patterns of domination and submission. They advocate both an end to the sufferings of women and the beginnings of genuine gender equity.

Benería and Roldán are representing the situation of a group of women in Mexico City in the early 1980s. Many of them are either illiterate or skimpily educated. Most of them are married. Their vision of the world burnishes the role of wife and mother. They work

[1]Ester Boserup, *Woman's Role in Economic Development* (London: George Allen and Unwin; New York: St. Martin's Press, 1970), p. 5.

vii

very, very hard. Part of the "informal economy," they do industrial homework. The subcontractor of a subcontractor of a subcontractor, each in search of cheap labor, gives these women jobs. They sew garments; pack sunflower seeds and metal sponges; assemble plastic bags and the pens their society has hardly taught them how to use. Their income can permit them some latitude in renegotiating their marriage contract, but they sense that the "insufficiency and lack of security do not offer any satisfactory long-run solution to their condition."

Although the scholarship of the authors is tough-minded and scrupulous, Benería and Roldán reject the complacencies of the role of the detached observer. They openly respect the courage, strength, and wisdom of the women of Mexico City. They mourn these women's sorrows. Suspecting economic growth alone as a panacea for those sorrows, they call for policies of development that recognize how much women matter. Because they care about equitable human relations as well as about the lives of one sex, they ask, too, for decentralized, democratic systems in which everyone can reveal her, or his, capacities for self-determination.

Another mark of Benería and Roldán's respect is the complexity of their interdisciplinary method. They look at a concrete, specific situation as holistically as possible. So doing, they see the interplay of the control of production and of sexuality; of socioeconomic forces and of single households; of piecework and motherhood; of the material world and women's consciousness. In brief, they stand at the trafficked crossings of class and gender.

The Crossroads of Class and Gender proves yet again how necessary such a double analysis is for any precise map of reality. Benería and Roldán show the ways in which capital investments incorporate and recreate artificially defined, hierarchically arranged gender traits. Because that capital is international, because it flows like the jet stream across national borders, it brings the "First World" closer and closer to the "Third World." Money, as well as the media, constructs the global village that Marshall McLuhan prophesied.

The Crossroads of Class and Gender speaks rationally, responsibly, compassionately. Because of those qualities, and because of the lives of which it speaks, it calls out to be read.

Catharine R. Stimpson

Preface

Despite all the work we do, there is still the idea that our work is not important because we don't bring money home or, with *maquila*, we make little money. When you work for a wage in a factory, you are more respected.

Doña R., Homeworker

We all came to the conclusion that we hadn't had a childhood, nor had we ever really been young because, as we were growing up we'd had the responsibility of feeding little brothers and sisters—it was like having a lot of children ourselves.

I, Rigoberta Menchu. An Indian Woman in Guatemala

Don't let them run over you, Nettie say. You got to let them know the upper hand.
    They got it, they say.
    But she keep on. You got to fight. You got to fight.
    But I don't know how to fight. All I know how to do is to stay alive.

Alice Walker, The Color Purple

In the course of our fieldwork in Mexico City during 1981 and 1982 there were days when we went home overwhelmed with human problems. Our visits to the homes of women engaged in industrial homework took us to a variety of very poor areas, often in the outskirts of the city, where densely populated *colonias*, or communities, have been spreading for twenty-five years. In many cases, families live in *vecindades*, or tenement houses, where a number of households, ranging from five to thirty, rent one unit each, under extremely crowded conditions. In some cases, each family unit is hardly separated by thin walls from the next. Individual privacy seems impossible under these conditions, and the lack of it appeared to be, at least from our relatively priviledged middle-class perspective, a fundamental problem at the root of many others. Our formal interviews were often intertwined with dialogue about daily problems: sickness, lack of public services—transportation, mail service, schools and health care—unemployment, unstable work conditions for some family members and inadequate incomes for almost everyone, unpaved streets and dangerous electrical installations, noise, leaking roofs, and inadequate, shared sanitary facilities.

Women had their own specific grievances: daily shopping difficulty in making ends meet; beatings inflicted by husbands, lovers and, at least in one case, by a drug-addicted son; male drunkenness; fear of rape (especially in the case of teenage daughters); prostitution and lack of adequate employment alternatives. "Estoy *muy* cansada, señorita" ("I am *very* tired, Miss"), Doña A. once said, as if summarizing the daily pain in one sentence. Although she was a woman our age, we had assumed her to be at least fifteen years older. She had a weak back and her feet hurt. Her husband had a regular job but she did not know how much he earned. Her teenage son was a casual worker in construction, and sometimes involved with drugs. Her hope for a more stable income was that her oldest daughter would get a factory job. She herself was making meager wages assembling metal sponges for dishwashing, and occasionally as a washerwoman. On the day of one of our visits, she had quarreled bitterly with her husband because she had brought home, on a temporary basis, two more children (both mentally retarded) whose prostitute mother (her sister) was unable to take care of them while working.

On days when our research shifted into social work (searching for legal aid services, special schools for handicapped children or psychiatric care), we carried scenes of these women's daily lives home with us. Some of the scenes were moving, some even haunted our dreams. We collected a wealth of data for our study, but we learned even more than that. We learned about the pain in these lives and the courage that it takes to face each day under incredibly difficult conditions. Despite the poverty around us, we were constantly moved by the humanity and dignity that we encountered—symbolized by the care that families took of one another and by the constant effort involved in keeping homes clean under adverse conditions or in growing the beautiful flowers that surrounded many shacks. We became aware of the pride in people's faces in spite of adversity and pain, of parents' love and care for their children, of their intelligence in designing strategies for survival, of their wisdom. We also became painfully aware of the hidden injuries of class and gender, of the intangible effects of poverty that can not be quantified: the sadness in a child's smile, the extreme narrowness of the horizons that life offers, the tears in the eyes of a young woman who understands the limits of her life, the psychological and physical repression required to cope with lack of space, the fear of a violent husband, shown in a woman's face, the tension created by the impossibility of getting away from the enveloping noises, the discomfort of living without basic services.

We cannot overstate the respect and admiration that we felt for many of the people that we met. Doña M., who headed a household of seven and often (when her mother joined them) of eight, lived under constant threat of eviction from her two-room, ground-floor dwelling. When we went to visit her, we could hear from a distance the racket she made as she sorted metal pieces for a battery factory while sitting outside her door. She was often helped by her children and mother. She was particularly proud of her oldest daughter for finishing secondary school and becoming a secretary. Doña M. saw it as her own accomplishment. Her energy and ability to carry on her family responsibilities were fueled by intelligence and determination. Her strength and optimism were a constant source of inspiration to us. She knew what her objectives were, but she was painfully aware of the obstacles in her way. She did not need planners and policy makers, or researchers, to tell her what she should do; as many other women and men that we encountered. Doña M. was ready to tell all of us what the obstacles were that prevented her from living the life she wanted.

We thank all the people who so generously agreed to share their lives with us, and we are deeply indebted for all we learned. We were often uncomfortable about the intrusion into their lives implied by our research. We want to express our genuine and deep appreciation by the only means that we have: that of reflecting the reality we saw and incorporating the voices we heard as accurately as possible in our account and our analysis. Throughout this book, we have preserved the anonymity of the respondants,—individual workers as well as firms—and names have been changed or simply not mentioned.

Almost three years later, the experience is still very much a part of us. We are painfully aware of the difficulty of expressing its fullness and of our debt to those whose possibility of being heard is constantly thwarted by existing economic, social, and political structures. We are aware also of the limitations of our narrowly defined academic tools for dealing with the richness and complexity of the reality to be described.

Thanks are due also to all those who made this study possible. The Ford foundation in Mexico funded the research on homework and paid Martha Roldán's traveling expenses for the completion of this book. Lourdes Benería was assisted by a grant from the Social Science Research Council and the American Council of Learned Societies for fieldwork on subcontracting and by a grant from Wenner-Gren Foundation during the writing period. We are also grateful for the support given by Nanneke Redclift, now at the University of Kent and formerly with the Ford Foundation of Mexico, and Bertha Hernández from the Program on Research of Women at the Ford Foundation in Mexico. Many thanks are also due to Regina Cohen and Gladys Gatica for their invaluable research assistance and to Constance Blake for helping with computer techniques. In addition, many other friends and colleagues have contributed their support, comments, and suggestions: Timothy Diamond, John Duggan, María Patricia Fernández Kelly, David Gordon, Sherry Gorelick, Robert Guttman, Heidi Hartmann, Martha Howell, Alison Jaggar, Rhoda Linton, Mario Margulis, Leonard Mertens, Ruth Milkman, Michele Naples, Hugo Radice, Helen Safa, Catharine Stimpson, Nelly Stronquist, Fiona Wilson, Kate Young, Marilyn Young, and the members of the Women and Development study group in New York City. Last but not least, we thank Jordi and Marc Benería Surkin for the time our work took away from them and for their understanding and openness.

One
Introduction and Theoretical Framework

This book grew out of our initial concern to understand the reasons behind the seemingly growing concentration of women in what has been called the "informal sector" of the Latin American economy. We were interested also in ascertaining the economic and political implications of this phenomenon, both for the women involved and for the evaluation of urban employment policies based on the optimistic promotion of that sector. Preliminary research into the subject was instrumental in narrowing the scope of our study to the more specific topic of industrial homework.

We were aware of the existence of this type of work in different areas of Mexico. Although information was not abundant, estimates of the number of seamstresses in the Mexico City garment industry ranged from 20,000 to 25,000 (Lomnitz, 1978; Alonso, 1979) and, according to newspaper reports, these may be conservative figures. In addition, scattered information we gathered during the planning period indicated the existence of homework in nongarment industries as well—toymaking, plastics, electronics and others. This was a relatively unexplored sector that appeared to be of increasing importance on a world scale. Moreover, since the large majority of the workers so engaged appeared to be women, the choice of homework as the focus of our study would allow us to deal with one of our primary interests; namely, the study of how class and gender are articulated in a concrete working and living situation. We perceived the possibility of exploring the connections between economic processes and the dynamics of social relations within the household. The setting in Mexico City, a large urban center of an industrializing country, provided the opportunity to study some aspects of the dynamics of an industrial labor market within the specific context of development problems facing a Third World country.

1

In the process of carrying out the pilot fieldwork, we realized the need to open our study to a wider perspective in order to capture more adequately the complexities of the issues. For example, it became increasingly necessary to analyze the placement of industrial homework within the larger economy in order to understand its articulation with other productive levels. What were the industries involved? What kind of tasks were sent out for home production? To what extent was homework connected with other levels of subcontracting? What were the labor-market dynamics generated by these processes?

At another level, we realized the need to explore the historical construction of gender and class, the nature of household exchanges, and forms of women's consciousness and struggles. In addition, we found ourselves short of analytical and conceptual tools to comprehend these phenomena. Consequently we felt the need for further elaboration of such commonly used concepts as class and gender.

The fundamental concern that ties these issues together is our attempt to develop an *integrated* analysis in which class and gender formation, struggle, and recomposition[1] are looked at simultaneously as necessary steps for an understanding of social reality. We are aware of the important role often played by race and ethnicity in determining this reality. Yet, given the homogeneous character of the population, these aspects did not seem to be directly relevant to our research problematic. However, our study is an attempt to explore the specific life situation and problems affecting a sector of Mexican working women. To the extent that we succeed in this endeavor, we are, in Bell Hooks's words, bringing "the margin to the center" by focusing our analysis on the experiences of women in a Third World country.

We therefore see our study as connected with two main bodies of literature. In the first instance, it is one of the growing number of studies dealing with how development, or the lack of it, has affected women. In another context, it addresses some concerns that emanate from feminist scholarship focusing on class and gender issues and from the need for feminism to deal with the experiences of Third-World women. It should be stressed that this is an interdisciplinary study combining economic, sociological, and anthropological perspectives. Its purpose is to transcend artificial boundaries between disciplines and, to the extent possible, capture the wholeness of the reality we want to describe. In the next two sections, we shall review various aspects of those bodies of literature that are of particular relevance to our study.

Women and Development

The literature on women and development appearing during the past fifteen years has made an important contribution to an aspect of development—its effect on women as workers and family members—that had been previously ignored by most social scientists. The publication in 1970 of Ester Boserup's *Woman's Role in Economic Development* represented the first important effort to break this tradition. It is perhaps for this reason, together with its timely publication in terms of the new interest in women's issues, that Boserup became the most quoted book on the subject of women and development. Although her contributions were varied (Benería and Sen, 1981), two of them were fundamental. One was to point out that all societies have developed a clear-cut division of labor by sex, even though what are considered to be male or female tasks varies considerably across countries—implying that there is nothing natural to this division. The other contribution was to show that economic development in the Third World has had a differential impact on men and women and that the impact on women often had been negative.

Numerous studies, with varying theoretical approaches and bearing directly or indirectly on the loosely defined subject of women and development, have appeared since 1970.[2] Although many problems regarding women's condition and subordination remain unsolved, we have learned a great deal about the realities facing women and their families in the Third World. Governments, international agencies and other institutions concerned with development have shown interest and allocated resources for projects dealing with women. The UN international conferences in Mexico City (1975), Copenhagen (1980), and Nairobi (1985) have been another expression of this interest. We have also witnessed the growth of women's networks and organizations at the community, national and international levels. In some cases, this has been accompanied by the mobilization of women from different class backgrounds, with significant political potential. In several Latin American countries, for example, women have participated as candidates in national elections and actively voiced their concerns.

These accomplishments have been parallel to an increasing interest within the academic community; courses and research on women and development or on gender and capitalist expansion have proliferated, and comparisons have begun to be explored between the historical experience of more industrialized countries and the current experience of industrializing countries (Elson and Pearson, 1981; Stolcke, 1983; Felton, 1986). Parallel also to all these efforts, numerous empirical studies and action-oriented projects have been generated during the past fifteen years, with most countries feeling their impact in one form or another. At the practical level of project design and implementation, a great deal of progress has been made since the mid-seventies (Buvinic, 1984; Chaney, 1985; Heyzer, 1985).

All this work in combination has resulted in a body of scholarship that is an important contribution to the literature on development, though often ignored in the mainstream. To illustrate with a relevant example, the emphasis women researchers place on household and family relations has provided an impetus for many studies around this topic dealing with a variety of themes.[3] First, there has been an interest in the question of women's participation in economic activities in and out of the household. This has generated various studies of labor-force participation rates and patterns of involvement in paid production according to family income levels, family life-cycles, types of household and other factors (Peek, 1978; Standing, 1978; Deere and León de Leal, 1982; García, Muñoz, and Oliveira, 1982). At the same time, a critical literature has emerged on the tendency for official statistics to underestimate women's economic activities and labor-force participation (Galbraith, 1973; ILO, 1978; Wainerman and Recchini, 1981; Benería, 1982).

A second area of interest closely connected to the first studies the sexual division of labor in the household in relation to the division of labor in subsistence and paid production work. Such studies have provided further insights into an analysis that previously focused solely on the labor market. Migration, for example, is influenced by the division of labor within the household. This, in turn, has a significant impact on future household dynamics and women's roles (Bukh, 1979; Pessar, 1982). In general, the household focus has provided detailed studies of women's paid and unpaid work and its connections with the outside economy (Alonso, 1979; Silva de Rojas, 1982; Spindel, 1982; Mies, 1982; Longhurst, 1982; Pessar, 1982; Netting, 1984; Phillips, 1985). As a result women's participation in economic activities has been further documented.

Third: emphasis on the household economy has contributed to

4

the literature dealing with survival strategies of families at different income levels (Bilac, 1978; Schmink, 1982; Tinker, 1985). This literature includes analysis of multiple-income families, income pooling, patterns of money allocation among family members and proletarianization (Roldán, forthcoming). In particular, the issue of female-headed households and their common occurrence in many regions of the world has received a great deal of attention (Buvinic, Youssef, and Von Elm, 1978). Fourth: emphasis on the household has also been used in fertility studies, analysis of social reproduction, population policies and migration (Margulis, 1980; Young, 1982; Oppong, 1978; Anker, Buvinic, and Youssef, 1983). Fifth: studies of income-generating activities in the home have added an important dimension to the ongoing discussion around the formal/informal or predominant/subordinate sectors of the economy. In particular, these studies have provided evidence of women's concentration in industrial homework and informal activities (SPP/UCECA, 1976; Connolly, 1982; IDS Bulletin, 1981; Roldán, 1984). Finally, a focus on the household, social relations within the family, and women's work has challenged our traditional understanding of proletarianization processes, labor mobility and the process of transition from precapitalist to capitalist forms of production (Rubbo, 1975; Medrano, 1981; Stolcke, 1983; Roldán, 1982).

These studies have made a significant contribution and have added new insights to a body of research that had placed little emphasis on the dynamics of the household and its connection with wider socioeconomic processes—showing the arbitrariness and insufficiency of analyzing the two areas separately. Studies of the household provide a basis for dealing with gender and class issues, even though not all authors have included a feminist concern in their analysis. This in fact was one of the dimensions missing in Boserup's book; namely, an effort to view women's role in the development process as conditioned by dynamics set up at the household level. Current work on the household adds a wealth of information about the differences and commonalities observed in different areas of the world.

A further illustration of the contributions made by the literature on women and development is provided by analysis of the impact that the new international division of labor has had on women's work. Numerous studies have illustrated the new employment of women as a source of cheap labor utilized by multinational and national capital in many areas of the Third World (Fröbel, Heinrichs, and Kreye, 1980; Elson and Pearson, 1981; Safa, 1981; Nash and

Fernández-Kelly, 1983). The intensification of investment on a world scale that has taken place since the mid–1960s and throughout the 1970s has resulted in new processes of proletarianization of women, particularly in the industries that have relocated from high- to low-wage countries.

Women are heavily represented in the industrialized areas of Southeast Asia, in the US-Mexican border industries, and in the numerous free-trade zones that have attracted multinational capital to many Third-World countries. This is a pattern differing from the employment generated by multinational investment in previous decades. The new employment of women has been the result of the massive transfer of labor-intensive production from the more industrialized countries to the Third World, made possible by the new technologies as well as the ability to fragment productive processes, the reduction of transportation costs, and the advances in modern communications. These studies have raised numerous questions that need further investigation: for example, regarding the extent to which women's employment has increased relative to men's. The analysis in chapter 3 deals with the reasons behind this increase in women's employment as it applies to Mexico. Discussion of the persistence of these trends in the 1980s is beginning to emerge given the development of new technologies and their effect on, and amount of, labor employed (O'Connor, forthcoming).

Writings on women and development since 1970 represent, first, a challenge to the assumption that the development process affected men and women in the same way. Second, they have added new perspectives and themes to development concerns, in particular those with a gender dimension. Third, they have been instrumental in projects and strategies for change that specifically incorporate women's concerns. To be sure, these contributions have been made in terms of differing theoretical frameworks and political visions. It is our intention to point out some of the limitations and shortcomings that have become evident to us in an overview of that literature.

Several problems seem particularly important. In the literature on modernization theory, one problem has to do with a model implicit in the analysis equating development with a growth-oriented process wherein capitalist institutions are taken as the norm. Some of the development literature in the past decade has rejected the assumption that economic growth per se, under these conditions, necessarily trickles down to all sectors of the population.[4] With regard to women, it has been argued that their subordination in the development process cannot be attributed to their marginalization from that process, as suggested by Boserup (1970), but to a variety of factors that have generated this marginalization. Some of these factors are gender-related; others derive from a pattern of growth that systematically generates acute class differences and social hierarchies (Benería and Sen, 1982).

A second problem comes from the assumption that capitalist penetration into Third-World countries has a dynamic of its own, independent of its specific socioeconomic and historical context. In our view, each development process needs to be understood in conjunction with preexisting patterns of accumulation and relations of subordination/domination that have conditioned and are in turn conditioned by that process. For example, as illustrated by Mies in a case study of lacemakers in India, caste and traditional practices of seclusion of women, as well as the region's specific connection with the international market, have helped to determine conditions under which women have been included in paid production. Moreover, there is no single pattern of development. Capitalism does not necessarily follow a unidirectional path toward the elimination of noncapitalist forms of production and increased proletarianization (Meade, 1978; Stolcke, 1983; Benería, 1983; Spindel, Jaquette, and Cordini, 1984). It may instead follow a variety of forms in a continuum ranging from the re-creation of noncapitalist forms to varying degrees of labor absorption in the so-called informal and formal sectors of the economy.

A third problem is the tendency to *describe* the location of women in the development process without focusing explicitly on gender asymmetries and therefore explaining them. A mere description may point out differences between men and women within the household or in the work force, recounting the sexual division of labor and the hierarchies deriving from ownership of land and other resources, as well as from the access to education, wages, skills, and opportunities for advancement. Such description, however, is insufficient to explain the roots of gender differentiation and the generation of inequalities affecting women. As a consequence, strategies for change eliminating such inequalities and precluding the appearance of new ones cannot easily be formulated.

A fourth problem derives from the androcentric and ethnocentric assumptions underlying development models. They often represent a projection on to the Third World of conditions prevalent in industrialized countries. To illustrate, studies of family survival strategies usually take for granted a model of income-pooling based on

7

a nuclear-family household system, neglecting gender and generational hierarchies. In Chapter 6, we will show that such a model is inadequate to reflect the complexities of household interaction and the asymmetrical exchanges among family members. This problem is quite apart from the fact that the model may also be inadequate to explain the variety of household interaction in the industrialized world itself.

A fifth problem is the tendency to view women as passive recipients of change and victims of forces they do not generate or control. Women are often pictured as part of the reserve army of labor, being pulled in and out of the labor market merely as a result of capital's interests and strategies. This takes no account of women's own resistance and struggles that, while clearly subject to significant constraints due to their subordination in society, derive from a strategy of their own.

Finally, there is the problem caused by a general tendency to separate women and development issues in the Third World from those concerning women in the industrialized countries. This tends to objectify Third-World women as a separate category without emphasizing their connection with women in the industrialized world and the differences and similarities that exist between women across countries. Studies of the impact of the current restructuring of the world economy on women in both industrialized and Third-World countries are beginning to throw some light on these connections (Fröbel, Heinrichs, and Keye, 1980; Fernández-Kelly, forthcoming; Sassen-Koob, 1982).

Class, Gender and Analytical Dualisms

The connections between class and gender raise the old question of the relationship between economic systems—capitalism in the case of Mexico—and the subordination of women. To be sure, not all feminist approaches pose the question in such a way; in particular, radical as well as liberal feminism tends to reduce emphasis on class inequalities generated by the productive system. The opposite problem is represented by those who apply traditional Marxist concepts directly to "the woman question" or reformulate them for the purpose of analyzing women's issues.[5] In the latter case, the main emphasis is on understanding the material basis of women's oppression—as understood within the Marxist tradition—often disregarding ideological aspects of the social construction of gender. Consequently, a straightforward use of Marxist concepts tends toward economic reductionism, resulting in the subsumption of gender hierarchies under class inequalities. In addition, this approach neglects a fundamental message of radical feminism; namely, that women's subordination is based on male control of women's sexuality, procreative capacity, and ideology. Although we do not subscribe to the radical approach, given its relative neglect of economic structures and class differences and its often ahistorical view of social reality, we think that no analysis can ignore the basic contributions of radical feminism.

The effort to explain women's subordination as the result of the interplay of class and gender has come from what Jaggar has called socialist-feminist approaches.[6] The question has often been posed either as an interaction between a given mode of production and a sex-gender system (Rubin, 1975) or as an interaction between capitalism and patriarchy (Hartmann, 1976; Sokoloff, 1980; Eisenstein, 1979). This approach has been crucial in pointing out the shortcomings of traditional Marxism in dealing with women's subordination. While traditional Marxism viewed "the woman question" as the result of class inequalities as conventionally understood, socialist feminism (or Marxist-feminism) credits the oppression of women with a dynamic of its own that has not been captured by traditional Marxism (Hartmann, 1981). The result has been a conception of two semiautonomous systems—the sex-gender system, or patriarchy, and the mode of production system, or capitalism—which are viewed as interconnected and mutually reinforcing.

There are advantages to this formulation. First, it emphasizes the importance of distinguishing between gender and class relations in a way such that both sets of relations become fundamental to an understanding of women's subordination. Second, it makes clear the insufficiency of the traditional analysis of "the woman question," which focused on class inequalities and the material, and neglected the asymmetry between the sexes in all other spheres of social life. Third, if the two systems are semiautonomous, this implies that patriarchy might be maintained throughout different modes of production or that the disappearance of capitalist institutions does not necessarily imply the elimination of patriarchy. Fourth, strategically the implication is that feminist politics do not necessarily coincide with conventional forms of struggle around class inequalities, even though commonalities exist to the extent that both systems often reinforce each other.

Yet, as pointed out by other authors, there are problems with this formulation. One is that the concept of patriarchy tends to be used in an ahistorical way, as if it applied to all societies, without specifying the historical reality in which the concept is immersed. Another closely related problem, is the difficulty of studying the interplay between capitalism and patriarchy as systems—or between any mode of production and patriarchy—without falling into dualistic analyses (Young, 1981). The specificity of real life does not present itself in a dualistic manner but as an integrated *whole*, where multiple relations of domination/subordination—based on race, age, ethnicity, nationality, sexual preference—interact dialectically with class and gender relations.

Our objective as social scientists and feminists is to capture the dynamics of this totality without losing sight of its different elements. In discussing Hartmann's dual systems, Ferguson and Folbre (1981) have argued that despite the fact that "capitalism and patriarchy are separate and semi-autonomous systems," they are also "wedded in conflict." We need to go one step further: reality presents itself not so much as a marriage in conflict but as a product with traits inherited from both systems and also from the multiple factors mentioned above.

Although class and gender may be analytically distinguishable at a theoretical level, in practice they cannot be easily disentangled. The problem before us is to build a unifying theory and analysis in which material and ideological factors are an integral aspect of our understanding of gender subordination, while women's subordination is an integral part of our understanding of economic and social reality. Strategically, this implies that class and gender must be dealt with simultaneously as part of the struggle towards eliminating exploitation in general and the oppression of women in particular.

As feminist scholarship has proceeded, a more integrated analysis is emerging both theoretically and empirically (Sen 1980; Phillips and Taylor, 1980; Elson and Pearson, 1981; Cockburn, 1981; Stolcke, 1981; Eisenstein, 1983, Goldberg, 1983; Wilson, 1985). A pioneer work at the theoretical level was that of Barrett (1980) which represented an effort to build a feminist theory that would challenge and at the same time benefit from Marxist analysis. Since the central Marxist categories of exploitation and appropiation, as traditionally understood, are neutral with respect to gender, for Barrett this implies rejecting economism as an explanation of gender relations by emphasizing ideological aspects in the social construction of gender which are embedded in the material. Thus, while a tacit assumption of Barrett's work is the usefulness of Marxism as a basic framework for the analysis of women's oppression, the objective is to "identify the operation of gender relations as and where they may be distinct from, or connected with, the processes of production and reproduction understood by historical materialism" (Barrett, 1980, p. 9). The nondualistic nature of this analysis is obvious: while borrowing heavily from radical feminism for the purpose of understanding the ideological aspects of gender formation, the analysis incorporates basic Marxist concepts and methods that are useful for an understanding of women's subordination; and while using a Marxist approach, it avoids economism by emphasizing the role of ideology.

The role of ideology in Barrett's work has been criticized because such formulation requires the analysis of how gender ideology itself gets constructed and because this analysis of this ideological realm leads to a degree of dualism (Brenner and Ramas, 1984). At the theoretical level, this may in fact be inevitable, even if reality is a unified whole. We agree with Barrett that, in the last resort, the question is not strictly theoretical but also historical in nature. That is, we need to examine a specific reality to understand how ideology and the material interact and how class and gender are interconnected and socially constructed. In this sense, dualistic thinking can be confronted only through historical analysis.

Furthermore, to the extent that Barrett's work is grounded in the conditions prevalent in Britain, it is not directly applicable to Third-World countries. The great variety of experiences that characterize women's lives in the periphery requires a special effort to conceptualize a paradigm to include all factors having an influence on the complexity of their subordination. This is still the challenge before us.

Definitions and Objective of the Study

We find it necessary at the outset to clarify our interpretation of the basic concepts of gender and class used throughout the text. Although both concepts are widely used in the literature, they are seldom defined. Yet, different uses of these concepts imply different visions of reality and different political strategies. We use gender in the usual way of most feminists: to differentiate it from sex and indicate its social rather than biological origin.[7] Gender may be defined as a network of beliefs, personality traits, attitudes, feelings, values, behaviors, and activities differentiating men and women through a process of social construction that has a number of distinctive features. It is historical; it takes place within different macro and micro spheres such as the state, the labor market, schools, the media, the law, the family-household, and interpersonal relations; it involves the ranking of traits and activities so that those associated with men are normally given greater value.[8] Ranking, and therefore the formation of hierarchies, in most societies is an intrinsic component of gender construction.

The outcome—and the means—of this construction is the asymmetrical and *structured* (institutionally defined) access to resources generating male privilege and domination[9] and female subordination. Gender relations so conceived give rise to feminist politics that focus on "long-run gender interests" and goals to do away with male domination. These goals include equality before the law, women's economic and psychological self-reliance, the abolition of a gender-based division of labor, women's control over their sexuality and reproductive capacity, and the eradication of male violence and coercion over women.[10] Since, however, gender is constructed simultaneously with a multiplicity of relations—such as class, race and ethnicity—each historical analysis may show that women perceive long-run gender interests differently and according to their own life experience (see Chapter 7 for an elaboration of this point).

With regard to the conceptualization of social classes, it must first be pointed out that there is no consensus on a definition within the literature. In broad terms, however, it is possible to distinguish between those authors who consider the common location of individuals within the process of production as the essential factor for class definition and those who emphasize the cultural and historical dimensions of class formation.[11]

Among the first group, economic ownership and possession of the means of production are the most frequently used definitional criteria, to which Portes (1984) adds modes of remuneration as a relevant dimension. According to these authors, the application of these formal criteria makes it possible to identify contradictory economic interests that define social classes, their basic political orientation, and their "class project," that is, an objective and global mode of organization of social life.

These exclusively structuralist definitions have been criticized by the second group of authors. This group points out that neglect of the cultural sphere and the social and psychological factors that influence class identity and solidarity results in lack of analytical power and is of limited use for political strategies. On the contrary, for these authors, classes are formed historically by their relationship to the economic foundation of society and also by coherent cultural existence, common social identity, and life-styles, features expected to originate from shared historical experiences through generations. This means that the links between economic class determination and class consciousness and action should not be taken for granted but carefully scrutinized.

We find the cultural/historical approach to class definition compatible with our theoretical perspective for three reasons. First, it does away with the economic reductionism of most structuralist analyses. Second, it leads to taking human agency, social perceptions and values, beliefs and forms of consciousness into consideration, and expands the sphere of class construction beyond the workplace. Third, it facilitates including in the analysis the dialectics of gender, race, and ethnicity that are of interest from a feminist perspective. However, there are two main problems with this approach. One is the little attention usually paid to the analysis of concrete production processes and their significance for class formation and struggles. The other problem is the conveying generally of an androcentric bias that does not consider the specific gender relation to the class system arising from women's reproductive roles and family dynamics, as shown by different authors. [12]

In order to remedy these shortcomings, in our view the analysis of concrete historical processes of class formation, recomposition, and reproduction must include a number of dimensions. First, it should include criteria of ownership and possession of the means of production (control over the labor process) and mode of remuneration, mentioned above. [13] This must be accompanied by the study of other factors that may call into question that assumed "common" relationship to the means of production and forms of class consciousness (again, those related to gender, race and ethnicity). In turn, this requires the study of the sexual division of labor and other hierarchies at the workplace and in the household; of subjective dimensions of class; and of forms of organization and struggle.

We now turn to our basic objective—to contribute to the understanding of why, how, under what conditions, and with what consequences women are incorporated into paid production. More concretely, we want to analyze a number of ways in which class and gender interact at the workplace and in the household. This includes, for example, the analysis of how women's participation in a given labor process is affected not only by previously existent gender hierarchies and work histories; it also reinforces these and creates *new* labor hierarchies based on gender. Jobs and skills, for instance, are subject to *gendering,* while social relations of production are being restructured at the workplace. At the same time, placement of women in specific labor categories as well as in their own occupational trajectories is a basic component in the social construction of gender. Similarly and at the household level, we will be studying how women's class insertion and control of their own income empowers them to renegotiate gender relations within the home.

The complexity of capturing this historical process of simultaneous class and gender formation and recomposition[14] has already been underlined; we do not pretend to deal with this complexity as a whole. Our study rather will concentrate on some dimensions of class and gender articulation in the spheres of the household and the workplace as they relate to the following focal points.

The first focal point has to do with how industrial homework and other types of female employment are connected with the wider issues of labor market and development dynamics. The second deals more specifically with the gender dimensions in these issues. Both of them raise some of the questions that are central to this book; for example, those concerned with conditions under which the incorporation of women in industrial work takes place. What is the connection between industrial subcontracting and women's employment? How can we explain the tendency for some tasks and clusters of activities to become feminized? How can women's lower wages be explained? Do wages respond to underlying economic forces or to gender dynamics or both? To what extent are women's gender traits used in the workplace and for what purpose? What role do women play in the articulation between the formal and the underground economy? Why is it that an overwhelming majority of homeworkers are married women with children?

Many of these questions lead to the old connection between the domestic and market sexual division of labor or between reproduction and production. They also raise the issue of the extent to which there is a *common* relationship of the working class to the means of production. As shown in Chapters 3 and 4, once gender is introduced into the analysis, the differences between men and women as workers—in terms of skill development, location in the production process, wages and working conditions—become more obvious. In fact, the workplace can be viewed as a locus in which gender can be used and re-created, with the implication that individual workers' relationship to the means of production is mediated by gender.

The remaining focal points of this study refer to the issues of fe-

male proletarianization, renegotiation of gender relations, and women's awareness of their subordination within the household.
These issues give rise to questions concerning women's specific
insertion in class relations, the nature of household interaction and
exchanges of resources, and the links of these with forms of
women's consciousness and struggle. What are the historical factors
explaining women's work strategies and their current insertion in
industrial homework? What is the difference between women's pre-
and post-marriage occupational and class histories? What is the
influence of family cycles upon women's patterns of wage labor? Is
it possible to talk about female proletarianization as an autonomous
process separated from male proletarianization? Is the concept of
household an adequate unit of analysis? Does this unit need to be
decomposed and, if so, how? What resources do household members exchange? Can we assume that all families engage in income-
pooling or that all adult members pool their incomes according to
their respective earnings? Are there differences between men and
women in terms of their expenditure priorities? Finally, to what degree does the wife's control over her income empower her in the
bargain of gender relations within the household? What are the control mechanisms that condition women's struggles within this
domain? Does paid work lead to a change in women's consciousness and perception of themselves? How are changes in family interaction linked to global patterns of class and gender relations outside the household?

These questions are taken up in Chapters 2 to 8. Chapter 2 includes a description of background data, of the general characteristics of the sample, and of the setting in which our research took
place in Mexico City; it also includes a description of our research
methodology. Chapter 3 analyzes the structure of subcontracting to
which homework is linked—providing a macro picture of the interconnections among firms and the different levels of production that
generate homework. It contains also an analysis of the dynamics of
women's employment at different levels of subcontracting. Chapter
4 deals with the nature of homework, the conditions under which it
takes place, reasons for the predominance of women in this type of
work, and its significance in terms of the discussion around the
formal/informal sectors of the economy. Chapter 5 examines family,
class, and gender histories to ascertain their influence on women's
insertion in industrial homework. It also compares wives' and husbands' proletarianization patterns, as mediated by the system of
household reciprocities, and locates this proletarianization within

the overall process of class formation in Mexico City. Chapters 6 and 7 explore the relationship between women's work strategies and patterns and the limits of women's renegotiation of gender relations within the home. Chapter 6 focuses on the asymmetrical exchanges of income and unpaid domestic labor among household members and analyzes the connections between these exchanges and the making and reproduction of class relations. Chapter 7 examines the links between the exchange processes analyzed in the previous chapter, the marriage contract and other mechanisms that constrain wives' struggles and attempts at control. Finally, Chapter 8 summarizes the findings of our study and their implications for policy and action.

Two
The Setting: Background Data and Methodology

This chapter provides general information about the setting for our study and contains a description of our sample. The objective is to describe rather than to analyze, in order to introduce the reader to basic data.

The current economic crisis associated with Mexico's external debt took a highly critical turn in the summer of 1982, at the time when we finished the fieldwork and data collection for our study. The study, therefore, captures the moment in Mexico's development when the economic problems that emerged clearly with the devaluation of the peso in August 1982 were just beginning to be felt. This time of transition was reflected, for example, in the interviews with firms' representatives reported in Chapter 3; while there was little talk of crisis during the summer of 1981, it was to become an urgent concern one year later.

As one of the so-called newly industrialized countries (NIC's), with a per capita income of US$2,270 in 1982, Mexico is ranked by the World Bank as an upper middle-income country. In relative terms, Mexico's per capita gross national product for that year ranked close to that of Brazil and Portugal and just below that of Argentina, Chile, South Africa, and Uruguay.[1] Despite uneven development and inequalities in distribution of resources and income, Mexico's economy grew rapidly during the 1960s and early 1970s. This was particularly true for the manufacturing sector; while the average gross domestic product growth was 7.6% for 1960–70 and 6.5% for 1970–80, the corresponding rate of growth for manufacturing was 10.1% and 7.1%. As a result, industrial production grew from 26% of the country's total product in 1950 to 40% in 1980 (Cordera and Tello, 1981). Industrial production slowed down, however, during the 1975–78 period, and strong inflationary pressures accelerated and continued during the vigorous recovery initiated in 1979.[2] These inflationary pressures, together with the sluggish growth of some key industrial sectors, were at the root of the difficulties that surfaced in the early 1980s.

Mexico's industrialization has been oriented toward import substitution, particularly of consumption goods. However, the highly uneven distribution of income and the lack of development of the rural sector have placed limits on the growth of the domestic market and on this industrialization. Following a typical Latin American pattern, ownership of the means of production is highly concentrated, particularly in industry (Cordera and Tello, 1981). One of the consequences of the concentration, together with the lack of absorption of a large labor supply, is an unequal distribution of income—as illustrated by the fact that in 1977 the lowest 20% of households received 2.9% of total household income while the highest 10% received over 40% of the total (World Bank, 1983, table 21). Other industries, and in particular those generating industrial inputs and capital equipment, have lagged behind—with important consequences in terms of reliance on imports for the provision of these basic inputs.

Mexico's dependent capitalism is typical of a peripheral country in which international capital, North American in particular, continues to play a fundamental role in development and industrialization.[3] Multinational firms produce more than a third of the country's industrial output, although the proportion has been as high as 40% in the capital goods sector, more than 60% for consumer durables, and 50% for the country's manufactured exports (Cordera and Tello, 1981; Jenkins, 1984). Furthermore, multinational firms are among the most dynamic sources of industrial growth and technology tranfers, though, at the same time contributing to the deficit of the external sector (Mercado, 1980; Soria, 1980; Minian, 1981). Dependency on foreign financing exists also in the national private sector—as illustrated by the huge external debt (US$2.3 billion in the summer of 1982) of "Grupo Alfa," a powerful Mexican conglomerate referred to in the past as a successful example of independent, national capital. This dependency is also reflected in our study. It will be apparent in Chapter 3 that multinational firms constitute a basic source of subcontracting that filters down to middle-size and small firms providing industrial piecework at the household level.

Another characteristic of Mexico's industrial development is its oligopolistic nature and its geographical concentration in a few states and cities. Mexico City is the largest industrial center and absorbed the lion's share of industrial growth until 1970. At the end of the 1950s, the metropolitan area accounted for 42.7% of the country's gross industrial product; by 1970, this figure was still almost 40%, while transport and service industries showed similar levels of concentration in the metropolitan area—30.9% and 49.6% respectively (Garza, 1976). In particular, Mexico City concentrates in its center the production of consumer durables, chemical products, electric and electronic equipment, and parts and assembly for the automobile industry. Subcontracting links and the decentralization of production to the level of homework must be viewed within this larger industrial setting; subcontracting offers also a micro picture of the connections among multinational capital and Mexican firms.

During the 1960–70 period, Mexico City experienced one of the highest rates of population growth in the world, due particularly to the immigration rate from other areas of Mexico. It has been estimated that, by 1970, about 35% of the total population in the metropolitan area and over 50% of those over 20 years of age had not been born in the city (Muñoz, Oliveira, and Stern, 1971). These immigrants also contributed heavily to the City's natural population growth (Goldani, 1977). As a result, the constant flow of in-migrants into Mexico City has contributed to the making of the industrial labor force and to the existence of a large labor reserve whose overflow swells the so-called informal sector. The population in our sample of households with homework illustrates the process by which in-migrants have been incorporated into different types of economic activity.

Our study captures a moment of transition from a period of growth to one of crisis in Mexico's development. Reliance on oil to finance imports, and the decrease in oil prices together with the acceleration of inflationary pressures, intensified the foreign debt problem. By 1982, this debt had accumulated to US$50 billion, while the debt service represented 29.5% of the country's exports (World Bank, 1984). The resulting pressure on key imports of capital equipment and other industrial inputs constituted a bottleneck to national development. As the pressure on the peso mounted, the flight of capital increased, to avoid the consequences of a probable devaluation. As a result of all these factors, the recovery of 1979 came to a halt in 1982, and the crisis, as stated above, became clearly manifest with devaluation of the peso and freezing of dollar accounts in August of that year.

At the time, fieldwork for our study was about to finish, and signs of the economic crisis were evident. For example, some of the subcontracting arrangements described in Chapter 3 resulted from the need to replace domestic production for imports. On the other hand, subcontracting orders for some consumer goods were reported not to flow as regularly as before. Yet it was too early to evaluate the overall effect of the crisis on the dynamics of subcontracting.

Areas Visited and Types of Homework

Our interviews with homeworkers were carried out in fifteen *colonias* or neighborhoods, located in different areas of Mexico City and the metropolitan area, which extend itself into the bordering state of Mexico and constitute an urban continuity in terms of economic activity, transportation and other services. The exceptions were three cases from the town of Chalco, within the state of Mexico. The map on p. 21 shows the general location of the boroughs and counties in which the colonias are located (shaded area). The map does not indicate the location of the subcontracting firms interviewed which tended to be spread throughout the metropolitan area. In general, immediate contacts with the homeworkers or "jobbers," took place in the area where homework was done.

Table 2.1 includes a detail of the colonias where homework was located and the different types of homework encountered. Although our sample was not representative, it covered a wide geographical extension. Different types of homework did not concentrate in one specific area but were scattered throughout the colonias in the sample.

General Characteristics of the Sample

The number of women homeworkers interviewed reached a total of 140—belonging to 137 households with a total population of 870. The average household size was 6.35, which is close to that found by García, Muñoz, and Oliveira (1982) for Mexico City as a whole. For the purpose of our analysis throughout the book, we use a common definition of household: a set of people that share a living space and a budget, usually, although not necessarily, on the basis of kinship relations.

Table 2.2 defines the concepts used to classify households and provides a breakdown according to family composition and average size. The proportion of nuclear households in the sample is almost 74% while that of extended households is close to 26%, and only one household is a single person. Extended households were based on kinship relations except for three cases that included non-kin

Research Site in Mexico City and Its Metropolitan Area

members. On the other hand, Table 2.3 shows that 56.1% of the households were within earlier phases of the family cycle, while 43.9% fell within the advanced phases. Relevance of these categories to the sexual division of labor in the household and the incorporation of household members into wage labor will be explored in Chapter 6.

What needs to be stressed here is the concentration of women

Table 2.1   *Geographical Distribution and Types of Homework*

Colonia	*Types of Homework*
Mexico City	
Tacubaya	Assembly of plastic flowers; packing cloth
Moctezuma	Plastic polishing (various products); assembly of staples and pens; packing sweets; quality control (socks)
El Rosario	Assembly of toys; packing metal sponges
Atzacoalco	Packing sunflower seeds; garment
Morelos	Assembly of plastic bags; garment
Iztacalco	Garment
Atzcapotzalco	Garment
State of Mexico	
Metropolitan area	
Lázaro Cárdenas	Quality control (metal pieces for batteries); assembly of toys; plastic polishing; textile finishing; electronic coil-making.
San Andrés Atoto	Textile finishing
El Capulín	Assembly of cartons; textile finishing.
El Molinito	Packing of metal sponges; textile finishing.
Altamira	Electronic coil-making
Outside metropolitan area	
Town of Chalco	Sheet metal riveting and making parts for antennas; assembly of latches.
City of Netzahualcoyotl	Garment

Table 2.2   *Household Size by Types of Household Composition*
             (N = 137)

Type of Household	Definition	Average Household Size	%
Nuclear	Reproductive couple with or without unmarried offspring		
Complete	Both partners living in the same household with or without unmarried offspring	5.95	64.23
Incomplete	Partnership terminated through death or separation; with unmarried offspring	5.38	9.50
Extended	Nuclear family, complete or incomplete, plus one or more individuals that might be married kin-offspring or married/unmarried individuals (kin or not)		
Type I	With single individuals (kin or not)	6.12	13.13
Type II	With other nuclear families (kin or not), one of which defines the phase of the family cycle	9.00	10.21
Type III	Combination of I and II	10.50	2.19
Single-person household	Individual living alone	1.00	.72
Total			99.98

homeworkers in nuclear households within the earlier family cycles. As will be analyzed in Chapter 4, this is connected with the compatibility of homework with child care and other domestic responsibilities; that is, with the gender-based division of labor that assigns such responsibilities to women. It is therefore not surprising that our sample includes a relatively high proportion of young nuclear households, a higher proportion, in fact than the 61.8% found for Mexico City as a whole (García, Muñoz, and Oliveira, 1982). However, women homeworkers here include not only wives from nuclear households but also heads of households and single daughters.

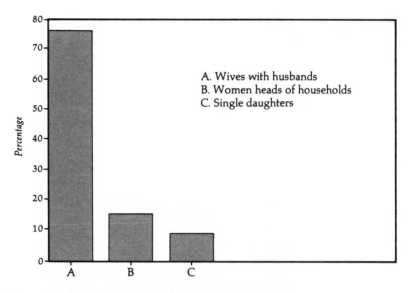

A. Wives with husbands
B. Women heads of households
C. Single daughters

Figure 2.1: *Household Gender Roles of Workers in Homes*

Figure 2.1 shows the breakdown of women interviewed according to their households' gender roles. Women with husbands represent the majority (76.42%) of those interviewed. At the time of fieldwork, 15% were living in consensual marriages, an arrangement viewed as less than socially desirable by the women themselves and most common among the urban subproletariat and people of rural origins. Their ages ranged from 19 to 64, with the greatest concentration in the 21 to 30 and 31 to 40 categories, representing 71% of the total number of wives. Their educational level was low: 60% of the wives had either zero schooling or had very little schooling. The great majority (72%) were either illiterate or had completed only 1 to 3 years of school. As to their migrant status, the majority of the wives (70%) came from rural areas, particularly from the states of Michoacán, Oaxaca, Guerrero, Guanajuato and the estate of Mexico—most of them having arrived in Mexico City during the 1960s and 1970s. Their reasons for migrating were always related to search for employment on the part of their parents, themselves, or their husbands. Nearly 70% of the wives had arrived in Mexico City after age 12; 67% of those arriving in the 12 to 20 age group were single women looking for urban employment.

Heads of households represented 15% of the total in the sample and included older women—71% above 40 at the time of the interviews. Given the low wages from homework, it is not surprising that the percentage of women heads of households in our sample is relatively small, since homework normally constitutes a complementary source of income rather than an adequate source for family subsistence. The educational level of this group was the lowest in the sample; only one of them had completed primary school and, among those that did not complete it, 90% either were illiterate or had 1 to 3 years of schooling. They had migrated from rural areas (62%), and from the states named above; 62% of them arrived at the

Table 2.3 *Household Distribution by Phase of Family Cycle*

Type of Household	Definition	(%)
1. Earlier Phases*		
a) formation	Couple without offspring	2.9
b) expansion	Complete or incomplete nuclear families only, with children under 7	45.9
c) plausible expansion	Complete or incomplete nuclear families with male and/or female offspring between 7 and 17 and 7 and 15 respectively	7.3
2. Advanced Phases**		
a) fission/expansion	Complete or incomplete nuclear families with offspring 18 or above for males and 16 or above for females plus children under 7	13.9
b) fission	The same as above but without children under 7	22.7
c) replacement	Complete or incomplete nuclear families with all offspring 18 or above for male or 16 or above for female	7.3
Total		100.00

*In the case of extended households, the phase is determined by the family nucleus to which the homeworker belongs.

**The ages of 16 for females and 18 for males have been chosen to separate the earlier from the advanced phases as a conventional marriageable age for both sexes in Mexico.

age of 21 or older and were already either heads of households or had husbands. As elsewhere, these women heads of household had to deal with the greatest hardships in terms of daily economic struggle for survival and the heavy burden of nonshared responsibility for bringing up their children and for other domestic problems. This was particularly true for women at the earliest stages of the family cycle who had recently been separated, deserted by their husbands, or widowed. Only two of the women in this category were able to support their household with wages derived exclusively from homework. The rest of them had to resort to other sources of income as well, mostly such personal services as washing and ironing, part-time work in small neighborhood eating houses, or other occasional cash-earning activities. Those who were older or sick had to resort to family help for cash or sharing in an extended household.

Finally, data on daughter homeworkers place them at the opposite end from heads of households in terms of age, education, and migrant status. Their age ranged from 13 to 20 and nearly 60% had concluded primary school education or were attending secondary school; none was illiterate. In terms of their migrant status, only 25% had not been born in Mexico City. We might ask why daughters engage in homework, given better opportunities in the labor market for the more educated and younger females. The reasons given ranged from the use of income from homework to pay for part of their school expenses to a need for replacing the mother in domestic and child care responsibilities (using homework as a way of reconciling the conflicting roles of household and paid production), to dealing with such special problems as physical disability.

Despite variations in our sample, the majority of households were working-class and low-income. Weekly average income, including that from homework and all wages from other household members as reported by the homeworker, was of approximately $2,400 Mexican pesos or US$109;[4] 72% of husbands earned a wage that ranged between the legal minimum of 1,260 Mexican pesos (US$57.27) and twice that amount. Approximately 64% of husbands had stable jobs as wage earners or as owners of small stores, implying that, although we are dealing with sectors of the urban poor, the households in our sample do not belong to the poorest "marginal" population with indirect links to the formal economy.

This is reflected, for example, by indicators of consumption levels: 15% of the families owned their homes, even though the dwellings were very small (1–3 rooms) and in poor condition. Overcrowding was a typical and in some cases severe feature of daily life in most of the households. Practically all homes had radio and television but barely more than 50% in a subsample (N = 56) had refrigerators and only a small percentage owned consumer durables such as washing machines and record players (11.11% and 6.06% respectively in a subsample of 99). In other words, the typical household in our study had a reasonable degree of economic stability to meet basic needs at a low standard of living; in most cases, it required the essential contribution of the wife's wages, however small, to make ends meet and the need for cash was often severe.

Research Methods

From the outset, we viewed our study as "committed research" in the sense of being "for" women rather than "on" women.[5] To the extent that we succeeded, women became subjects rather than objects in our research. Also we saw our interdisciplinary research as a dynamic and dialectical process rather than a way of picturing a static structure. Thus, the final set of questions included in the questionnaires and interview guide was heavily influenced not only by findings in our pilot research but also by changes in our perception of the issues.

Our study relied on data collected through a variety of techniques—including formal and informal intensive interviews and partial participant observation during fieldwork. All 140 women answered a first questionnaire dealing with general information about homework, conditions under which it is carried out, household information, occupational trajectories of the women interviewed, unpaid housework, and the women's perception of their own work and family situation. This questionnaire was agreed on after a two-month pilot study that changed quite radically our initial research framework and questions. For example, it became increasingly clear that our suspicions about the existence of nongarment homework were justified since different types of this work were found. Thus our first questionnaire, oriented towards garment work, was adapted to cover other varieties of homework as well.

A second questionnaire and interview guide, generally taped, was used for a subsample of 53 wives and 7 heads of household. This subsample was chosen for the purpose of focusing on the wives' specific predicament, after realizing their predominance in homework. The second interview dealt with domestic budgets, intrahousehold resource allocation, survival mechanisms, decision-making power, conjugal relations, and norms and values relating to the women's situation as working wives and mothers.

In carrying on these interviews, we visited the homeworkers several times and consulted them whenever doubts and problems of interpretation arose during fieldwork. It was in fact through their patience in explaining why they thought the way they did, and what were the sources of their hesitations and fears, that we began to unlearn our outsiders' view and became attuned to our subjects' horizons and their understanding of reality.

Our study is based on a nonprobabilistic, purposive sample. Due to the underground nature of homework in Mexico, we had no initial information about the universe of homeworkers. Given the illegality of homework and the level of confidentiality required to gather information—particularly on earnings, budgets, and marital relations— it would have been impossible to obtain access to reliable data without the contacts that first provided the ground for developing rapport with the interviewees. These contacts were obtained through a variety of sources that ranged from local health center personnel to school teachers to personal acquaintances. Once a homeworker or several of them were found in a neighborhood, it was possible to find others, either through the same jobber or through friends, relatives, or neighbors. Searching for an initial contact for different types of homework often turned out to be a time-consuming and trying experience. Using much of the time and energy allotted to our fieldwork, this problem resulted in limiting the number of interviews in our sample to fewer than we had planned.

Data on subcontracting above the level of homework was collected through visits to 67 firms of various sizes; formal interviews included managers, technicians, or professionals from each firm. Whenever possible, the visits included a tour of the production process, which for some firms was repeated during the summers of 1981 and 1982. This often allowed for probing of data as well as for gathering information about the firm from its different representatives.

Here too we were not dealing with a random sample, since the list of firms was based on their direct or indirect connections with the homeworkers interviewed. We worked from the bottom up; that is, the jobber or firm distributing homework was the first level of subcontracting visited, and these provided the information for visits to other subcontracting firms. There were exceptions to this sequence; in cases where small firms were reluctant or unwilling to provide information about larger subcontractors, we succeeded, in a few cases, in contacting the larger firms directly, thus gathering information from the top down. Not all subcontracting chains were completed because of some firms' unwillingness to give information or grant interviews.[6] This was particularly true where production was at the borderline of illegality, but it was also encountered in a few large multinational firms. Also, not all types of homework were linked to subcontracting chains; a small number of operations, such as the packing of sunflower seeds, implied only a contract between the producer/distributor and the homeworkers.

Given that the universe of homeworkers in Mexico City is not known, we may ask how extensive homework is in that industrial center. Conceptually, this type of work is part of what is loosely defined as the informal sector. Several studies on this sector have documented its importance in Mexico City; according to one of them (SPP/UCECA, 1979), based on a survey in 1976–77, the percentage of the population in that sector was estimated to be 35.3% of the total labor force. Homework was ignored in the survey probably due to its underground nature and the difficulties of gathering information about it. If it had not been ignored, it could have included only many of the productive units of our study; namely, firms with five workers or less, located at the lower end of the subcontracting chains. The study, however, does not shed any light on the prevalence of homework in Mexico City.

Studies dealing specifically with homework have concentrated on the garment industry (Avelar, 1977; Alonso, 1979; Connolly, 1982). Mexican newspapers also report frequently on the existence of garment-industry homework and denounce the exploitation of seamstresses in sweatshops.[7] It seems clear that homework is a common phenomenon in that industry. Alonso, for example, estimated that for the city of Nezahualcoyotl (de facto, a part of Mexico City), garment homeworkers in 1976 could be found in as many as 10% of the homes. These estimates, although rough, document what seems to be a widespread occurrence in the garment industry. There are also indications that homework can be found in states and locations other than those reported in our study.[8]

There was less information, however, about the not-so-traditional, nongarment homework included here. Practically no information was available about it at the time when our investigation began. It is not possible to draw any conclusions from our research about the prevalence of these types of homework. Yet our data suggest that the use of homework for non-garment industrial work was on the increase, at least at the time of our fieldwork. Although it is difficult to make generalizations from our study, there is no reason to believe that our sample is unrepresentative. In any case, our findings open a window to a complex reality that is little known, raising a series of interesting questions that can be answered only by further research.

(Above) Doña M. answering questions while working. *(Right)* Doña M. sorting out metal pieces used in making batteries.

Doña T. outside her home in a *vecindad*.

Flowers and bushes outside a shack: girls with sad eyes facing the future.

(*Above*) Outskirts of Mexico City: crowded spaces with tangles of electrical wires and TV antennas. (*Left*) An unpaved street showing the ravages of the rainy season.

(Above) Makeshift homes and unpaved streets. *(Right)* A child enjoying the morning sun.

Three

Subcontracting Links and the Dynamics of Women's Employment

This chapter offers a macroframework within which to situate industrial homework by analyzing the shift of production through various subcontracting levels. It provides also the framework for analysis of how subcontracting affects women's employment. The need to present this picture became gradually more obvious as interviews with homeworkers proceeded, and questions about their relationship with the wider economy reappeared. Where did their work originate in the last resort? What were the key points of articulation between the formal economy and the semilegal or underground activities that typified homework? What were the reasons behind subcontracting and the employment dynamics that it generated, and what were the implications for labor—women workers in particular?

The first part of this chapter concentrates on the mechanics of subcontracting. Our sample of firms allows us to illustrate connections among different productive units ranging from the piecework carried out in the household to small workshops, middle-size factories, and large national and multinational firms. The second part of the chapter analyzes the tendency for women's employment to increase among the firms studied and explores the reasons behind this. Included here is an analysis of the feminization of some tasks and job categories, and of the use made by employers of "gender traits"—assumed or actual—in hiring women workers.

Subcontracting Links

The literature on industrial subcontracting distinguishes between two types of business arrangements: one that contracts out production without providing raw materials and another that provides raw materials and other inputs (Watanabe, 1983). The first is often called horizontal and the second vertical subcontracting. In Mexico, vertical subcontracting is normally referred to as *maquila,* or "domestic maquila" in the case of homework. It consists generally in processing work or production for another firm under very specific contract arrangements, with design and other product characteristics included. It affects mostly labor-intensive tasks resulting from fragmentation of the production process so that different parts can be carried out by different firms. In Mexico City, maquila does not usually represent export-processing activities, but largely production for the domestic market and therefore quite different from the export-oriented subcontracting prevalent along the US-Mexican border.

Vertical subcontracting was found to predominate in our sample of firms. In most cases, particularly for the smaller firms and for homework, this type of subcontracting amounts to a putting-out system that, as Murray (1983, p. 81) has defined for the case of Italy, is "the transfer of work formerly done within a firm to another firm, an artisan workshop or domestic outworkers." Table 3.1 shows the distribution of firms by industry and size. The relatively small proportion of large and medium-size firms in the sample is due to the pyramid structure of subcontracting, where one large firm deals with a large number of subcontractors, even for the same type of product.[1] Most subcontractors produce exclusively for other firms. Yet there are cases—particularly among medium-size firms—in which they also produce final goods for the market (for example, small toy manufacturers who produce their own toys and also subcontract work from larger firms). Thus, although 40.3% of the firms in the sample sold directly to the market (i.e., they represent the final level of production) 25.4% among them also produced intermediate goods for other firms. Overall, 75% of the firms in the sample were engaged in some form of subcontracted production of intermediate goods.

Among the industries listed in table 3.1, garment work represents the type whose traditional subcontracting, either to workshops or to homework, was well known. Of the other kinds of work, although maquilla may be new and involve new products, none included the type of subcontracting related to high-tech production for export typical of the border industries. In all but two cases, production was geared towards the domestic market and, in these cases, the amount exported was very small.

The importance of non-Mexican capital in generating these link-

Table 3.1   *Number of Firms by Industry and Size*

	Number of workers in firm						
	19 or fewer	*20–99*	*100–299*	*300–999*	*1000+*	*Total*	*%*
Electrical/							
electronics	3	2	2	3	—	10	14.9
Consumer durables	1	—	1	3	5	10	14.9
Cosmetics	1	2	—	2	1	6	8.9
Plastics	6	9	2	0	—	17	25.4
Metal	2	3	—	3	—	8	11.9
Garment/Textiles	5	1	—	—	1	7	10.5
Other*	5	3	—	—	1	9	13.4
Total	23	20	5	11	8	67	99.99
%of total	34.3	29.8	7.5	16.4	12.0	100.0	

*Glass, toys, food and decoration of glass and plastic containers.

ages is quite clear: although only 11 firms (16.4%) were multinational, more than 69% of the remaining firms were under subcontracts with multinationals. Figure 3.1 illustrates a typical subcontracting chain of four levels that ranges from a multinational capital to homework. Production in this case is subcontracted from a large multinational to increasingly smaller firms—the last level in this case being homework distributed from a workshop operating illegally in the basement of the owner's home. Employment at the last two levels is occasional and follows the patterns associated with the informal sector. Workers in firm C were paid minimum wage without fringe benefits, while homeworkers received an average wage equivalent to one-third of the minimum.

Watanabe (1983) argues that subcontracting in Mexico tends to be limited to two, or a maximum of three, levels involving mostly large and middle-size firms, with a low degree of involvement on the part of small units. As a result, he argues, Mexican subcontracting, unlike Japanese, does not take the form of a pyramid with a small number of large firms at the top and a large number of medium and small-size firms at the bottom. Instead, the Mexican structure narrows down in the second and third levels like a diamond-cut. However, his sample of forty-six firms was mainly in metal-engineering subcontracting from the automobile industry. It included also, as our study did, some producers of electronic and electrical appliances. Our observations differ from his in that we found three and four levels of subcontracting to be common. This disparity is probably due not only to the different industries studied but also to the cases in our sample in which production was either underground or at the borderline of legality, thus adding one or two levels to a subcontracting chain. For example, levels 3 and 4 in figure 3.1 represented the type of units not present in Watanabe's study. As a result, the structure in our sample is more like a pyramid—with a larger number of units as firm-size decreases, with some narrowing only at the level of medium-size firms in the 100 to 299 workers' category (see figure 3.2).[2]

The pyramid structure just described does not of course imply that Mexican subcontracting resembles the Japanese system using numerous, highly productive small firms on which the model of low

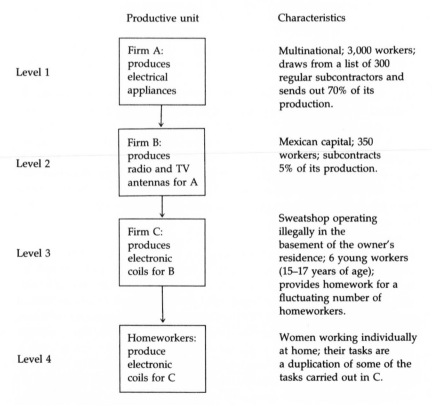

	Productive unit	Characteristics
Level 1	Firm A: produces electrical appliances	Multinational; 3,000 workers; draws from a list of 300 regular subcontractors and sends out 70% of its production.
Level 2	Firm B: produces radio and TV antennas for A	Mexican capital; 350 workers; subcontracts 5% of its production.
Level 3	Firm C: produces electronic coils for B	Sweatshop operating illegally in the basement of the owner's residence; 6 young workers (15–17 years of age); provides homework for a fluctuating number of homeworkers.
Level 4	Homeworkers: produce electronic coils for C	Women working individually at home; their tasks are a duplication of some of the tasks carried out in C.

Figure 3.1: *Typical Subcontracting chain*

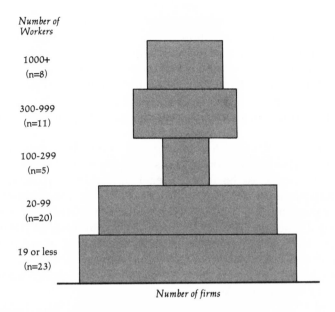

Figure 3.2: *Number of Firms According to Size*

labor cost relies. It does imply, however, that subcontracting in Mexico has penetrated spheres of production not previously documented and that there is at work an incipient subcontracting system performing functions similar to those attributed to the Japanese model.

From the perspective of the literature that emphasizes the formal/informal sector division and the articulation between those sectors (Portes, 1983), it seems clear that the key points in this articulation are at level 3 (or its equivalent in other chains). These are the points of contact between the legal and illegal operations and/or between the formal and informal activities—depending on the definition of these sectors (see Chapter 4). This articulation takes a variety of forms that can be summarized, according to our sample, as three basic types. The first, *direct articulation*, corresponds to cases in which a regular firm sends out production to informal settings without the use of intermediaries. This procedure can be found among small firms that have direct contact with illegal workshops or even homeworkers; it applies rarely to large firms. An exception in our sample was a large textile factory of 1200 workers that was giving piece work to prisoners and to nuns in charge of an orphanage.

The second type, *mediated articulation*, takes place through a jobber. The mediator's function consists merely in establishing the connection between the legal and illegal operations. No production takes place at the jobber's level although, in many ways, he or she performs an indirect supervisory role for activities that are subcontracted. The jobber, in many cases, also performs other functions such as distribution, transportation, and gathering of materials and products.

Finally, *mixed articulation* takes place when the connection between legal and illegal production is centered in a workshop where production combines legal and illegal operations. To illustrate: a workshop produces plastic parts for different firms: the store front is a legal operation; i.e., paying taxes, minimum wages, and meeting other legal requirements. At the back of the building, an oscillating number of women are hired to do plastic polishing at wages below the minimum and without fringe benefits. The workshop also sends work to homeworkers in the neighborhood—depending upon the amount of work available.

In all cases, however, this articulation is part of a highly integrated system of production segmented into different levels and of an overall process of accumulation that encompasses all of the levels. In this sense the conceptualization of the formal/ informal dichotomy is not very appropriate—at least insofar as the two sectors are viewed as separate and independent of each other.

Reasons for Subcontracting and Firm Hierarchies

Why and under what circumstances do firms send out production? What are the factors affecting this process? In the case of a country like Italy during the 1970s, decentralization of production, of which subcontracting is part, has contituted a global strategy to relocate production—as a response to a variety of factors ranging from industrial relations to technology and state legislation.[3] For each country, however, the approach to subcontracting will depend ultimately on the factors that affect profitability. Although much more needs to be known about subcontracting (in Mexico and elsewhere), our data make some generalizations possible not only regarding these questions but also concerning the types of output affected.

Among the reasons given by firms for subcontracting, the most prevalent was the *lowering of labor costs*—the first reason in 79% of

Table 3.2   *Average Monthly Wages for Manual Workers by Subcontracting Level, 1981*

Levels	Chain A	Chain B		Chain C	
	Wages*	No. of workers	Wages	No. of workers	Wages
1	12,000	2,500	11,000	25,000	11,000
2	8,500	50	5,880	20	3,000
				(illegal workshop)	
3	5,880	5	1,776	n.h.	
		(homework)			
4	1,776	—		—	
Wage ratio	6.75:1	6.19:1		3.67:1	

*Wages are in 1981 Mexican pesos—23 pesos to $1.00.
n.h. = no homework in this chain.

the cases. This is because savings can result from wage disparities existing among various subcontracting levels. As illustrated in table 3.2, the ratio of average monthly wages (not including fringe benefits) for manual workers between the firm at level 1 in chain A and homeworkers (corresponding to figure 3.1 and to tasks of plastic polishing) was estimated to be 6.75:1. Chains B and C further illustrate these wage scales, in this case for two chains in the cosmetics industry of two and three production levels and wage ratios of 6:19 and 3.67:1 respectively. The largest drop in wages takes place at the point when production goes underground. (If this level was eliminated, the wage ratio for chains A, and B would be 2.04, and 1.87 respectively.)

It can be argued that productivity may be lower at lower levels of subcontracting and that wage ratios therefore may reflect productivity ratios. Unfortunately, there are no available data to evaluate this issue. Given the labor-intensive character of subcontracting, however, there is no reason to believe that significant disparities in productivity exist, particularly for the more unskilled tasks. Even if there were some disparities, the resort to subcontracting indicates that wage differences more than compensate for productivity differences. To the extent that productivity is the same and wages lower—or that wages more than compensate for lower productivity—labor costs are reduced and profits increased, implying a higher rate of exploitation.

From this perspective, subcontracting is clearly a shift of production in search of cheap labor. Following Braverman (1974), it can be argued that this process of decentralization responds to the dictates of the Babbage principle: namely, the reduction of labor costs through changes in the division of labor. This is made possible by the fragmentation of tasks and the use of workers associated with lower skill and lower wages (deskilling). Although Braverman focuses on the division of labor within the capitalist firm, this approach can be applied to an analysis of the division of labor among firms—as in the case of subcontracting.

The literature on the new international division of labor, for example, has made use of this analysis to understand processes of fragmentation/relocation on a world scale (Brighton Labor Process Group, 1977; Fröbel et al, 1980). To be sure, emphasis on the Babbage principle does not exclude the possibility that firms can lower production costs by other means, particularly through technological change.[4] Whether firms resort to subcontracting or to the introduction of new technologies will depend on the relative price of labor and capital investment and the ongoing dialectic between capital and labor. But it seems clear that subcontracting responds to a cheap-labor strategy of lowering costs.

From a different perspective, it can be argued that subcontracting takes advantage of an existing labor-market fragmentation in which the most clear-cut division is between the legal and the underground economy with its corresponding sharp drop in wages, disappearance of fringe benefits, and deterioration of working conditions. The literature referring to employment in the Third World tends to pose this fragmentation within the framework of a formal/informal sector division, to which we will return in Chapter 4.

In addition to lowering labor costs, sending production out is done for other reasons. These reasons, as provided by firms, can be summarized as follows:

A. Production of parts is highly specialized and can be obtained at lower cost by firms concentrating on a few products. This is the case particularly when the number of parts required by the subcontracting firm is relatively small and does not justify the investment required by internal production. In other words, the objective is the lowering of fixed costs.

B. When production is cyclical or unstable, subcontracting offers the possibility of transferring the risk and avoiding the problems caused by fluctuations of production such as layoffs and the costs associated with a temporary increase in production. To illustrate, a small subcontractor working for large companies in the cosmetics industry listed from 30 to 60 workers as the oscillating number of employees working according to availability of contracts. Only the supervisory and clerical personnel had permanent contracts.[5] Similarly, the toy and garment industries offered numerous examples of this type of subcontracting.

C. In the case of family businesses or medium-size firms controlled by an owner/manager, the avoidance of growth was a factor mentioned for keeping control of the enterprise. As one manager put it, "further growth would require a more sophisticated system of accounting, a larger bureaucracy and the loss of control on my part." Faced with a trade-off between a high degree of control and further expansion, this type of entrepreneur seems to be opting for control. Hence, the permanence of firms in what Garofoli (1978) has called the "peripheral" area of the economy (small, specialized units of production) which differs from the "central" area of large firms and the "marginal" area of informal and relatively "underdeveloped" productive units.

D. A related factor in the development of subcontracting is the avoidance of labor conflicts and, in particular, of unionization among small firms whose number of workers is about to exceed 20, the limit above which unionization is required by Mexican law. The most explicit case of this type was a family business subdivided in five separate legal entities under the ownership of different family members, each with fewer than 20 workers.

Other factors mentioned as influencing decisions to subcontract were transportation costs, the ease with which tasks can be fragmented from the overall production process, and low requirements of quality control. The extent to which subcontracting takes place, therefore, varies substantially with the weight of these factors, even for the same firm. For example, in 1981 a large multinational firm producing household appliances was subcontracting an average of 80% of its production in Brazil and 60% in Mexico.[6]

The overall picture emerging from a close observation of subcontracting links is that of a hierarchy of firms along the lines of a pyramid. Although segmented by subcontracting levels, its interconnected units form a continuum in the productive process. In addition to wage differentials, this hierarchy can be observed in other terms, relating to working conditions, access to financial and other resources, levels of technology, and work stability. Working conditions—in terms of such factors as working space, light, services available for workers, safety measures, and temperature levels—deteriorate as we move down the pyramid. With similar motives (while restrictions against firing workers in Mexico are quite severe) many firms make frequent use of the legalized procedure of hiring workers for just 28 days, after which they do not need to guarantee employment; for many workers, this results in intermittent or occasional employment.

The hierarchy has other dimensions, such as the dependency of medium- and small-size firms on larger enterprises and of Mexican firms on multinational capital to obtain production contracts. As mentioned earlier, the great bulk of subcontracting in our sample ultimately came from multinational firms—exceptions being mainly in the garment, food, textile, and some metal-sector industries. A close look at these links presents, in fact, a view of the form of dependent development of newly industrialized countries in the Third World, which Mexico typifies (Evans, 1979; MacEwan, 1985). As an engineer from a firm of 50 workers producing mainly auto parts put it, "we need the multinationals to generate work and employment." Large firms tend to enjoy monopsony power, and there is intense competition among small subcontractors to obtain work from such firms. The result is often resentment on the part of the smaller firms against what a manager called "the princely tendencies of the large firms that can impose their own terms."

Finally, subcontracting implies also that a given firm at the top of the pyramid has a number of options, beyond the internal structure of the firm, regarding its division of labor and location of production. That is, subcontracting expands the mechanisms by which the firm's demand for labor can be met and increases the range of choices regarding the conditions under which labor is hired. To put it differently, subcontracting amounts to the firm's access to a more flexible labor supply. An obvious parallel exists between these processes and the "informalization" of production resulting from the growth of the underground economy during recent years in the more industrialized countries (Sassen-Koob, 1982). Yet theoretical models dealing with the division of labor within firms, including Braverman's, tend to emphasize internal hierarchies only. Our analysis implies that these models need to take into consideration the expanded options offered by the *macro* hierarchy of firms generated from subcontracting arrangements.

The Dynamics of Women's Employment

In this section we analyze the implications of subcontracting in terms of sex composition of the work force. There are two aspects to this analysis. One is the extent to which we find in our own sample of firms the tendency observed in many Third-World industrialization processes towards a growing employment of women. There is, for example, increasing evidence that the latest phase in the internationalization of capital since the mid-1960s has resulted in the employment of a high proportion of women (Fröbel et al. 1980). A high concentration of women workers can be found not only in the more traditional industries such as garments and textiles; women are also employed increasingly in the electrical/electronics, metal, chemical, and other industries (Safa, 1981; Elson and Pearson, 1981; Nash and Fernández-Kelly, 1983).

Some of these studies have called particular attention to the concentration of women workers in the export-oriented industries in free-trade zones and areas, such as the US/Mexican border, with a heavy concentration of foreign investment. Similarly, authors dealing with decentralization of production in industrialized countries have pointed out the tendency towards the employment of women, particularly in putting-out industries (Goddard, 1981; Allen, 1981; Garofoli, 1983). The question here is the extent to which this trend towards an increase in female employment can be observed also in an industrial center such as Mexico City, which is basically oriented towards the national market, and in which national capital plays an important role, coexisting with multinational investment.

The second aspect of this analysis is the need to examine patterns of women's employment and reasons behind the feminization of some tasks. We will see that the proportion of women in the workforce increased as we moved down the lower segments of the subcontracting pyramid. Given that, within some firms, there was a tendency to replace men with women in certain tasks, a subsequent question is why and how this is happening? At the theoretical level, labor-market segmentation analysis, as suggested earlier, offers a useful framework for understanding wage differentials and the employment of women associated with subcontracting. This type of analysis has been proved useful to analyze segmentation by gender, and evidence suggests that job segregation and differences in the characteristics of jobs normally assigned to women are important factors in explaining gender asymmetry in the labor market (Steven-

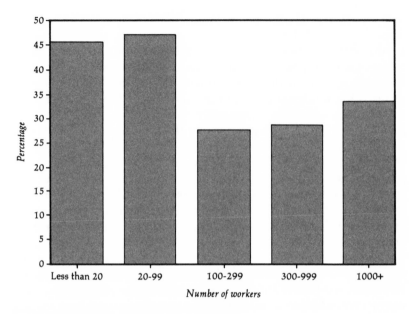

Figure 3.3: *Proportion of Women by Firm Size*

son, 1985; Blau, 1975, Ferber and Spaeth, 1984). Segmentation analysis, however, offers a *description* rather than an *explanation* of women's labor-market conditions; describing where and under what conditions women are located in the labor market does not necessarily explain why.[7]

In order to pursue the question beyond a description of women's location in the subcontracting chains, our research involved close observation, whenever possible, of each firm's labor process. In observing the organization of production, we kept in mind the theoretical framework associated with Braverman (1974) and the literature that has either elaborated or criticized his approach (Brighton Labor Process Group, 1977; Elger, 1979; Edwards, 1979). Our emphasis is on the analysis of how the cheap-labor strategy of subcontracting unfolds with respect to gender differentiation; to what extent is there a gendering of jobs and occupations and, if so, how does it take place? Is there deskilling in the process of substituting women for men? What are the firms' motives for hiring women? How are women's lower wages justified? What type of characteristics differentiate women and men as workers?

Within our sample of firms, we found two major tendencies. One has to do with the percentage of women employed by firm size. As shown in figure 3.3, this percentage is higher, on average, among firms with fewer than 100 workers than among the larger firms. That is, the smaller firms tend to be more feminized, and this feminization was practically complete for homework. The apparent exception was in the case of firms with more than 1000 workers. The ratio of women to men in this case, however, is very likely to be overestimated because of the type of industries included. Some of the large firms to which we were unable to gain access belonged to the automobile and metal sectors; the low percentage of women employed in these sectors would have lowered our figures for the group of firms of over 999 workers. Overall, the trend shows the percentage of women employed to be higher as employment becomes progressively less formal and as it approaches and crosses the borderline of illegality.

On the other hand, we found a tendency for women's employment to increase at each level of subcontracting and firm size. Table 3.3 shows that over 40% of the firms reported a tendency to employ a higher proportion of women during the three preceding years or under plans current at the time of fieldwork. The trend towards an increase in female employment was found particularly among firms whose work force was already 30% or more female. The higher ratio of women in firms with fewer than 100 workers, implies a further intensification of feminization of these firms. In some cases, this trend was taking place rapidly. To illustrate, a firm of 50 workers

Table 3.3   *Female Employment*

(1) *% of women in the firm's workforce*	*(2)* *Number of firms**	*(3)* *Number of workers employed*	*(4)* *% of all firms reporting that report an increase in the proportion of women employed***
10% or less	12	2,892	25.0
10–29%	9	2,154	33.3
30–49%	12	4,639	41.6
50% or more	26	4,085	53.8
Total	59	13,770	

*For firms that registered an increase in the proportion of women employed between the summers of 1981 and 1982, the table refers to the figures given in 1982.
**During the past three years or under current plans.

producing and assembling plastic goods under subcontracting arrangements had shifted from 25% to 75% women workers in one
year. This change had been parallel to the restructuring of the labor
process with the introduction of more automatic machines and a
moving line for assembly work. The manager expressed optimism
about the employment of women. As he noted, the trend was new;
this was also pointed out by other observers. [8]

It is interesting to note that this trend and the corresponding
emergent favorable attitude of management toward the employment
of women was found also in industries such as metal that previously had employed very few women. For example, a metal firm (a previous multinational now controlled by Mexican capital) had shifted
from zero to 20% female employment in a period of three years. The
shift had taken place after a series of tests showed women to have
higher productivity than men. In particular, they were found to be
more productive in assembly tasks requiring "a high degree of concentration, patience, and physical immobility for long periods of
time." Similarly, women were clustered in these type of tasks where
they replaced men. Women were also found to be more productive
in some types of supervisory work such as quality control. Yet,
management had decided against replacing men with women because "men did not take well the directives coming from women in
positions of quality control". Another example was that of a
manufacturer of electrical equipment with ambitious plans for expansion as a result of joining ventures with an Italian multinational:
from employing no women (other than clerical personnel), the firm
had plans to begin hiring them, particularly in a new plant of 600
workers outside of Mexico City. One year after the first interview,
the old plant (of more than 100 workers) did not employ women as
production workers but the new plant had a 40% female workforce.

Several related issues require further investigation: why women's employment is increasing, what factors affect this trend, and
what types of jobs women are filling. To begin with the last question, it is useful to consider three types of job categories. In the first,
women replace men without any change in the nature of the job. To
illustrate, in a cosmetics multinational of 2,500 workers, women
have been replacing men in accounting, sales, and middle management; for most of these jobs, there appears to be no change in job
content and degree of responsibility associated with it. In some
cases, however, a subtle distinction has been introduced when the
same job is subject to a redistribution of supervisory tasks. In such
cases when jobs are feminized, a new supervisor has been appoint-

ed and the relative responsibility and ranking of the job has decreased.

Second, there are instances in which the nature of the job changes through the introduction of new technology or the restructuring of the labor process, or both. Introduction of automatic plastic injection machines to replace manual machines is often accompanied by the placement of women in care of the machine, a job that had been previously performed by men. In the same way, introduction of a moving line or conveyor in the assembling of consumer durables is for many firms an opportunity to replace men with women. In both cases, there is a degree of deskilling taking place (see below) even when the change is not accompanied with a lower wage.

Third, there are jobs defined as female from the outset; this has been the case in the traditional female industries such as garment and textiles but can also be observed in new industries such as electronics. In these instances, the increase in the employment of women results from the dynamics of subcontracting generating new jobs rather than to women being substituted for men.

In all three cases, gendering of jobs and skills is taking place. However, the question of why women are hired needs to be investigated further. Feminists have often pointed out that women's work in the labor market tends to concentrate in the production of goods and services that had previously been provided within the household or in tasks that are a projection of their child-rearing activities. This might be the case for garment and textile work as well as for jobs in the service sector. Given that hiring can be observed in traditional and nontraditional women's tasks, however, more general conceptualization of the reasons behind the increase in women's employment is necessary. Our data lead us to conclude that there are several types of factors behind this increase, and that they can be classified within two general categories: 1) women's lower wages, and 2) assumed characteristics of women workers.

Lower Wages for Women

Given the same productivity on the part of men and women, lower wages for women may be the result of wage discrimination or occupational segregation. In our study, wage discrimination—unequal pay for equal work—was difficult to detect because interviewees (mostly middle-to-top management, other professionals and technicians, or heads of workshops and owners of small firms) would not report it. However, there were indirect indications of its existence. To illustrate, an executive from the personnel department of a large cosmetics firm pointed out that "for each job, there is a minimum and a maximum salary—depending upon seniority, productivity and other factors. Women tend toward the minimum and men toward the maximum; women, in particular, see their salary as a complement to family income and accept lower pay." Similar situations were detected in other firms, affecting particularly young women workers. The extent of this type of discrimination, however, can not be systematically documented from our data.

In contrast to the limitations encountered in the reporting of wage discrimination, the clustering of women in specific jobs of relatively low pay was widespread and commonly reported because, firms tend to see the lower pay as justifiable for a variety of reasons—lower skill and fewer requirements for physical strength were reasons most commonly given. For example, a large firm producing electrical appliances had women clustered in the assembly of parts for the production of irons, fans, radio and TV sets. The assembling of parts and the finishing of irons was done by women and fans by both men and women, although performing different tasks. Radios and TV sets had women assembling the minute parts—coils, and wires attached to the screen, for example—while men concentrated on the final stages of assembly.

The assembly of larger electrical appliances, such as refrigerators and washing machines, was entirely men's work. Women usually worked sitting down, within very limited and crowded spaces, while men's working areas were more spacious and allowed physical mobility. Although all the work was assembly, the clustering of tasks by gender was associated with lower pay for women.

This type of wage differential was prevalent in firms where women and men were segregated in clusters performing different jobs. It was consistently justified by pointing out that men's tasks required greater physical strength and mechanical knowledge. Yet, when asked why they hired women for assembly work (and for other tasks), employers stressed women's "greater dexterity" and "manual ability". These characteristics, while clearly recognized as skills, were not seen as deserving the same reward as physical strength and mechanical ability. This points to a core problem in the male/female wage gap: *the artificiality of skill definition.* By what criteria are some skills ranked as superior to others? Why is it that women's jobs are defined in such a way that they tend to be placed at the bottom of skill hierarchies and below male jobs? Our analysis suggests that these criteria need to be scrutinized—very much along lines leading to comparable-worth criteria in the United States.

Lower wages for women are also associated with part-time or intermittent full-time employment, both of which are more prevalent at the lower levels of subcontracting. Homework is the most prominent example of highly unstable female work that is also consistently the lowest paid. Temporary and intermittent employment, such as that based on twenty-eight-day contracts, also tends to fall heavily on women, particularly those who are young and single. [9]

To summarize, the increase in female employment associated with lower wages can take place mainly through three types of changes: a) the shifting of production to lower subcontracting levels or labor-market segments; b) the restructuring of the production process and changes in the nature of jobs leading to redefinition of new job clusters as female; c) defining tasks as female in new industries, such as electronic coil making. All three types of changes were at work in our sample of subcontracting and offer the most plausible explanation for the increase in women's employment.

Assumed Characteristics of Women Workers

When asked about the reasons for hiring women, firm representatives hardly mentioned lower wages. Instead, they referred to specific qualities of women as workers. Table 3.4 shows the breakdown of the most frequent answers to the question "What advantages do you see in hiring women?" Each of these answers needs some clarification. First, the most common example of reliability was women's lower rate of absenteeism, particularly on Mondays when absenteeism among male workers is very high because of weekend drunkenness: a minority of employers mentioned an absentee rate

Table 3.4   *Reasons Reported by Firms for Hiring Women (Most Frequent Answers)*

Reported characteristics	% of firms
1. Reliability and work stability	47.4
2. Careful manual work	27.8
3. Discipline and patience	21.4
4. Ability to follow orders	15.9
5. Productivity	4.5
6. Less troublesome	3.8

as high as 30%, but the problem was mentioned in many cases. In the electronics industry, turnover rates are reported also to be lower among women (Bancomer, 1981). Some employers mentioned that single mothers are among their "best workers" because their responsibility as heads of households implies that they cannot rely on anybody else for family subsistence (even when they may rely on the extended family for child care).

Second, "more careful manual work" mostly referred to the handling of objects: when assembly work is involved, women are said to have more patience and greater dexterity in meticulous work and handling small parts. This is of course the traditional nimble-fingers argument that was alive and well among our sample of respondents as well as elsewhere in Mexico. In the June 1981 newsletter published by one of the largest Mexican banks, the argument goes as far as to affirm (with no evidence) that women's "dexterity in both hands is 75% greater than men's" (Bancomer, 1981). This, argued in relation to women's assembly work in the electronics industry—where 80% of the workforce is female—is written in the spirit of new discovery of the advantages to hiring women workers.

Third, with regard to discipline, patience, and ability to follow orders, the answers given clustered around two types of examples, one being that women more than men are able to sit for long periods of time without becoming restless. The other was that women tend to be less mechanically inclined and do not touch the machines when they break down, thereby reducing the risk of damaging equipment or slowing down the production process. This implies that with the confinement of mechanical knowledge to a supervisor, control over the machine and the labor process becomes more centralized, suggesting that, in this case, there is an element of deskilling in the process of substituting women for men—the new worker being preferred because she does not exercise the same degree of mechanical control over the machine. A process of centralization of knowledge is therefore taking place, very much along the lines described by Braverman, with the feminization of this type of task resulting both from technical factors and from the assumptions made by employers about women workers.

Fourth, although the proportion of firms that mentioned women's higher productivity is small, this answer is of particular interest in terms of breaking gender stereotypes. It can also explain the cases in which the replacement of men with women did not, according to the firm, imply a lower wage.

Finally, women are said to be less troublesome than men in terms of demands concerning wages and working conditions and in their involvement with union activity. Although only a few employers mentioned this factor, the information gathered is likely to be biased because questions dealing with unions were usually a source of tension in the interview. In any case, this factor, together with women's self-discipline and tendency to follow orders, has much in common with the stereotype of women as "submissive and docile workers."

These answers provide, on the one hand, an *explanation* why women are preferred in general or viewed as particularly suited for some jobs. On the other hand, the answers may be viewed as a *rationalization* for placing women in specific tasks and job clusters—the real reason for hiring them being their lower wages. In both cases, the responses reflect common stereotypes about women, or "gender traits" resulting from the social construction of gender in a patriarchal society. The answers raise the question also as to whether these are *actual* or *perceived* characteristics.

A question remaining about the increase in women's employment has to do with why it is taking place in this particular period of Mexican development. Although, it is not possible to generalize from this study, on the demand side our data point toward two reasons. The first is the need to tap new sources of cheap labor to lower labor costs, particularly in a period of economic crisis. This would of course apply to labor-intensive maquila production that typifies our subcontracting chains. Second, a trickle-down effect seems to be at work, resulting from the increasing employment of women by multinational firms in Mexico and elsewhere. As mentioned earlier, firm representatives pointed to the successful employment of women elsewhere to explain their own decisions to hire them—suggesting the existence of an emulating mechanism. [10]

On the supply side, at least two factors seem to be at work. One is that women's work outside of the household is becoming more acceptable, as the traditional opposition to women's paid work, especially in the case of married women, has subsided. As the female head of personnel in a large cosmetics firm put it, "the taboo of not employing married women has practically disappeared." [11] The other is that in a period of economic crisis and high unemployment, women's paid work becomes part of family strategies of income pooling. This is clearly the case for homework, as argued throughout this book, and there is no reason to believe that the same strategy does not apply to work outside of the home.

Women's Employment and the Social Construction of Gender

In this section, we explore the use of gender in the workplace as a source of differentiation between men and women workers. We have seen that employers point to characteristics attributed specifically to women to explain or rationalize the hiring of women for specific jobs. These gender traits may be acquired through a long process of socialization or gender formation—ranging from learning to work with nimble fingers by sewing and embroidering at home to being socialized to please and serve, follow orders, and accept subordinate positions. Because they are socially acquired, such characteristics are not natural or universal but specific to a given society, race, or ethnic group and affected by other factors such as class and level of education; they derive from ideological constructs and can obviously change through time. In addition, and as suggested earlier, gender traits may be actual or perceived. Women who have learned to use sewing machines at home as part of their training can translate this knowledge into actual skills at the work place. The important question is what this use of gendered skills implies for women as workers. On the other hand, gender traits may be perceived or falsely assumed, without corresponding to an actual differential skill between men and women. That women are more disciplined or less troublesome as workers may be an example of an assumed trait. As other authors have argued, women's docility may be a mirage that can disappear even in the face of authoritarian structures (Heyzer, 1982).

To illustrate how gender traits can be used in the work place, table 3.5 summarizes what our analysis suggests in terms of correspondence between gender formation and the assignment of women to specific tasks and positions. Given the fluidity of gender formation and the continuous restructuring of the production process, this correspondence should not be viewed as unidirectional or static. First, gender traits can be used as an ideological tool working in opposite directions: what, under specific circumstances, justifies calling a given task a "female job" or a given occupation a "female occupation" may change over time or across cultures and economic conditions. History has showed repeatedly that a high level of unemployment, or the return of men from war, for example, can be used as justification for male employment as long as women are viewed as having their primary area of concentration in the household.[12] Second, gender can be used and reinforced at the workplace but it can also, as Elson and Pearson (1981) have argued, be decomposed or broken down. In the first case, gender is used to intensify the asymmetry or discriminatory treatment between the sexes—as when a job is feminized while its relative wage decreases. In the second, gender asymmetry diminishes or gender categories break down as in cases of equal pay for equal work or women's penetra-

Table 3.5   *Gender Traits and Women's Jobs*

Socially Acquired Gender Traits	*Use of Gender Traits by Firms*
1. Concentration of women in reproductive activities; work outside of the household viewed as secondary for women, with dependency on a male income-earner as the norm.	a. Women's income viewed as complementary and not primary; lower wages for women justified by employers and incorporated in women's expectations. b. Part-time and short-term employment more likely among women.
2. Manual dexterity passed on among women from generation to generation: sewing, lacemaking, embroidery, arts and crafts.	Manual dexterity used in female jobs—assembling, plastic polishing, garment work—and by many industries: electronics, textiles, metals, cosmetics, garments.
3. Household activities are tedious, repetitive, and, in poor households, done in crowded spaces; this requires discipline, ability to deal with frustration, commitment, and persistence.	a. Assembling of small parts is tedious and repetitive, and done within crowded spaces. b. Women are hired because they are less restless than men: "they can sit down for longer periods of time."
4. Patriarchal households and schools teach women to be obedient and to follow orders; inititative and assertiveness become more a male than a female trait.	a. Women are hired because they are assumed to follow orders better than men. b. Women are placed in subordinate positions in a hierarchical labor process. c. Women are assumed to be less active in unions.
5. Cultural and gender socialization in Mexico has resulted in a higher incidence of drunkenness among men.	Women preferred because men's rate of absenteeism on Mondays is very high.

tion of male jobs. This phenomemon in turn is likely to affect gender relations in other spheres such as the household; that is, the interaction between the two is dialectical.

The following quote from an economist in the sales section of a home appliances firm with 250 workers provides a poignant example of how gender is reinforced at the workplace:

> Women are at lower levels in production and are paid less because employers understand that their wages are for their individual needs whereas a man has to cover more expenses, particularly if he is married. There are few women who can move beyond the level of unskilled work; a woman has the burden of her children and has no time to get an education to be promoted. For promotions we look for men. It is assumed that a woman is dependent, even if only from a psychological point of view. Given that she has no time to educate and advance herself, she knows that she cannot aspire to more. Women's opportunity to distinguish themselves depends also on their beauty; a beautiful young woman working on a conveyor line might become a secretary because of her looks. A young woman better prepared but less beautiful will find that promotion more difficult and she will have to compensate by greater efficiency in the job. In men we only look for efficiency and loyalty.

This statement indicates that such gender traits as beauty can take material forms such as a higher wage and promotion. Gender, therefore, is imbedded with work and integrated in the hierarchical structure of production. To put it differently, an integration between ideological and material processes takes place. In this sense we agree with Cockburn (1981) that gender differences and their corresponding relations of domination and subordination are created at work as well as at home and in other spheres of interaction. This leads to the conclusion suggested in Chapter 1 that men and women do not have an identical relationship to the means of production because gender has an impact on the conditions under which workers are incorporated into the labor process and these conditions, in turn, have an impact on gender.

In a hierarchical labor process such as that generated by a capitalist organization of production, criteria need to be designed to assign workers to the different echelons of the labor structure. While such criteria as educational credentials, experience, and seniority are conventionally accepted without much questioning, use of gender (or race) is viewed as discriminatory unless accompanied by some form of rationalization. This is the function that the use of gender traits can play; i.e., they provide a basis for this rationalization by suggesting an association, even if a socially constructed one, between specific jobs and the skills attributed to men and women. This does not mean, however, that women play the role of passive victims or that contradictions do not emerge; the "young woman better prepared but less beautiful," for example, is likely to be conscious of the discriminatory treatment inherent in the type of promotion practices made explicit in the quoted passage. Whether or not this consciousness is translated into action will depend on a series of factors that range from the woman's own security as worker to the political convictions and support mechanisms available to her at work and outside.

Conclusions

Although it is difficult to generalize from our study, industrial subcontracting seemed to be on the increase in Mexico City at the time when fieldwork took place; while almost half of the firms reported an increasing tendency to send production out, none of them reported a general tendency for maquila work to decrease (despite temporary decreases). More research is needed to determine the extent to which there is also in Mexico a geographical dispersion of production as well as subcontracting that involves small artisan firms. To be sure, the economic crisis of the mid-eighties is likely to have had a significant impact on the restructuring of these processes.

We have argued that subcontracting makes use of market segmentation and facilitates the shift of production to lower-cost segments. In particular, it provides a way of shifting employment towards the more informal and underground sectors of the economy. From an economic perspective, the clearest break in the continuum occurs when production goes underground. This implies that a conceptual distinction emphasizing the legal/illegal or formal/ underground divisions in the economy can establish clearer boundaries than the formal/informal sector breakdown. This is because illegality—and its corresponding sharp decrease in wages and other costs resulting from the absence of regulation—represent a major shift in the conditions under which production takes place. In any case, subcontracting widens the options of the firm that sends production out and implies access for capital to a progressively more flexible labor supply.

It can also be argued that the shift of production toward informal and underground units gives the system a great deal of flexibility in terms of expanding and contracting productive capacity in the small-business sector. In addition, and as suggested by different authors, given the high proportion of active labor in the informal sector in Third-World countries, this flexibility may be important to build an infrastructure of small firms that would provide a basis for growth.[13] The positive aspect of this sector is that it stimulates the development of small businesses that are more adaptable to economic conditions prevalent in the Third World and creates the basis for fostering and channeling entrepreneurial skills and developing productive forces in general.[14]

There are limits, however, to this optimistic view. At least for the small business associated with subcontracting, the development of a small-business sector is highly dependent on the large firms in which it originates; it will be self-sustaining only to the extent that the general development of the country is so. In addition, the permanence of small businesses in the market is constantly threatened by the competition of larger firms and the tendency towards economic concentration. From labor's perspective, decentralized production under the circumstances described for our study implies a recomposition of the industrial working class (or a new composition) toward the more marginal workers and with an important gender dimension. This serves to intensify labor's weaknesses rather than its strengths, which should derive from labor's contribution to accumulation. At the lower echelons of subcontracting, this intensification results from the precarious conditions under which production takes place, including wages that can drop to way below the legal minimum and a high degree of job instability. The invisibility to which workers are subject makes them politically if not economically marginal. In fact, the development of this sector is built precisely on labor's general vulnerability.

With respect to women's employment at all levels of subcontracting, our analysis also points to the need to raise in question and struggle with the issue of how skills are defined and redefined in order to identify any gender component in the definition. This amounts to a comparable-worth argument based on the assumption that the location of women in low-paid jobs is not due as much to women's skills and preference for these jobs as to employers' placement of women workers.[15] That is, our analysis indicates that placement is heavily influenced by employers' decisions, implying that the weight is on the demand rather than the supply side.

The implications of our analysis go even further. Comparable-worth policies assume a given hierarchy in the structure of production and its corresponding division of labor, regardless of gender. These are essentially liberal policies aiming at eliminating gender differences within the existing structure. Yet, there is no need to assume a given hierarchical productive structure; it can be reduced by the elimination of the capital/labor relation or through the flattening of the labor pyramid—brought about by institutional and political change and/or by changes within firms and productive units toward more cooperative and democratic forms of production. One of the reasons for the stubbornness of the male/female wage gap is that, while it is being narrowed in some occupations, the labor process is restructured and new jobs are created such that women are placed at the bottom of a constantly re-created labor hierarchy. To return to a Braverman framework, this re-creation yields to two basic dimensions in the capitalist labor process; namely, the need to control labor from the top down and the tendency to minimize the wage bill. The introduction of new technologies and the restructuring of production facilitate the process of, as Braverman puts it, "dividing the craft" in order to cheapen its individual parts. The employment of women facilitates this process. In this sense, our analysis suggests that women are likely to benefit from a reduction of hierarchical divisions since it would reduce the need to use gender traits to differentiate workers and justify or rationalize their location within that hierarchy.

Moreover, to the extent that there is a social and political aspect to productivity, as argued by many authors,[16] productive arrangements that increase workers' control among middle and small subcontracting units could provide an avenue to raise productivity and wages. Although this might decrease the extent of subcontracting—given the reduction of wage differentials—it represents an alternative that would have the advantages of a decentralized and flexible small-business sector without the negative aspects outlined above.

It is for these reasons that policies dealing solely with male/female differences without questioning the structure of production, although very important, are bound to have limited results. Once this structure is questioned, a feminist policy aimed at the elimination of gender inequalities in the labor market becomes an integral part of a general goal of eliminating class exploitation and establishing a more egalitarian division of labor.

Four
The Nature of Industrial Homework

During the past few years, industrial homework has been rediscovered by researchers for a variety of reasons. First, the new decentralization of production that has taken place within the more industrialized countries, and the growth of an underground economy, particularly since the 1970s, have resulted in a new interest in the subject. Studies in such countries as Italy (Garofoli, 1978 and 1983; Goddard, 1981; Murray, 1982), England (Allen, 1981), and the United States (Gutmann, 1977; Tauzi, 1982; Sassen-Koob, 1982) have raised many questions about the extent and the significance of this type of decentralization for the economy as a whole. In addition, this process has a multinational dimension and affects also the countries on the periphery (Fröbel et al., 1980; Nash and Fernández-Kelly, 1983; Portes and Benton, 1984). Second, given the predominance of women workers in industrial homework, it is no coincidence that some of these studies have been carried out as a result of an interest in gender issues. This is the case for the more industrialized countries as well as for the Third World (Moser and Young, 1981; Banarjee, 1981; Alonso, 1981; Mies, 1982). The process therefore affects the center and the periphery, even though differences between the two exist in terms of the extent and significance of the phenomenon.

A number of theoretical and empirical questions need to be explored in order to understand the significance of this process. To what extent, for example, can it be argued that homework is simple commodity production or, alternatively, a form of wage labor with "disguised proletarization" of the labor employed? What kinds of articulation exist between the larger economy's organization of production and the industrial work inside the home? What implications do studies of homework have for the analysis of the so-called informal sector? Can any comparison be made between the putting-out system that predominated during the Industrial Revolution and the variety of settings in which homework is carried out today?

In exploring these questions, we will first analyze data on the conditions under which homework is carried out. Second, we will deal with the gender issues raised by the fact that it is mostly women who concentrate in this work. Finally, we will analyze more theoretical issues regarding the nature of homework and its part in the overall production process. In particular, we will deal with the significance of our analysis for literature that has been concerned with the informal sector. The focus of this chapter is, therefore, on the economic aspects of homework, its significance, and its linkages with the larger economy. The analysis of data is based on the interviews with the 140 women workers described in Chapter 2.

Work and Pay

Figure 4.1 includes a breakdown of the types of homework analyzed. It can be observed that the larger percentage of workers in our sample was concentrated in plastic polishing and assembly. The work was done for different industries, as described in Chapter 2; it

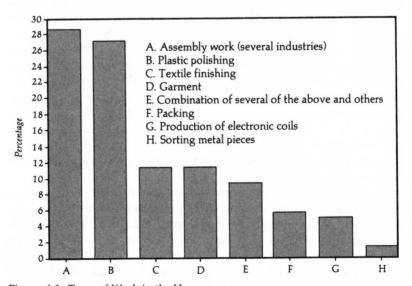

Figure 4.1: *Types of Work in the Home*

Table 4.1   *Average Hours Worked and Earnings*

1. Average work-hours per week	
a. Main homeworker	24
b. Other household members (N = 100)*	22
2. Average earnings *equivalent to 48-hour work-week (Mexican pesos)*	
a. All homeworkers (N = 130)	444.00
b. Garment workers (N = 17)	1,010.00

*Based on 100 households in which this help was provided. Of the rest, there were 30 cases in which the main homeworker did not receive any help and 10 without sufficient information.

included a variety of products such as plastic containers for the cosmetics and pharmaceutical industries in the case of plastic polishing, or toys, cartons, and flowers in the case of assembly. Only a small percentage (11.4%) of cases are from the garment industry since, as mentioned earlier, garment homework is more traditional and better known; these cases were included mostly for comparative purposes.

Work is distributed to the homeworkers daily, weekly, or by quota. As can be observed from figure 4, 2a, work is received either through a jobber (in about 50% of the cases) or directly from the factory or workshop. The percentage of cases in which work is provided directly by a factory is in fact surprisingly high (over 27%). The workshop plays an intermediary function since it is a productive unit and at the same time a distributor of homework; it often operates at the borderline of legality and under very poor working conditions.[1]

The types of industrial homework consisted mostly in very simple and unskilled tasks, labor-intensive, with minimum use of capital or production tools. As figure 4. 2b shows, in more than 25% of the cases the work performed did not require any tool; this was so, for example, in the sorting of metal pieces for batteries or the assembly of cartons. In other cases such as plastic polishing, the tool (a special kind of knife to cut plastic) was extremely simple. With the exception of the sewing machines used by garment workers, the most sophisticated means of production encountered were for electronic coils; these consisted in either a pedal-induced machine the size of a can opener that the workers attached to the kitchen table or a slightly larger manual machine requiring electricity for lighting. The breakdown in figure 4.2b also shows that the tools used were

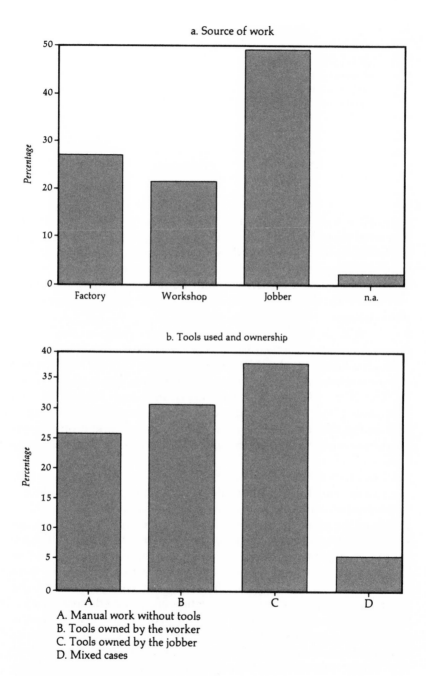

Figure 4.2: *Contractual Relations*

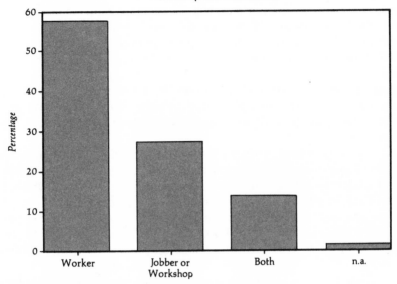

Figure 4.2: *Continued*

either owned by the worker or by the jobber, and, in a small number of cases, by a combination of both or by hiring them.

The number of hours worked, working arrangements, and form and amount of pay varied considerably from one case to another. Although in some cases materials were transported to and from the workers' homes by whoever provided the work, the majority of workers had to do the transport themselves (see figure 4c), a job that was very arduous because most of them did not own private means of transportation. Materials used and the products themselves were protected generally through severe rules. In one case, weekly wages were not paid if the merchandise was damaged; in another, an amount estimated at five times the value of the merchandise was deducted from wages. These types of rules were imposed in an ad hoc fashion, without the existence of any contract specifying them in advance.

Work was unstable and offered no security—in a degree that is not quite captured by figure 4.3. These figures do suggest a certain instability by indicating that during the previous year the majority of the women had been working between one and five months and that almost 50% of them were either not engaged in homework or working less than six months. However, figure 4.3 also shows that more than 30% of them had been engaged in the same work between 1 and 5 years and almost 8% of them more than 5 years. But the figure does not indicate that even when working at the same type of homework during a given period, job insecurity continued in the form of unstable amounts of work, time of delivery, and assurance of its continuity with an amount sufficient to generate the needed income. For example, women in this category often did not know, on a given day, whether they would have any work; they had to wait until work was delivered to them in the morning.

Pay was based without exception on piecework—such as US$6.60 per thousand electronic coils, US$2.05 per box of metal battery plates sorted as "finished" or "defective," or from US$4.35 to US$15.22 per thousand polished plastic pieces (depending on their size and the type of product).[2] These are extremely low pay rates by Mexican standards although our estimates show a high level of variation in pay per unit of time and in the number of hours worked.

Table 4.1 shows that the weekly average time spent on homework was 24 hours for the main homeworker and 22 for other household members. The variation is very large—ranging from 5 to 72 hours/week for the main homeworker. According to our estimates, average wages from homework for the equivalent standard work week of 48 hours were $444.00 Mexican pesos or US$19.30. This is well below the weekly minimum wage of $1,470 pesos or US$63.9 prevalent at the time of fieldwork, representing less than a third (30.2%) of that amount and not bolstered by any other type of benefits. Only certain garment workers earned more than the minimum wage, although the average earnings in this work were $1010 pesos or US$43.91, also below the minimum.

The variation in average earnings per worker was very great also—and dependent on the type of homework and the number of hours worked. The lowest weekly average income of $145 pesos or US$6.30 was found among workers assembling plastic toys; the highest (of $2999.00 pesos or US$130.4) was that of a garment worker. This suggests a high degree of market imperfection; i.e., lack of information about work availability and prevalent market rates and the existence of market segmentation, which prevents wage equalization from taking place. In fact, 70% of the homeworkers interviewed had found the work through direct personal contact with acquaintances, relatives, or through a jobber or head of a local work-

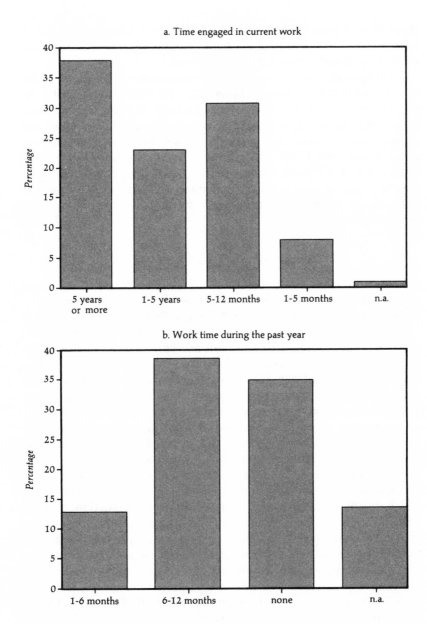

Figure 4.3: *Indicators of Work Stability*

shop; 22% of them had found it at the community level—in the market, the local shops, and the health centers. Only in one case had work been found through a newspaper ad.[3]

It is clear that wages received by homeworkers place them at the lowest end of the labor-market hierarchy. For the whole sample, the percentage of family income derived from homework averaged 25%.[4] This, however, is subject to a high degree of dispersion; the sample includes only two cases of women heads of household in which homework is the sole source of family income, while in 32 cases (22.8%) it represents less than 10% of that income. In addition, it must be kept in mind that these earnings derive from the work of the main homeworker and the help received from other household members.

Homework and Gender Relations

Despite the great variation in terms of tasks and type of industrial work included in our sample, some generalizations can be made regarding the work performed and the conditions under which it is carried out. Given the size and nonrandomness of our sample, these generalizations must be taken as suggestive and referring to nontraditional homework.

First, homework represents labor-intensive production that utilizes either very simple tools or none at all. Therefore it requires negligible capital investment and can easily be set up in the home.

Second, it is unskilled industrial work generated by the fragmentation of the labor process. The required tasks are extremely simple, repetitive, and monotonous and represent a small step in the overall process of production. It is, therefore, a typical "domestic maquila" or subcontracted production at the household level, which results from the search for lower costs of production, particularly labor costs.[5] This implies that it is not commodity production or artisan work since this would encompass all productive steps—from the raw materials to the finished product to sale in the market.

Third, homework is unstable work without any type of security; it creates a precarious dependency by the worker on the jobber or firm that assigns work, without any assurance that the work will be forthcoming. This dependency is reinforced by the fact that the supply of labor eager to do the work (including women and other family members) is well above the existing demand.

Fourth, as shown in Chapter 3, the work is carried out on the border of illegality and is therefore part of the underground econo-

Table 4.2   *Reasons Given for Doing Homework*

Reasons	%
1. Demands of care and domestic chores	37.9
2. Husband's opposition to work outside of the household	5.0
3. Lack of alternatives	15.7
4. Combination of the above	24.3
5. Other reasons, including age and health	12.8
6. N.a.	4.3
Total	100.0

my, not because domestic piecework is outlawed in Mexico but because legal productive requirements are not met. These include not only the payment of minimum wages but also fringe benefits, taxes, and the observance of other legislated work regulations. This lowering of the costs of production implies, other things being equal, higher profits and a higher rate of exploitation. In some cases, other nonlabor costs are also passed on to the worker, such as cost of the use of electricity, of services normally provided at the site of production and, for workers that own their own tools, of productive resources.

Finally, most of the domestic pieceworkers are women; our sample included only two exceptions. Yet, as has been pointed out, women receive considerable help from other household members. Most of this help is provided by female household members, while husbands, sons, and other male relatives assist on a sporadic and temporary basis. Children's help is often required in the poorest households, while adult female members' help is commonly found in extended households. In this sense, the main homeworker exercises the role of managing available labor power within the household.

There are several reasons for the predominance of women in this work. Some of them have to do with the characteristics of labor demand, which limits the alternatives available to women; illiterate women, for example, often mentioned their inability to find factory work because factories require a minimum level of literacy. As table 4.2 indicates, lack of alternatives as a reason for concentrating on homework was mentioned by more than 15% of the women. Most of the reasons, however, have to do with the women's role in reproduction and the corresponding construction of generic functions that assigns childcare and domestic work to women as their primary responsibility and is used to rationalize the husband's opposition to women's work outside the household. The result is a gender-based division of labor and social relations within the home that limits women's alternatives and choices. This is not to say that, given the possibilities available, women themselves do not choose the combination of homework and domestic chores as the best alternative. These alternatives and choices are also determined by their occupational histories, as we will analyze in Chapter 5. There is, therefore, an ideological and a material component in these choices; the two are highly integrated and can hardly be separated.

The Nature of Homework

At the conceptual level, homework involves a mixed organization of production in which capital takes advantage of the prevalent social and economic relations within the household. The jobber, the workshop, or the factory gives the materials to the worker who is paid by the piece wages for the work, but has no control over the product since it is returned to the jobber. There is appropriation of labor on the part of the jobber, much along the lines based on capitalist relations of production. As Marx noted, industrial work done at home becomes "an outside department of the factory, the manufactury, or the warehouse" (p. 461).

The worker has some control over the labor process, however, in terms of schedule and combination of domestic and industrial work, using other family members, and work intensity. This control clearly is limited; an indirect control on the part of the jobber, workshop, or factory is exercised by way of setting up work quotas and deadlines as well as through different forms of quality control. Very low wages also tend to have a speedup effect—to the extent that workers have an income target to reach. In addition, women's ability to control their own pace and schedule is limited by their household responsibilities. Yet, when production is shifted out of workshop or factory, the firm obviously loses a degree of control in terms of supervision and organization of the productive process. For this reason, it seems appropriate to view this form or work as capitalist production based on a partial proletarianization of labor and based also on the social relations of subordination/domination prevalent within the domestic unit.

A special case is garment industry work because it presents greater conceptual complexity. Although our subsample of workers with garment industry tasks was small, the patterns observed are similar to those found by J. A. Alonso (1979) in his larger study of the Nezahualcoyotl area in Mexico City. Some aspects of the garment work done at home are comparable to what has been described for other industries; the tasks represent a small part of the fragmented labor process that leads to the final product (sewing buttons, seams, buttonholes, and the like). In most cases, however, an important difference exists in that the main worker owns the sewing machines. These are relatively expensive machines, particularly in comparison to the tools used in other types of homework.[6] Another difference is that the level of skill required by garment work is higher than in other types of homework; this is in fact one of the typical cases in which the industry, as argued by Elson and Pearson (1981), uses women's traditional skills, transmitted from mothers to daughters without any formal training.

Two consequences result from this. One is that garment homework is more stable and better paid even though, in our sample, the pay is still only 68.7% of the legal minimum. The other is that some seamstresses that own their machines tend to employ young women who are paid either time or piece wages. Thus the seamstresses can exercise direct control over their "employees," contrary to the indirect control hold by the jobber.[7] We have then a situation in which the worker who has semiproletarian status vis-à-vis the jobber, workshop, or factory establishes relations of production of a semicapitalistic character with other workers. Although control over the product and the provision of raw materials remains with the jobber, ownership of the machines allows the main worker to accumulate a surplus, no matter how low-paid the piecework. There are then two levels of labor appropriation—at the jobber's level and at the level of the worker who owns the machines.

In sum, several factors need to be considered for conceptualization of these productive processes in terms of their similarities to and differences from commodity production:

a. ownership of the instruments of production
b. control over the labor process
c. control over the product and the process of labor appropriation
d. direct contact with the market, either to purchase inputs or to sell the product
e. the use of wage or family labor
f. noncontractual mode of remuneration; i.e., the use of time or piece-wages

Simple commodity or traditional artisan production, for example, imply ownership of the means of production, control over the labor process along with cooperative work and a minimum degree of job fragmentation, control over the product together with direct contact with the inputs and product markets, and the utilization of nonwage labor. In no case can we argue that all these factors apply to homework. Instead, homework has the following characteristics: a) ownership of the means of production in some cases but not in others; b) a relatively high degree of control over the labor process; c) no control over the product and no direct contact with the market; d) the use of piece wages as the form of remuneration. Similarly, despite the different characteristics of garment homework, neither can it be classified as simple commodity production nor is it likely that the workers might become independent producers, given their dependency on the jobber and their lack of direct contact with the market.

Quite the contrary, all types of homework analyzed present the common feature of being the lower echelons of a segmented market and a fragmented labor process. As shown in Chapter 3, homework is often connected, directly or indirectly, with firms of different sizes representing national and multinational capital. Thus, the electronic coils produced by some women on their own kitchen tables become a part of several products—from microphones to radio and TV antennas—that undergo as many as three or four levels of subcontracting. Similarly, plastic polishing for a local workshop is but a step in the production of fans and other electrical appliances by a large multinational firm. Viewed from this perspective, homework becomes an integral part of the overall processes of production even if hidden behind the curtains of illegality and mixed forms of production. This has clear implications for the significance of the so-called informal sector, which will be examined below.

A different question is how this type of domestic industrial work compares with the putting-out system of earlier European capitalism that represented an intermediate system between guild and capitalist production. Some similarities can be pointed out, such as concentration within the household, the employment of predominantly female labor, and the conditions under which the work takes place (for example, the role of jobbers and the predominance of piece wages). Yet, some differences between the two clearly exist:

First, the putting-out system was controlled by commercial capital whereas domestic piece work in Mexico today is controlled by industrial capital. Even within the garment industry where many workshops have practically shifted all their production to individual homes, the role of the firms is not purely commercial; they still concentrate a few key productive levels, such as cutting and finishing of products.

Second, the accumulation process initiated by commercial capital in Europe facilitated the development of national industrial capital. In the Mexican case, these processes of production contribute to accumulation of both national and multinational capital; there is a new important dimension that connects industrial homework to the ongoing accumulation on a world scale. This difference between some types of homework in the Third World and in the more industrialized countries may still persist. Yet, the process of internationalization of capital affecting both groups of countries may gradually erase this difference, as the more industrialized countries are also subject to industrial activity not controlled by national capital.

Third, the putting-out system engaged independent producers who, at least initially, owned the means of production. It was closer to a system of simple commodity production but with loss of control over the product. As the system evolved, the independent producers' direct contact with the inputs market was also gradually lost—thus bringing the system closer to the characteristics observed in Mexico today. This transformation had already taken place when Marx wrote that "This modern so-called domestic industry has nothing, except the name, in common with the old-fashioned domestic industry, the existence of which presupposes independent urban handicrafts, independent peasant farming, and above all, a dwelling-house for the laborer and his family" (1967, p. 461). What we observe in Mexico City today is also the result of this transformation although based on the specificity of an industrializing Third-World country.

Homework and the Informal Sector

Given the described characteristics of homework, the analysis above is relevant in terms of the literature that has conceptualized the economy along dualistic lines connected with the differences between the formal/informal or dominant/marginal sectors (Singer, 1970; ILO, 1972; SPP/UCECA, 1976). Initial formulations of the informal sector emphasized its connection with the marginality of the urban poor, their economic activities, and their precarious location within the larger economy. The SPP/UCECA study defined it in terms of factors such as level of earnings, the nature of a job contract, the access to medical services, the type of social services received, and affiliation to labor organizations. It also defined all productive units of five or less workers as being part of the informal sector. Subsequent studies have emphasized the conceptual problems and shortcomings derived from these dualistic divisions (Bromley and Gerry, 1979; Connolly, 1982). For example, they have pointed out the high level of integration and mutual dependency between the two sectors and the important role played by the marginal sector for the functioning of the larger economy. Other authors have incorporated these criticisms in their analysis and expanded or modified the concept accordingly (Portes, 1983 and 1984).

According to these definitions, homework must be viewed as part of the informal sector. Yet, our analysis reinforces the arguments of those who have pointed out the artificiality of the formal/informal division; the types of homework analyzed in our study clearly represent production *directly integrated* with the formal sector through subcontracting links. As shown in Chapter 3, what is produced at the household level is a fragment of a final output finished and sold in the formal sector.

This division can lead to conceptual confusions, as pointed out by Scott (1979), and to contradictory implications for policy and action. Thus, in our study the informal sector would include the various types of domestic piecework described, but also the jobbers who use family labor at home, and the workshops that hire wage-labor and operate illegally. All of these would be classified as part of the informal sector alongside artisan work or simple commodity production. The conceptual confusion has several dimensions. One aspect is that when these different agents of production are included within the general concept of informal sector, no distinction is made between their different class categories. Yet, it is important to distinguish between the owner of a workshop and his or her wage workers, and between these and family labor, and each of the categories of domestic pieceworkers. The distinction is essential for understanding the process of labor appropriation and the dynamics created by conflicting class interests. The distinction is helpful also in clarifying some puzzling empirical studies that have found higher average earnings for workers in the informal sector than for their counterparts in formal employment (López et al., 1982). As Portes (1983) has pointed out, this effect is due to the upward bias in earnings resulting from the inclusion of entrepreneurs, merchants, and selfemployed artisans in the informal sector.

Another aspect of this conceptual confusion has to do with the *nature* of the classification between informal and formal. Banarjee (1981), for example, has stated that the division between formal and informal sectors is a way of classifying the labor market rather than the economy. Our study indicates that such a classification tacitly refers also to dimensions other than the labor market, such as the structure of the overall labor process (subcontracting levels) and the ability of capital to lower other (nonlabor) production costs by shifting certain productive steps to the underground economy. That is, if we are to persist in this conceptualization, it should be clear that it refers to a variety of economic and social factors that interact with the labor market; limiting its relevance to the latter only obscures its overall significance.

This is not to say that the conceptualization of the formal/informal sector division may not be useful. It is particularly meaningful for the purpose of emphasizing the underground or unregulated nature of many activities, and it is probably for this reason that it continues to be used in the literature. The connection and the links of mutual dependency between the two sectors, however, need to be underlined.

From the perspective of economic policy, our study suggests that it would be naive to expect that any of the productive units engaged in homework might constitute the base for further development toward promotion of the small enterprise as has been suggested for the informal sector as a whole (ILO, 1972). At the general level, we agree with Gerry (1979) that such development is doubtful because of the degree of dependency of the informal on the formal sector and the tendency of the former to be absorbed by the process of economic concentration. In particular, industrial homework represents an extreme case in which any autonomous development is very difficult because of the very nature of this type of work whose gravity center is located at other levels of production.

A different issue regarding the literature on the informal sector is that important gender dimensions have been ignored. It should be no surprise that women are heavily represented in industrial homework. Their role in reproduction and their primary concentration in domestic work makes them likely candidates for tasks that can be carried on within the household. In addition, society's and women's own perception of themselves as secondary income earners prepares them for involvement in unstable and low-pay jobs. This reduces women's choices, a fact that has not been well developed in the literature.

For example, Davies (1979), while pointing out that many workers in the informal sector are "wage-labourers-in-waiting" (that is, waiting to become wage workers whenever they can get a job), emphasizes that a good proportion of them (50% in his sample) are actually not "in-waiting"; instead, he argues, they deliberately chose to work in the informal sector. He does not, however, differentiate between men and women or between different types of work within the informal sector itself. Our data indicate that many homeworkers would prefer to work in the formal sector in order to have more stable and better-paid work with fringe benefits. Yet they also make clear that they chose to engage in homework as a result of their strategies for combining different roles and objectives. That is, women's choices are highly limited and conditioned by their domestic role, which, as will be shown in Chapter 5, affects them differently according to their place in the family life cycle. Within this context, it is difficult to view them as "wage-labourers-in-waiting."[8] As table 4.2 indicates, the reasons for the lack of choice were related either to *direct* limitations—ranging from husbands' opposition to outside work to the care of children—or to *indirect* limitations, such as the lack of employment alternatives, resulting from class and gender traits. The highly restrictive constraints on these women were in fact the bases for our overwhelming conclusion about lack of choices.

Given that reality, an immediate question has to do with the possibilities for action and legal protection for the workers. Short of radical changes related to ownership, control, and contacts with the market, what can be recommended that would improve the plight of homeworkers? Efforts to enforce existing laws affecting industrial homework are likely to fail. In addition to the difficulties of enforcement because of the dispersion of jobbers and households, any implementation of minimum wages or other legal requirements resulting in an increase in cost of production is likely to eliminate homework. This would happen because such measures would erase the differential cost advantages of domestic production that is the basis for its existence. On the other hand, any attempt at joint action on the part of the workers is quite inconceivable as long as their work is illegal; their tendency is to remain invisible for fear of losing the work. Paradoxically, the implementation of the law would amount to the loss of the only source of income available to many of the workers.

The gloomy outlook derived from these contradictory objectives is reinforced by the fact that industrial homework, in the last resort, does not offer women any adequate solution to their subordination, economic dependence, and possibilities for advancement. The work is not only based on existing social relations and the sexual division of labor within the family, but reinforces them. And although it is important in providing women with some income of their own—and with the possibility of partially renegotiating the marriage contract—its insufficiency and lack of security do not offer any satisfactory long-run solution.

Conclusions

The existence of industrial homework in Mexico City and other Third-World countries shows tendencies similar to those that have generated the growth of the underground economy in the industrialized world. At the root of homework is the search for cheaper processes of production, particularly for the labor-intensive tasks that generate considerable savings in labor costs. Moreover, homework contributes to increasing flexibility in labor supply by using a pool of labor that adjusts to demand requirements without any regulation of hours or length of period worked. This process may have two dimensions—one representing a shift of production from larger to smaller units and the other a shift from the large industrial centers to those of less industrial concentration, including rural areas, as in the case of Italy (Garofoli, 1983).

In the Third World, these tendencies are built on preexisting large reserves of labor generated by the dynamics of development and the processes of migration and proletarianization of labor. Given that wages are lower than in the more industrialized countries, the incentives for firms to send out production would appear to be lower. Yet, to the extent that profits decline and the pressure of the market is felt, firms are likely to make use of the existing mechanisms offered by the informal sector in order to lower costs of production. However, while the current informalization of production in the more industrialized countries is new and builds on the labor reserves created by high levels of unemployment, in the Third World, this informalization represents a continuation of old problems generated by the inability of capitalist development to absorb existing labor reserves.

In either case, homework responds to a strategy of *accumulation* and an *income-generating* strategy for capital and workers respectively. In this chapter, we have argued that gender plays a significant role in these strategies. In terms of accumulation, women homeworkers represent the cheapest source of labor; in Mexico City, they constitute an unlimited labor reserve as a result of their primary concentration in domestic work and childcare. This concentration derives from a powerful "ideology of domesticity" that affects individual development and goals, resulting in a limitation of their working alternatives and ability to choose, and from individual and household economic strategies for survival. All of these factors converge in creating the conditions that result in the extremely low level of wages found among homeworkers. Although conscious of their exploitation, their willingness to engage in this type of work results from the household's strong need to generate new sources of income. For women, it represents access to income over which they have full control. It also represents an income-generating strategy as well as a search for a lower degree of dependency on other household members.

Five

Class, Gender, and
Work Trajectories

In the preceding chapters we have analyzed how capital incorporates and recreates gender traits throughout the work process, the subcontracting mechanisms and industrial homework itself. This means that the expansion of capital implies, simultaneously, the formation of a working class fragmented along gender lines and a new phase in the social construction of gender brought about by the process of proletarianization itself.

This chapter will explore some features of this intertwined construction of class and gender relations by focusing on family, class, and gender experiences in search of historical milestones to help explain women's current insertion in industrial homework. This background will also prove useful for understanding how women, in their daily lives, experience and define the articulation of those relations and how they, as purposeful (although constrained) human agents, devise work and other strategies to renegotiate aspects of gender relations within the household. The analysis will focus on two key areas: first, relationships existing between class of origin and educational level on the one hand, and premarriage occupational and class trajectories, on the other; and second, the relationships between formal marriage, or consensual union and separation (if applicable), motherhood and postmarriage occupational and class histories.[1]

Usually, the many decisions affecting women's lives (such as schooling, beginning of or return to wage labor, marriage, as well as first cohabitation, separation, and later unions, motherhood and subsequent labor-market re-incorporation) are interpreted as falling within the individual or family domain; without any recognition of their class and gender dimensions. Our purpose here will be, first, to explore whether those decisions, which mark seemingly "personal" milestones in the lives of the women homeworkers, have influenced their long-term patterns of employment, and if so, what the consequences have been. Second, our intention is to point out, on the basis of women's family, class, and gender histories, some of the features of the proletariat and subproletariat of Mexico City—classes undergoing a fluid process of formation and recomposition.

Premarriage Phase

Class of Origin

Sociologists and political scientists usually give special importance to the individual's class of origin in their explanation of a number of variables, including educational level attained, type of socialization received, life options, and aspirations. The determination of that class is not considered problematical: the assumption is implicit that the person interviewed comes from a nuclear family (considered as synonymous with household), which is stable, with a single breadwinner—the husband or father—who as head is the one to determine the family's class position according to occupation of members and a cultural milieu that will remain basically unchanged throughout his existence. It is plausible that this static, ethnocentric and androcentric view of social classes had a greater empirical hold in the central capitalist countries, England for example, during the historical stage in which the industrial working class was becoming consolidated. Along with the rise in real wages and the granting of a "family salary" to the husband, this process allowed the wife to retreat into domestic life, with only sporadic periods of paid work. The outcome of this process was the system of domestic economy that Tilly and Scott (1978) call the "Family Consumer Economy."

In a peripheral capitalist country such as Mexico, however, where the male industrial proletariat is still in the process of formation, a reexamination of these assumptions seems in order.

The Definition of Social Classes / Class Determiner and Life-Stage of Origin. In the search for the class of origin of the women interviewed, a number of interrelated conceptual and empirical problems emerged: what definition of social classes to apply; who to select as the determiner of the young woman's class position, and which period in her life to single out as the one when class of origin was established.

All subjects of this study belong to the subordinated classes of capitalist society: the proletariat, the subproletariat, the petty bourgeoisie, and the peasantry, either in "pure" terms or in simultaneous articulation of several class positions.

The proletariat and subproletariat are similar in their lack of economic ownership and possession of the means of production. They differ, however, in how they are remunerated. The distinct feature of the proletarian is that the wage he or she receives is established by contract and is subject to existing labor codes. In Mexico, the proletariat is the sector made up of workers who have permanent jobs *(planta)*, earn legal minimum wages, have access to the social security system, and usually belong to the organized labor movement.

The distinction between legally regulated and casual wage employment is extremely important in socioeconomic and political terms. Entering into a formal labor relationship protects workers against arbitrary dismissal, and social security coverage represents an "indirect wage" composed of health programs, retirement benefits and various other insurance programs established by law (Portes, 1984). Belonging to the proletariat rather than to the subproletariat means, therefore, a substantial difference in terms of security and stability of family subsistence. When this class difference is further compounded by gender (as in the case of our sample) family dynamics are correspondingly affected. The formal relationship has political implications also since it supplies workers with minimal social and economic conditions—work stability, relatively high salaries, free time (in the case of males) to engage in union and political struggles traditional for the proletariat.

The subproletariat, on the contrary, receives casual rather than protected wages, does not benefit from a contractual relationship with employers, and does not have access to social security coverage. Forms of remuneration are multiple, including not only informally agreed-on cash compensation but also noncash forms such as food and shelter. Because wages are unstable and usually fall below the legal minimum, members of this class generally engage in a variety of other cash-generating activities (as do the women in our sample) and may also participate in the subsistence economy as peasants in the process of proletarianization. For the purpose of this study, and to clarify women's entrance into the subproletariat,[2] we find it useful to distinguish between different sectors: 1) *general-waged subproletariat:* employed in private enterprises or in the public sector and who thus stand a better chance of graduating into the ranks of the proletariat;[3] 2) *subproletariat offering personal services:*

working for private consumers as household servants, laundry women, chaffeurs, gardeners; 3) *autonomous subproletariat* offering services or selling commodities independently in the market (street peddlers, porters, shoe shiners, food vendors, weavers); 4) *subproletariat in industrial homework*, who have partial control over the labor process and ownership of the instruments of production in the case of garment homework. This suggests the presence of mixed or intermediate class positions within a continuum that ranges from full proletarianization to simple commodity production.

The third subordinated class is the petty bourgeoisie: direct producers of commodities or suppliers of services who own or possess some means of production that they utilize with help of unpaid family labor or a few waged workers hired under noncontractual arrangements. In the nonagricultural sector, the petty bourgeoisie is composed of small shopkeepers, workshop owners and subcontractors, and in the agricultural sector, contractors who hire out migratory gangs to agribusiness or, most commonly, to commercial farmers.

In our sample there are no instances of the "pure" rural petty bourgeoisie. Instead, there are examples of the peasant who combines subsistence agriculture with casual labor on larger farms or in the cities and may also venture into commercial farming at various stages in his life. When women referred to their male or female relatives as "peasants," they usually meant peasant owners of their land *(campesinos con tierra propia)*, who combined these other features. In our analysis "peasant" is taken to mean that particular figure articulating subsistence production, commercial agriculture, and some degree of semiproletarianization, and seeming to be typical of most of the Latin American rural scene (Portes, 1984).

The empirical determination of these definitions is especially complex because we have to resort to a cross section of historical processes and rely on the memory of the women interviewed as our only source of information for the period selected. This last caveat also applies to our next conceptual and empirical problem: the identification of the young woman's class determiner and the stage in her life to be defined as "of origin." In our opinion there is no simple solution to these problems.[4]

To explore the relationship between class of origin and level of formal education (and since the latter is usually related to access to and level of economic resources) we adopted the criterion of economic support. The individual who determines the young woman's class of origin will therefore be the one primarily responsible for her support during the period chosen as relevant. For the same reason, we have chosen the older childhood phase (eleven to twelve years old) as the crucial period of origin. The importance of this stage lies in the fact that at this time the educational future has been decided for most of the women interviewed. If the woman has already begun formal education, during this period it is decided whether she will complete elementary school, begin her paid occupational trajectory (if she has not begun already)[5] or devote her time to household chores making it easier for other family members to work outside the home. The adoption of an economic criterion for the person who determines class and the selection of the older childhood phase as the period of origin, however, set limits on who may become class determiners, since this responsibility may fall on different individuals according to the period selected: birth, infancy, first or second childhood, adolescence. Also the class determiner may change because of his/her sickness, unemployment, abandonment, nonfulfillment of obligations, or death. On the other hand, the determiner may not change, but his/her situation may—from the birth of the woman interviewed to the period of origin chosen.

A common pattern in our sample is that of a father who was a peasant or an agricultural day-laborer when the woman interviewed was born, but who later migrated to Mexico City and got a job in a factory, opened a small shop, or more commonly, joined the capital's subproletariat. Generally, these occupational changes imply changes in class situation as well; these in turn can mean different educational opportunities for daughters, though of course, this depends also on the daughter's position in the age and gender hierarchies of the household of origin.

Another common pattern appeared where the same class determiner had multiple class insertions simultaneously or successively during the period of origin. The father might be a peasant and owner of a small grocery store in town; or he might be a peasant undergoing proletarianization as an agricultural day-laborer during the harvest season, and a construction worker in Mexico City during the remainder of the year. In these cases, we chose the class situation that the woman interviewed considered most important. Finally, when both parents worked for wages at the same time we had to decide which was the class determiner. Usually it was assumed that the mother's income was simply a complement to the father's, making the latter the class determiner. To assume a priori that responsibility for the household's subsistence rests on the father without inquiring into the importance of the mother's contribution (or that of other members of the family) would make us guilty of androcentrism. But the empirical determination of such a fluid situation is a complex task, and Señora Cuca's history is a case in point.

Cuca's mother was "stolen" (*robado*, taken by force) by her father, whom Cuca believes to have been a peasant who was already married and had children in another town. Cuca is the fruit of that "robbery," and her childhood unfolds amid successive changes of residence that result from her father's occupational shifts. Finally, her mother tires of this situation, leaves the father, takes the girl to live with her maternal grandmother, and gets a job as a domestic in Mexico City; from there she continues to support her daughter until her own death during childbirth. The grandmother, herself a very poor peasant widow with two children to support, starts working as a day laborer. Cuca stays home, taking care of her baby brother and wishing "someone would give me breasts so I could feed my brother, since my granny doesn't have any money to buy food." When Cuca is 10 years old, her grandmother takes her out of school and sends her to work as a domestic in town: "She was very old and couldn't support my brother anymore, so she needed my wages." She stayed in town for another year before being called back to help Granny at home. What is Cuca's class of origin? We arrive at different determinations depending on which stage of her life (first year, first or second childhood phase) is given priority: her father was first a peasant and then presumably a member of the urban autonomous subproletariat; her mother and Cuca herself belonged to the same class, but in the personal services sector; her grandmother was a semiproletarianized peasant. Each of these class positions corresponds to objectively different urban and rural realities and may have exerted correspondingly different influence on the education of the women interviewed. According to our chosen criteria, we consider the grandmother to have been the peasant class determiner, while we bear in mind once more the fluidity of the processes of class formation and recomposition and the difficulty in discerning their specific features.

Empirical Determination of Class of Origin. This kind of complexity underlies the data presented in Table 5.1, which shows distribution of the women interviewed according to class of origin and class determiner.

Table 5.1 shows that only 11% of the women belong to the proletariat; within the nonagricultural sector the subproletariat (26.2%) predominates, while peasants (31.7%) predominate in the agricultural sector. The majority of the class determiners are fathers

Table 5.1   *Distribution of Wives by Class of Origin, Class-Determining Individual, and Number of Mothers in Paid Work (%)*

| Class of Origin | % | Class-determining Individual | | | Nonclass-determining Mothers |
		Father	Mother	Other	
Nonagricultural Sector					
Proletariat	11.2	12	10	—	7
Subproletariat					
General-waged	17.8	20	—	—	34
Personal services	8.4	—	80	33.33	—
Petty bourgeoisie	15.9	15	10	33.33	21
Agricultural Sector					
Subproletariat					
General-waged	13.1	16	—	—	28
Peasants	31.7	35	—	33.33	7
Other: armed forces	1.9	2	—	—	3
Total (N:107)	100	100	100	99.99	100
% of total		87.9	9.3	2.8	29.8

(88%), but there are also 10 mothers and 3 other relatives (a stepfather and two grandmothers). Among the male classes determiners, we find a diversity of class and occupations. In contrast, of the 12 women class determiners, 80% belong to the subproletariat in personal services, the poorest and most unstable sector of the working class. It also should be noted that close to 30% of the mothers of the women interviewed, although not heads of households, worked for wages during the period of origin. The mothers' class position reveals the same concentration in the autonomous and personal services branches of the subproletariat that their daughters will exhibit a generation later, and during an identical phase in the expansion of the family life-cycle. The majority of these mothers are sellers of clothes, food, and articles for the home, or maids and washwomen; a minority are domestic outworkers, agricultural day-laborers, and workers in *fondas* and restaurants.

To summarize: within the nonagricultural sector, the class origin of the majority of the women interviewed is the general-waged subproletariat (if the class determiner was the father) or the subproletariat in personal services (if the class determiner was the mother). Within the agricultural sector, the majority are very poor peasants and in the process of semiproletarianization as construction workers in the cities and/or day-laborers. We can conclude, therefore, that only a small number of women—those whose class of origin is the proletariat, the urban petty bourgeoisie, or the middle peasantry—come from modest households, which nonetheless have a relatively stable level of income. The economic precariousness of the rest of the households is reflected in the educational level reached by the majority of the women interviewed.

Educational Level. According to our initial hypothesis, we expected that, within the nonagricultural sector, the homeworkers whose class of origin was proletariat or petty bourgeoisie would have higher levels of formal education, given the stability and higher level of income usually associated with those class positions.[6] We expected this relationship to hold also within the agricultural sector, when comparing the educational level of women of the former classes, with that of women of the agricultural subproletariat or peasantry. This hypothesis is confirmed by data in table 5.2.

As shown in table 5.2, 92% of the women with proletarian origin, and 71% from the petty bourgeoisie finished elementary school; it is from these classes that we find a majority of the industrial homeworkers—those who have taken technical and vocational work (especially commercial, secretarial and beautician's courses) or have high school education. The only university student of the sample comes also from the petty bourgeoisie. The lowest educational levels are found among the women whose class of origin is the subproletariat in personal services (almost 90% of whom did not complete elementary school), the agricultural subproletariat, and the peasantry.

It should not be assumed, however, that a direct relationship always exists between class of origin and level of education. The hypothesis assumes that the higher the level of income and work stability of the male head of the household, the greater his contribution to the common household fund, which in turn facilitating a higher educational level for his daughter. But this assumption is not borne out in many cases, due to the father's nonfulfillment of obligations, alcoholism, absence and/or temporary desertion of the home. Also, women's position in the household age hierarchies connects their eventual educational level with the occupational changes of the head of the household and the possible economic contribution of other members of the family group. The historical/geographical context of the period of origin is also important with regard to access to

Table 5.2 Distribution of Wives by Class of Origin and Educational Level (%)

| | Primary School Not Completed | | | | Primary School Completed or Higher | | | | | | |
Class of Origin	Illiterate	1–3 years	4–5 years	Sub-total	No High School	Primary and Technical School	High School*	High and Technical School	College**	Sub-total	Total
Nonagricultural sector											
Proletariat	—	8	—	8	52	8	16	16	—	92	100
Subproletariat											
General-waged	5	32	21	58	32	—	—	5	5	42	100
Personal services	22	45	22	89	—	11	—	—	—	11	100
Petty bourgeoisie	—	23	6	29	29	18	18	—	6	71	100
Agricultural sector											
Subproletariat											
General-waged	14	43	29	86	14	—	—	—	—	14	100
Peasants	18	41	20	79	18	3	—	—	—	21	100
Other: armed forces	—	—	—	—	50	—	50	—	—	100	100
% of total (N:107)				60						40	

*Incomplete in two cases.
**Students at the time of fieldwork.

school, this especially affecting older women with peasant or agricultural day-laborer background.

We lack systematic data on the influence of gender on the relationship between class of origin and educational level, but Cohen's research (1983) on patterns of gender socialization for a subsample on industrial homeworkers indicates a strict sexual division of labor in the family of origin. Girls were assigned housework responsibilities and child-minding at an early age, and traditional domestic values were inculcated during the women's childhood. These findings suggest that many girls are passed over in selecting household members to receive an elementary education. Simultaneously, through differential socialization, girls acquire gender traits influencing the character of their adult proletarianization.

In sum, the relationship between class of origin and educational level is affected by the nature of family interaction and its internal hierarchies—at different stages of the family life cycle—as well as in its historical and geographical context. Thus, the educational level of the women interviewed forms part of an extremely complex set of decisions that includes also her immediate or eventual entrance into the labor market, and her possible role as a substitute mother for younger brothers and sisters. All the decisions vital for her future were adopted during her childhood and almost always were beyond her control. It is possible that economic need has not always been so urgent as to require girls to leave school immediately, but especially in rural areas, women's education does not seem to have been valued highly by parents, or in many cases by the girl herself. Together with economic need, this attitude encourages her early entrance into the labor market, and the end of her formal schooling.[7]

Work Trajectories before Marriage. As shown in table 5.3, 75% of the sample of women engaged in paid work before marriage. Given the connection between women's class of origin and level of education, is it possible to ascertain any relationship between these and their typical occupational and class histories in the premarriage stage?

Table 5.3 shows the class position of the 75 wives who worked when single at the prenuptial "moment"; the time of the first consensual union, or religious or legal marriage. Only 11% of these women belonged to the proletariat while close to 90% belonged to the urban subproletariat, mainly in the general-waged (45%) and personal services (36%) sectors.

With two exceptions, the rest of the permanent workers had an elementary education and, in the case of the secretary and the beautician, had completed a technical course. The owner of the beauty

Table 5.3   Class Position of Wives Who Worked When Single: At Time of Marriage, by Class of Origin, and Level of Schooling

Class Position at Time of Marriage. The groups are: **Proletariat** = (1)*, (2); **Subproletariat** = General-waged [(3), (4), (5)], Homework, Personal Services, Autonomous; **Petty Bourgeoisie**.

Class of Origin and Level of Schooling	Proletariat (1)*	Proletariat (2)	General-waged (3)	General-waged (4)	General-waged (5)	Subproletariat — Homework	Subproletariat — Personal Services	Autonomous	Petty Bourgeoisie	Total
Non-agricultural sector										
Proletariat										
Less than primary	—	—	—	—	—	—	1	—	—	1
Primary/higher	1	1	3	2	—	—	—	—	1	8
Subproletariat										
General-waged										
Less than primary	2	—	4	—	—	—	1	1	—	8
Primary/higher	—	—	3	—	—	1	3	—	—	7
Personal services										
Less than primary	—	—	3	—	2	—	1	—	—	6
Primary/higher	—	—	—	1	—	—	—	—	—	1
Petty bourgeoisie										
Less than primary	1	—	1	—	—	—	2	—	—	4
Primary/higher	2	—	2	1	1	—	—	1	—	7
Agricultural sector										
Subproletariat										
General-waged										
Less than primary	1	—	2	—	1	—	6	1	—	11
Primary/higher	—	—	—	—	1	—	1	—	—	2
Peasants										
Less than primary	—	—	6	—	—	1	10	—	—	17
Primary/higher	—	—	—	—	1	—	2	3	—	3
Total	7	1	24	4	6	2	27	3	1	75
% of total	11		37		8	3	36	4	1	(100)

Note: "Marriage" indicates legal or religious marriage or consensual union.
*(1) = manual proletariat; (2) = nonmanual proletariat; (3) = manual subproletariat; (4) = nonmanual subproletariat; (5) = seamstresses in workshops.

salon, the only petit bourgeois woman in the sample, had completed a beauty course and a high-school education.

The subproletariat, in contrast, shows greater heterogeneity with regard to women's educational levels. Let us look first at general-waged subproletariat. Its nonmanual category is made up of four workers: a typist, a secretary, a nurse and a telephone operator. All of them had completed primary or high school and had taken commercial, secretarial, or first-aid courses. Within the manual categories we find that about half of the women had experienced occupational shifts between different sectors of the urban subproletariat—in particular from personal services to general-waged activities—a pattern of mobility that the women considered a professional advance. This is understandable if we take into consideration that 56% of the women in this sector had not completed elementary school.

The subproletariat in personal services is characterized by its low educational level (only 15% of the women completed elementary school) and by its class background, almost all of them having origin in the agricultural subproletariat or peasant class. They are also women who began to work intermittently at an early age as domestic servants or agricultural day laborers before migrating to Mexico City. Shifting between temporary jobs and household responsibilities implied that most of these women had little or no schooling (were in fact illiterate) or attended school infrequently when they were back home before entering the house of a new mistress *(patrona)* who, as a rule, did not send the young girls back to school. (This pattern is exemplified by Doña Soledad's early work history; see Appendix.)

By way of synthesis, we can say that within a given class of origin, decisions concerning women's level of schooling appear to have played a fundamental role in their premarriage occupational and class trajectories. Women who are illiterate or have completed only two to three years of schooling remain within the ranks of the subproletariat in personal services. Those who went a little beyond this minimum level might have a chance of upward mobility into the general-waged subproletariat as seamstresses in workshops, waitresses, or cooks in restaurants or fondas. Increasingly an elementary school diploma has become a prerequisite for work in factories and in general for membership in the proletariat. Nonmanual activities require additional qualification: a high-school education or diplomas from specialized technical schools. Our findings coincide therefore with those reported on a general level for Mexico City by García, Muñoz, y Oliveira (1982).

What implications do these processes have for the reproduction of class and gender relations? Given that educational level is closely related to class of origin and its internal divisions, it acts as a mechanism for the reproduction of the differences within and between classes from one generation to another,[8] while simultaneously separating women from one another. In our sample, daughters of the proletariat or the petite bourgeoisie, with primary or high-school education, had greater access to the nonmanual or manual proletariat than their peers from the subproletariat in personal services, the agricultural subproletariat, or the peasantry. Level of schooling and labor trajectories not only reproduce class inequalities, but also gender hierarchies, through the sexual division of labor prevailing in the various processes of incorporation into wage labor.

This is shown first in the horizontal division of labor caused by women's concentration in "feminine" activities that reinforce gender and are usually of lower status and are more poorly paid than masculine occupations. The listing of jobs held by young women showed them in branches traditionally associated with women or that constituted an extension of their domestic role: seamstresses, personal services, beauticians, and preparers and servers of food in restaurants. In industry they were concentrated in those branches that required manual skills and the patience commonly associated with the female "nature"—(manufacture of clothing, assembly of toys, condensors, and television and other machine components).

Secondly, the vertical sexual division of labor also contributes to the process of gender re-creation or reinforcement. None of the manual or nonmanual wage earners in our sample held supervisory positions or had progressed beyond the lowest stratum of the occupational pyramid. In this way women's entrance into the proletariat or the subproletariat typically reproduces gender hierarchies at the heart of the working class itself.

Women in our sample, therefore, participated only indirectly in the making and consolidation of the industrial proletariat of Mexico City—a class position that was monopolized by males—during the sixties and seventies. Moreover, given that the income of young, single women is usually appropriated by the household of origin, one may legitimately ask to what degree their premarriage subproletarianization contributed to the proletarianization of fathers and brothers or to the reproduction of the peasant economy. We do not have data to clarify this question. Our data does suggest, however, that through women's subproletarianization in personal services and as general-waged earners during a period of increasing male proletarianization, the gender gap was increasing at the same time as the fragmentation of the working class was strengthening along the same gender lines.

After-Marriage Phase

Marriages and Husbands

There are a number of reasons why young women who come from economically and emotionally deprived homes seek escape from the limitations of their life by cohabiting or marrying.[9] On the one hand, there are factors related to family dynamics embedded in the class and gender histories previously described: the reality of a daily family life that most women described as lacking in affection, companionship, and communication with the parents, carried on in an atmosphere of verbal and often physical violence in the household; young women have wanted to forge a minimum space within which they could better control their lives. This they have hoped to find as wives and mothers in their new homes. Some sought economic security and masculine protection, others affection, if not love. On the other hand, the features of the majority of the work trajectories described dead-end occupations, with neither intrinsic attraction nor contractual and social security; this helps to explain why the alternative to such jobs—marriage or cohabitation—has appeared more logical and appealing in their eyes.

The age at which these women first cohabit or marry oscillates between 14 and 23 years. In each social class and educational level, the average age for marriage of women who worked when single is higher than that of those who did not.[10] For the first group the average varies from sixteen and a half years for women of general-waged subproletarian origin to 23 years for those of peasant origin. For women who did not work when single, the average is fifteen and a half years for those from the subproletariat in personal services and nineteen and a half for those of peasant origin.

Who are the husbands of the women interviewed? Table 5.4 shows their distribution according to educational level and class position at the beginning of the period of consensual union or marriage.

It can be seen that 25% of the husbands belonged to the proletariat, compared with only 11% of the women who worked when single (as seen in table 5.3). Also, four of the husbands (com-

Table 5.4   Distribution of Husbands at Time of Marriage, by Class Position and Level of Schooling (%)

| | Nonagricultural Sector | | | | | Agricultural Sector | | | | |
| | Proletariat | | Subproletariat | | Petty Bourgeoisie | Subproletariat | Peasant | Other: Armed Forces | Unemployed | Total |
Level of Schooling	Manual	Nonmanual	General-waged	Autonomous		General-waged				
Less than primary	4.6	—	30	1.9	—	3.7	3.7	—	—	43.9
Primary	11.0	—	15	1.9	0.9	—	0.9	4.7	0.9	35.3
High school or Technical	5.6	1.9	2.8	—	2.8	—	—	4.9	0.9	18.9
College	—	1.9	—	—	—	—	—	—	—	1.9
Total (N:107) % total	25		51.6		3.7	3.7	4.6	9.6	1.8	100.00

pared to only one woman) had nonmanual occupations: an engineer, a bookkeeper, an administrative employee, and the supervisor *(encargado)* of a tortilla shop.[11] Fifty-two percent of the men belonged to the nonagricultural subproletariat (compared with 88% of the women); however, they belonged to different sectors from the women. Among subproletariat men, the majority (93%) are general-waged workers among whom there exists greater possibility of attaining occupational stability. In contrast, fifty-two percent of the women belong to this sector, but the personal services sector—which does not exist among men and which offers no chance of professional advancement—makes up 41% of the female subproletariat (table 5.3).

As for the educational level of the men: 44% of them have not completed elementary school (compared with 60% of the women—table 5.2). Within the wider sector who completed elementary school or have more education, 52% had reached an intermediate level—secondary or technical—and two had attended a university—an electronic engineer and an advanced law student—at the time of the interviews. The general educational level is, therefore, markedly superior to that of the women.

Finally in terms of age, the men (with one exception) are older than the women, age differences ranging from a few months to 15 years, the average being four years.

In summary, the men, in terms of such indicators as educational level and class position, were better off than their wives. To be sure, half of them did not have job stability, but they held positions that would allow them to achieve it later. This was not the case among the women in the sample. The men were older and had greater educational and economic resources at the time of marriage, a situation that influenced the resulting marital interaction. We shall return to that in Chapters 6 and 7.

Postmarriage Work Histories

The onset of consensual union/marriage or motherhood (which for all wives who were also mothers took place within the first year of the marriage/cohabitation) marks the interruption of paid work for 80% of the women who had worked when single.[12] If we include also those who had not had a prenuptial paid activity, we find that marriage/imminent motherhood takes 87% of the women interviewed away from the labor market.

This situation should not be interpreted as proof that in every case the men wanted to or were able to support their wives; instead, it should be considered the initial expression of some of the reciprocities understood between spouses—economic provision by the husband, unpaid domestic work by his wife. In the case of the men with job stability, and especially in those relationships where the age difference was greatest, the new couple was able to rent a room in a *vecindad* and live independently. This was not the case for the majority, who had to bring a bed or mat and sleep in their parents' home. For at least half the wives, quitting work did not mean economic independence in the new family nucleus, but rather the possibility of joining forces with another preexistent household/ family group and sharing expenses. Therefore, at the beginning of the period of consensual union or marriage, the formation of an extended household represented a form of struggle for economic survival that facilitated the wife's temporary withdrawal from the labor market. This interruption was generally short-term: in 71.7% of the cases re-entry into paid work occurred in the midst of the formation or expansion of the new family nucleus. This finding conflicts with the assumption that the withdrawal of women from the labor market is supposedly greater at this stage (not counting unpaid farm work carried out by peasants' wives). Marriage and motherhood in particular therefore, have not prevented women's reincorporation into paid work, but have influenced patterns of employment.[13]

Two different work trajectories should be distinguished, each one corresponding to half of the women interviewed, as indicated in table 5.5.

The first work trajectory is made up of 54 women who began their postmatrimonial labor in some type of industrial homework[14] and were still working at home at the time of our fieldwork, in some cases, industrial homework was combined with other remunerated activities (see table 5.6).

The second work trajectory includes women with an occupational history preceding homework. Table 5.5 shows the class position corresponding to the first labor-force insertion after marriage and previous to homework. This includes those women who did not interrupt their remunerated work when they married, although they might have changed the type of activity (see note 12).

Only two workers (3.5%) belong to the manual proletariat, working in a leather and lampshade factory for 11 and 15 years respectively. Two seamstresses are petty bourgeois owners of a sewing workshop, which they later closed to continue as garment homeworkers.

91

Table 5.5   Wives' Class Position after Marriage, by Class of Origin and Level of Schooling

Class of Origin and Level of Schooling	Subproletariat	Proletariat	General-waged		Subproletariat		Petty Bourgeoisie	Total
	Industrial homework	(1)	(2)	(3)	Personal Services	Autonomous		
Nonagricultural sector								
Proletariat								
Less than primary	—	1	—	—	—	—	—	1
Primary/higher	10	—	—	—	—	1	—	11
Subproletariat								
General-waged								
Less than primary	5	1	—	1	4	—	—	11
Primary/higher	5	—	1	—	1	1	—	8
Personal services								
Less than primary	2	—	2	—	3	1	—	8
Primary/higher	—	—	1	—	—	—	—	1
Petty bourgeoisie								
Less than primary	2	—	2	—	—	1	—	5
Primary/higher	5	—	1	—	1	4	1	12
Agricultural sector								
Subproletariat								
General-waged								
Less than primary	4	—	2	2	1	3	—	12
Primary/higher	1	—	—	—	—	—	1	2

								Total
Peasants								
Less than primary	14	—	1	—	11	1	—	27
Primary/higher	5	—	—	1	—	1	—	7
Other: Armed forces								
Primary/higher	1	—	1	—	—	—	—	2
Total	54	2	11	4	21	13	2	107(100%)
Total wives with occupational trajectory previous to homework	—	2	11	4	21	13	2	53(100%)
% of total	—	3.5	21	7.5	40	24.5	3.5	

NOTE: Class position is that of the first labor-force insertion after marriage and previous to homework. (1) = manual proletariat; (2) = manual subproletariat; (3) = seamstresses in workshops.

Table 5.6   Current Class Position of Wives and Income Level, by Class of Origin and Level of Schooling

Class of Origin and Level of Schooling	Subproletariat						Petty Bourgeoisie	Incomes*				Total
	Homework	Homework, waged	Homework, personal services	Homework, autonomous	Homework, autonomous, sewing	Homework, other	Homework	(1)	(2)	(3)	(4)	
Nonagricultural sector												
Proletariat												
Less than primary	1	—	—	—	—	—	—	1	—	—	—	1
Primary/higher	10	—	—	—	—	—	1	10	1	—	—	11
Subproletariat												
General-waged												
Less than primary	6	—	4	—	1	—	—	10	—	1	—	11
Primary/higher	4	—	1	2	1	—	—	8	—	—	—	8
Personal services												
Less than primary	4	—	2	1	1	—	—	7	—	1	—	8
Primary/higher	1	—	—	—	—	—	—	—	1	—	—	1
Petty bourgeoisie												
Less than primary	3	—	—	2	—	—	—	5	—	1	—	5
Primary/higher	6	—	2	2	—	2	—	10	1	1	—	12

Agricultural sector

	(1)	(2)	(3)	(4)							Total
Subproletariat											
General-waged											
Less than primary	9	1	1	—	—	1	—	11	1	1	12
Primary/higher	2	—	—	—	—	—	—	2	—	—	2
Peasants											
Less than primary	17	—	3	4	—	2	1	25	1	1	27
Primary/higher	6	—	—	—	—	1	—	7	—	—	7
Other: armed forces											
Primary/higher	1	—	1	—	—	—	—	—	1	1	2
Total	70	1	14	11	3	6	2	96	6	5	107 (100%)
% of total	65.4	0.9	13.1	10.3	2.8	5.6	1.9	89.7	5.6	4.7	

*Incomes: (1) = less than minimum wage in 1981; (2) = equal to minimum wage in 1981; (3) = up to twice the minimum wage in 1981; (4) = more than twice the minimum wage in 1981.

The remaining women belong to the urban subproletariat, in which are concentrated 93% of the women with a postmarriage labor trajectory prior to industrial homework. Within the subproletariat, the most important sector is personal services, followed by general-waged and autonomous workers (43%, 31% and 26% respectively). We will examine some examples of the activities of these women to clarify the nature of postmarriage trajectories.

The subproletariat in personal services includes maids paid by the hour and washerwomen. The autonomous subproletariat comprises women who sell beauty products, blankets, clothes, food, sweets and fruits on their doorsteps, vegetables in their houses; who prepare and sell *quesadillas* and popsicles, give shots and meals to boarders, weave doilies and dolls, are independent seamstresses and in one case, a beautician without a salon. Finally the general-waged subproletariat includes manual workers in a tortilla shop, a print shop, on the subway, in fondas and markets, plus 4 workers in sweets, knitted wear, and razor blade factories and 4 seamstresses in workshops.

It should be pointed out that 40% of all the women with occupational history previous to homework had other labor insertions after those detailed above and prior to homework. In three cases these insertions involved a change in class position, from proletariat in a factory to subproletariat in personal services; from the autonomous subproletariat to petty bourgeois positions (owners respectively of a hardware store and a grocery store).

In the remaining cases, changes in employment were restricted to shifts between sectors within the same subproletariat. Doña Lucía's trajectory illustrates these various shifts before she undertook industrial homework. She was first a casual worker in a sweets factory; this position was followed by autonomous activities (selling tortillas in the street); casual wage-labor again (in a peanut factory); personal services (washerwoman for several periods); and one more autonomous activitiy this time selling *elotes*, ears of tender corn.

The two types of postmarriage labor trajectories previously mentioned; i.e., industrial homework as first job (although it may appear combined with others at present) and an occupational history preceding homework contribute to the making of the subproletariat in industrial homework as originated in the subcontracting networks studied in Chapter 3.

Table 5.6 shows the class position and total incomes of the wives at the time research was done. It will be noted that 65.4% are homeworkers only. The remaining women (with the exception of two who articulate a double class-insertion as owners of a hardware and grocery store and as homeworkers) combine several activities within different sectors of the urban subproletariat, in particular the personal services and autonomous categories described above.

The incomes those multiple activities produce is very small as well as unstable. Almost 90% of the women in our sample earned an income lower than the legal minimum wage.[15] It should be noted that higher incomes derive either from better remunerated kinds of homework, such as sewing, lace cutting, or metal selection, or from multiple labor insertions. The beautician, for example, now does plastic polishing during her children's vacation, goes as a beautician to women's homes, works as an independent seamstress, and does laundry work twice a week.

The instability of the incomes is explained in part by the nature of homework and the other activities women engage in. Instability results also from the frequency with which the women wanted to or could engage in them, according to their varying labor strategies at different phases of the family cycle.

Both aspects, the macrosocial context and the concrete reality of the household microcosm, help to explain the short-term nature of the industrial homework subproletariat. Among the women whose postmarriage labor trajectory begins with some sort of homework, almost 90% have been on the job either for less than a year or between one and five years. Among women with an occupational trajectory that precedes industrial homework, we find practically the same distribution.[16]

To recapitulate on the influence of marriage and motherhood upon the work trajectories of the women interviewed, let us start by pointing out certain common features. First, except for permanent jobs that grant and require continuity and strict fulfillment of schedules, and those of the general-waged subproletariat, in particular temporary work in factories, the majority of the occupations are characterized by flexibility of schedule, so as to accommodate daily contingencies, the birth of children, and sudden changes caused by family emergencies. The conciliation of paid work and maternal/domestic demands is thus facilitated. The personal service activities include domestic work by the hour (not live-in) and work for laundresses, who, though leaving home, do not have to adhere to the strict schedule of a factory or workshop. Autonomous activities offer the same advantage and in many cases are carried out at home, on the doorstep, or at worst, on the corner; this is the case for women who feed boarders, sell sweets, fruits, and ice cream;

who knit, make floral arrangements, etc., or who work as independent seamstresses and in their own workshops.

A feedback mechanism seems to operate in these cases. Factory owners tend to prefer young single women, whereas married women with children, unless urged by economic need (for example at periods when they head the household), prefer more flexible schedules at this stage of their lives.

A second, closely related feature has to do with the intermittency of women's paid work insertions. Wives/mothers enter the labor market for short periods of time, or carry out several paid activities simultaneously.[17] What they do depends on their definition of family needs, the quality of conjugal relations (including temporary or long-term separation of the couple) and the multiplicity of circumstances characterizing family interaction at each stage of its vital cycle.

The relationship between paid work and the urgency of family problems is mentioned in practically all cases of women with an occupational history previous to industrial homework. Urgent economic need is felt during the husband's sickness or unemployment, or because of the husband's nonfulfillment of obligations or more or less extended absence (for example, in the United States in the case of former agricultural day workers or peasants). The wife must therefore assume the position of head of household. An increase in household expenses caused by more dependents—elderly parents who must be helped or children whose schooling requires increased spending—not only necessitates but also justifies this working prior to industrial homework and in jobs outside the home.

It is important to emphasize that this more or less urgent economic necessity cannot be deduced simply at any given time from the class position and income of the husband. For example, the nonfulfillment of obligations on the part of two husbands from the proletariat brought about reentry into the labor market of their wives (one of them in an advanced stage of pregnancy) during the first year of marriage, even though one husband was a nonmanual worker with an income above the legal minimum. In the last analysis, the need for successive labor entries and withdrawals by the working class wife/mother cannot be derived from a knowledge of the class position and income of the husband, or from the phase of the family cycle, or from the number of children she has. All these elements are part of a concrete network of family exchanges in which intrahousehold patterns of income allocation and control and women's own labor strategies play a fundamental role; they necessitate an examination at the microsocial level and in terms of internal household hierarchies.

Third, in the case of women with high-school and/or technical education, jobs held in the course of their postmarriage labor trajectories erased differences in education and prior professional experience, (with the possible exception of the seamstresses and one of the beauticians). This pattern of "deskilling," which sacrifices the possibility of personal advancement and economic reward, represents another cost that marriage and motherhood exact from the better-educated women in our sample.

It should be noted that at this stage there are no nonmanual, waged positions, either permanent or temporary, and there are twice as many women in the subproletariat in the personal services and autonomous sectors as there are in the general-waged subproletariat. Also at this stage, the autonomous subproletariat, practically nonexistent in the prenuptial phase, begins to emerge.

Analysis of the postmarriage labor trajectories, therefore, makes clear the influence exerted by women's definition of conjugal/ maternal roles upon the occupational options they pursue. Premarriage differences in terms of class of origin, level of schooling, and prior work history fade in the face of gender, which has systematically encouraged women's postmarriage involvement in industrial homework and the lowest-paid sectors of the urban subproletariat. The pre-homework careers and the entrance into homework of women with no prior occupational history, and those with higher educational level, show that homework limits the work potential of the women interviewed to its lowest common denominator (with the possible exception of some seamstresses). Besides, as was the case during the premarriage stage, gender is also reinforced by the prevalent horizontal and vertical sexual division of labor, as well as by the possibility of dovetailing paid work and domestic demands.

Yet, the influence of gender on postmarriage trajectories should be qualified according to its class context. As will be detailed in the following chapters, women may make homework the unique component of their labor strategy only when their husbands' better-paid proletarianization and subsequent financial contribution are high enough to constitute the basis of household reproduction. In other words, the class and gender gap not only takes place at a societal level; it appears also in a concrete way to shape family dynamics and the economic dependency of wives inside the home. To substantiate this claim, it is useful at this point to look at husbands' and wives' differential labor insertion during the postmarriage stage.

Proletarian Husbands and Subproletarian Wives

Table 5.7 shows the distribution of husbands according to present class position and level of income.[18]

Half are proletarians, including six in the nonmanual sector. If we consider that there are also five retired husbands who belonged to the proletariat, then 55% of all husbands belonged or belong to this class, as compared with 1.9% of the wives in the same postmarriage stage (see table 5.5).

The subproletariat includes 30.6% of the husbands, 72.7% of whom belong to the general-waged sector, as compared to .9% of the wives (See table 5.6). Of the remaining husbands, 7.4% belong to the petite bourgeoisie, owning taxis, hardware stores, and furniture and tin workshops; 5.5% are low-grade members of the military or the police force.

The income of nearly three-fourths of the husbands is concentrated in a range that runs from around twice the legal minimum wage to only 14% who receive less than the legal minimum.

It can be concluded, therefore, that although a minority of the husbands earn less than the legal minimum and have no job stability, for the majority of them the postmatrimonial stage has meant an advance in terms of proletarian membership and level of income. Half of the husbands have joined the Mexico City proletariat of migrant origin, having been absorbed by industries or enterprises expanding during the sixties and seventies. Others, such as members of the petite bourgeoisie and the armed forces, receive incomes that are relatively stable, high in the first case, and stable, although not so high, in the second. If we take into account that 86% of the husbands receive incomes equivalent or superior to the legal minimum and 90% of the women, whatever number of remunerated activities they carry out, are unable to reach this legal minimum, the economic superiority of the husbands is clear. The meaning of this economic prodominance and its implications for family dynamics will be analyzed in Chapters 6 and 7.

Conclusions

Analysis of the pre and postmarriage work histories of the women interviewed stresses the complexity of the factors influencing the processes of female proletarianization. This complexity can not be adequately grasped if analysis is restricted to the immediate conditioning factors of wives' entrance into paid work. In our view, one

Table 5.7   Distribution of Husbands by Class Position and Level of Income (%)

| Level of Income | Nonagricultural Sector | | | | | | | | | Agricultural Sector | | Other: | Total |
| | Proletariat | | | Subproletariat | | | | | Petty Bour-geoisie* | Peasant | Retired** | Armed Forces | |
	(1)	(2)	(3)	General-waged	Personal services	Autono-mous	(4)	(5)					
Less than minimum wage***	—	—	—	8.4	—	1.9	—	0.9	—	0.9	1.9	—	14
Equal to minimum wage	22.4	—	—	9.2	0.9	—	1.9	0.9	0.9	—	0.9	0.9	38
Up to twice the minimum wage	18.3	0.9	3.7	2.8	—	—	0.9	—	2.8	—	0.9	3.7	34
More than twice the minimum wage	3.8	0.9	1.9	1.9	0.9	—	—	—	3.7	—	—	0.9	14
Total % of total (N:107)	51.9			30.6					7.4	0.9	3.7	5.5	100

(1) = manual proletariat; (2) = men who articulate two or more class positions; (3) = nonmanual proletariat; (4) = men who articulate two or more class positions; (5) = other.

*Comprising one case of articulation with another class position
**Comprising two cases of retired men currently in paid work
***Minimum wage: 1,260 Mexican pesos, or US$ 57.27 for 48 weekly hours, in 1981

must go back to the various milestones in a woman's life history, each one of which, by being defined within a particular context of class, gender, and family relations, progressively shapes the future class insertion. (See Appendix: "Three Typical Work Histories," as an illustration of these milestones.)

During the premarriage stage, class of origin, level of schooling and job experience, and skills interact and set the maximum limits women can attain with regard to class and membership in the manual or nonmanual proletariat. In the postmarriage stage, gender plays a decisive influence on women's insertion into the ranks of the lowest paid sectors of the urban subproletariat. However, gender role definition and enactment are not static. Women's labor strategies are also contingent upon their husband's own class insertion and upon family dynamics, including separation of the spouses from one another. Women's past and current skills, education, and professional training (themselves dependent on class of origin) are also contributing factors.

This continuous feedback between class and gender construction along a number of dimensions leads, in our sample, to the reinforcement or re-creation of forms of gender subordination at the workplace, especially in the postmarriage stage. Mechanisms of subordination comprise the vertical sexual division of labor and types of subproletarianization within the personal services, autonomous, and homework sectors, all of which use and reinforce gender traits. All these processes give the women fewer socioeconomic resources for the renegotiation of gender relations within the home and less possibility than the men of occupational mobility and entrance into the proletariat.

Let us now turn more specifically to processes of class construction and recomposition. The nature of industrial homework has been examined in Chapter 4. What is important to stress here is that the making of the subproletariat in industrial homework is not separated from but rather subordinately linked to other processes of female and male proletarianization.

Capitalist expansion and the simultaneous forging of the working class appear as a process differentiating along gender lines according to phases of the family life-cycle. In the same historical period, proletarianization tends to absorb the young, single and better-qualified women, while the wives/mothers and older women make up the subproletariat rendering reproductive support to the proletarianized male gender. At a later stage, however, capital discards these women, who are no longer young or they quit because of marriage or motherhood. Capital now absorbs other young and educated women, and the older ones may join the subproletariat, perhaps in the field of industrial homework through subcontrating networks or in the personal services or autonomous sectors. In other words, wifedom/ motherhood contributes to the division of women within the same working class. From a different angle, it may be said that women, by means of their work trajectories and strategies, supply labor for different processes of capital expansion and proletarianization according to the family life cycle, a conditioning factor that does not pertain to men. Neither is industrial homework separate from processes of male proletarianization in general and that of husbands in particular.

The comparison between the pre and postmarriage work of husbands and wives shows that the subproletarianization of women—who in their character of unmarried daughters, wives, and mothers, are differentially "expelled or retained" in the household they belong to—facilitates a different and generally higher paid labor opportunity for the husbands. *It is not a question of two autonomous processes of labor incorporation, that of the men in the proletariat and women in the subproletariat.* Out analysis suggests that if women who migrate to Mexico City are found predominantly in the subproletariat in personal services and in the autonomous sector (Leff, 1974 and 1976; Arizpe, 1975; García et al., 1979) this subproletarianization need not be independent, but may be articulated through household/family reciprocities to processes of proletarianization of males who thus strengthen their consolidation both in class and gender terms.

The historical conformation of Mexico City's proletariat is therefore a product not only of migratory waves from the hinterlands, but also of gender and generational "waves" of female proletarianization and subproletarianization of wives, heads of household, and daughters who facilitate the proletarianization of spouses, sons, or fathers. It can be argued, therefore, that a kind of "functionality" of gender subordination exists for capital, not only through cheap reproduction of labor power by means of the housewife's non-remunerated domestic work, but also through the subproletarianization of the wives in countries such as Mexico (and one can assume in other peripheral societies) where no family salary exists that would permit the reproduction of the worker and his family.

These considerations underline the heterogeneity of the proletariat of Mexico City, a product of the processes of proletarianization and subproletarianization that incorporate gender hierarchies in diverse phases of the family cycle. What would be the possible ramifications of such heterogeneity and gender reinforcement with respect to forms of organization, consciousness and struggles? We believe this constitutes a fundamental theoretical/political aspect, with implications yet unexplored. Some of them, as they relate to women's renegotiating strategies and struggles within the home, will be taken up in the following chapters.

Appendix: Three Typical Work Histories

1. Doña Soledad

Age: 45 years. Born in 1936 in Tulancingo, state of Hidalgo.
Class determiner: Mother—laundress all her life (subproletariat in personal services); father—deceased at the time she was born
Schooling: No formal schooling but she knows how to read and write.
Work History as a Single Woman (subproletariat in personal services)
Age:
6–8   Attended a paralyzed woman, washed her clothes and took care of her. Payment was food and clothing.

9–14   Worked intermittently as a domestic in several homes. Learned how to read and write by herself because she wanted to work in a factory in order to earn more.
Work History after first Consensual Union (subproletariat in personal services and general-waged sectors)

14–16	Ran away with her boyfriend; continued working as a domestic by the hour.	*First Partner:* 19 years old. Had not completed primary school. Construction worker (general-waged subproletariat).
17–24	Worked in a sweater factory for 8 years. Had 2 children. She was never made permanent. (They laid her off at the end of every month and signed a new contract a week later.) She decided to quit this job and migrate to Mexico City with her children.	Nonfulfillment of economic obligations begins. They did not get along. Leaves her for another woman.

Work History after Second Consensual Union and as Head of Household (subproletariat in the general-waged, personal services, and
industrial-homework sectors)

24–26	Arrived in Mexico City. Worked in a hospital for 10 years as a charwoman. Never made permanent ("I did not have the school papers they wanted").	
26–34	Began second and current consensual union. Continues working in the hospital. Has 4 more children. Soledad remembers that she earned good money during these years and that she had more decision-making power. ("It was not like it is now, with homework. Then it was different. When I wanted something I bought it. And I dressed my children as I wished.")	*Second Partner:* 22 years old. No formal schooling. No job skills. Did anything that came along. (autonomous subproletariat). Alcoholic, violent, with periodic nonfulfillment of economic obligations. Worked in California several times as a *bracero* (agricultural day-laborer). Brings presents home but Soledad supports the household during his absence.
35	Husband returned from California and made her quit the hospital job in order to spend more time at home. The children were still small and there was no one to feed them, and no one to take care of him either. ("So, out of respect for him, I left my job. He promised never to go back to the States and to give me a good *gasto* [household allowance]."	He begins to specialize in electricity, but he always has temporary waged work (general-waged subproletariat).
35–40	Starts taking in laundry. Birth of youngest daughter. Soledad got a kidney disease and could not wash clothes	

any longer, because it was too hard. ("But I have always worked because my husband's work is seasonal and I cannot stand by when my children go needy".)

41–45   Started industrial homework in plastics but is poorly paid. Now she does polishing in toys ("I have always worked out of necessity".)   Currently he works for subcontractors. He does not have social security coverage but with overtime he earns four times the legal minimum wage (general-waged subproletariat).

2. Doña Goya

Age: 33 years. Born in 1947 in Mexico City.

Class determiner: Father—casual worker in a company that transported produce to the market (general-waged subproletariat); mother: laundress all her life (subproletariat in personal services).

Schooling: second year of elementary school

Work History as a Single Woman (subproletariat in personal service)

Age:

8–14   Worked intermittently as child carer and domestic in several homes. She also substituted for her mother at home. Father was an alcoholic.

Postmarriage Work History (subproletariat in personal services and industrial homework sectors).

15   Stopped paid work when she married. The couple lived with her parents and shared expenses. Had 6 children during this period. Her mother helped them, if needed, so: ("no habia motivos para trabajar afuera y los niños eran muy chicos"). ("There was no need to work outside and the children were too small.")   *Husband:* 30 years old. First year primary school. Factory worker (proletariat). Factory closed and he changed to other jobs before getting his current job. Factory worker (proletariat).

25–29	Because of increasing school expenses she started taking in washing. She also worked as domestic in the same neighborhood. She has 4 more children: a total of 10.	
30–33	Started industrial homework (assembling toys) helped by 8 of her 10 children. She also continues working as a laundress and domestic. Both jobs give her more stable and higher earnings than homework.	He continues working in the same factory.

3. Doña Rosa

Age: 28 years. Born in 1953 in Puerto de Veracruz, state of Veracruz.
Class determiner: Father—owned a grocery store (petite bourgeoisie); mother—helped in the family store.
Schooling: High school and secretarial course
Work History as a Single Woman (nonmanual general-waged subproletariat)
Age:

14–17	Worked first as a typist and later as a secretary. She liked her job very much.	

Postmarriage Work History (subproletariat in industrial homework and autonomous sectors)

| 18 | Quit her job when married. They moved from Veracruz to Mexico City. Her husband had promised to let her work once married, but later forbade her to look for a job as a secretary. Her in-laws with whom they lived, also thought that a good wife and mother should stay at home, unless poverty obliged her to work for a living. | *Husband:* 22 years old. High-school education (nonmanual proletariat; encargado [supervisor] of a tortilla shop). |

18–25   Two children.

25   Started homework; quit after
           3 months because of
           husband's opposition and
           poor pay. But she enjoyed
           having some economic au-
           tonomy (*"Me gusta tener lo
           mio"*).

26   Started selling clothes and   He has kept the same job all
           blankets to friends and   these years and has been
           neighbors, intermittently.   promoted twice.

28   She continues selling blan-
           kets and has started home-
           work (assembling coils). A
           friend provides her with the
           work. She accepts it only 3
           times a week, to keep up
           with proper standards of
           housework. She would like
           to get a part-time job as a
           secretary but is afraid of
           husband's opposition.
           Wants to be retrained be-
           cause she has lost her skills.
           With income from home-
           work she bought a typewrit-
           er to practice typing in her
           spare time.

Six

Class, Gender, and Asymmetrical Exchanges Within Households

In preceding chapters we pointed out the feedback that exists between the processes of class and gender conformation as they appear in our sample. But we do not maintain that there exists a perpetual cycle of functional re-creation and feedback between both relations of domination. The working women interviewed are not passive bearers of class and gender relations. As workers confronting a particularly unfavorable bargaining situation, women do occasionally resist and struggle on an individual or collective basis. As gendered subjects they also develop strategies to create minimum spaces of control over their lives. But what are the conditioning factors, boundaries, and links between forms of struggles that women develop within the domestic domain? Is it safe to assume that wives' access to an autonomous income will automatically empower them in the bargaining of gender relations within the household? And how do changes in family dynamics relate to society's class and gender relations in which these women are embedded?

These issues will be the subject of this and the following chapter.[1] We shall start unravelling the complex links between those processes, beginning with the "decomposition" of the household unit in terms of patterns of income allocation and control. We shall next relate these patterns to homeworkers' work strategies and exchanges of unpaid domestic work (according to level of marital reciprocity); to the phase of the family life-cycle, and to kinship composition of different households. Finally, we shall refer to the links between the processes studied and the conformation and reproduction of class relations in society at large.

109

Decomposing the Household Unit

In recent years in Latin America, a growing interest has focused on the household as the key entity for the understanding of a wide gamut of phenomena, as has become evident in several kinds of analysis: the participation of men and women in the work force (García, Muñoz y Oliveira, 1982); demographic behavior (Burch, Lira, and López, eds. 1965); reproduction of labor power (Singer, 1977; Margulis, 1982); and survival strategies of different social groups (Bilac, 1978; Schmink, 1982). The variety of disciplines interested in the household[2] (sociology, anthropology, demography, economics) and the contrast among the theoretical paradigms in each of the investigations notwithstanding, in our judgment they all coincide in the vision of the household as a single entity, with the the assumption that the family roles supporting the vision are complementary.[3] By way of example, studies on survival strategies (mentioned above) present the family as an interest group, without internal fissures. It would appear that the family is an active social agent that rationally chooses survival mechanisms (among which figures the incorporation of members into the labor market) in order to insure the standard of living and the reproduction of its members and its class, survival mechanisms maximizing the interests or benefits of each and every one of the family members.

It is undeniable that, insofar as they focus on the household family as an entity conditioning the incorporation of men and women into the labor market, those studies represent a significant advance over the conceptualization of the male and female labor force as aggregates of isolated individuals—the most typical example being the information derived from census reports. At the same time, from a feminist perspective, the analyses given by mainstream Marxist sociology, anthropology, or economics all suffer from the same bias: the adoption of the household or family as unit of analysis along with the employment of classificatory categories; for example, in accordance with its sociodemographic elements (kinship composition, phase of the family life-cycle, sex of the head of the household) which, although essential, ignore the internal gender, class, and generational hierarchies.

Behind the facade of the monolithic household/family various underlying assumptions should be distinguished:

—The household/family as a whole makes decisions on marriage, fertility, migration, levels of schooling and consumption, and the incorporation into the labor markets of its members.

—The household/family is a corporate entity, and as such has shared and unique interests in any sphere of family interaction.

—If interests are shared and unique, so also are the needs to be satisfied by the courses of action of its members (incorporation in the labor market, housework, education, etc.), which benefit everyone in the same way.

—As a corollary to this interpretation, the individual income, salary, or earnings of the household/family's members all go into a common fund made up of proportional contributions. The allocative priorities of household resources are likewise similar.

Evidence is mounting from feminist anthropological, sociological, historical and economic studies to qualify or question these assumptions.[4] Although even a partial review of contemporary critical literature on the hegemonic concept of the household or the family goes beyond the limits of this chapter, we shall point out two main tenets. In the first place, this literature challenges the ideology of the "monolithic family," consecrated in the model of the bourgeois nuclear family and its gender division of labor as the only form of family—atemporal and functional within the capitalist system. It also rejects the concept of the biological or "natural" family. Instead it reclaims for social and historical analysis the multifaceted household/family arrangements prevalent within a given class and race: the gender division of labor, gender and generational hierarchies, motherhood, the construction of sexuality and gender identity—to name a few. In the second place, it requires the "decomposition" of the household/family entity to uncover its underlying structures that incorporate hierarchies of class, gender, and age.

In the light of this evidence it becomes necessary once again to question the validity of these assumptions in the Mexican case and, logically, the model of family or household on which that validity rests. But how can the household/family be defined and decomposed so that its internal hierarchies are exposed, while, simultaneously rescuing individual men and women as the constrained forgers of their own history? Also, how is the exclusively microsocial analysis to be transcended, in order to show the connection between household processes and society as a whole?

Neither theory nor feminist scholarship provides uniform criteria for "decomposition"; these criteria will vary according to the theoretical position and the ends pursued in each research.[5] In our case, we started by adopting the broad definition of household introduced in Chapter 2; i.e., a locus or social sphere made up of a number of individuals who share a common place to live and a budget.

In line with this definition, our point of departure in the "decomposition" of the households consisted in establishing the relationships that linked the components of the locus. All the cases were households based on kinship relationships. It was therefore fundamental to establish the role of the women interviewed within the system of family reciprocities—the marriage contract—and how this system was handled within the broader framework of wives' consciousness as "interpretation of the world." Secondly, we established the circuits of flow and distribution of domestic monetary resources, or the material base of family interactions.

Both aspects are dialectically connected, as we intend to show in the course of analysis. For simplicity, each aspect will be introduced separately. This chapter will give a detailed account of allocational patterns and their links with exchanges of unpaid domestic work, and in the following chapter, those links and other dimensions of conjugal dynamics will be seen through the lens of the marriage contract.

From the beginning of our research, the industrial homeworkers had pointed out time and again the importance they placed on the husband's regular and sufficient provision of housekeeping money to cover household needs. They talked about consequences when it was lacking and the role it played in their strategies for longterm security. They defended the meaning of marriage as economic support for themselves and their children, feeling they owed "respect" or deference to the responsible husband who fulfills his economic obligation.

In their eyes, the patterns of monetary distribution and control constituted the crux of a style of conjugal interaction and formed the basic pillars of household exchanges by means of their articulation in a whole series of reciprocities. These reciprocities were between the spouses themselves, their parents, and their children; they were expressed through sexuality, personalized attention, nurture, unpaid domestic work, as well as the opportunity and/or obligation of engaging in paid work by different members of the family group.

It is within this network of exchanges that wives' entrance into paid work and the limits of their renegotiating strategies may be understood. In effect, regardless of the impression of an outside observer regarding the pressure of economic need, a conflictive family context per se, or lack of employment opportunities in society at large, women saw themselves as constrained subjects devising work and other strategies to attain specific and general goals that included bargaining over given areas of conjugal dynamics. The allocation circuits and points of control, their tensions and conflicts, may be regarded in this light both as the outcome and the condition of power renegotiation between husbands and wives (and possibly other adult household members). They provide therefore, an appropriate starting point for uncovering women's renegotiating strategies, their priorities and limits. This discussion constitutes the first stage in our exploration of the concrete relationship between women's control of their earnings and the persisting or undermining of forms of male domination within the household.

Intrahousehold Patterns of Money Flows, Allocation, and Control

Before describing the distribution patterns themselves, it is necessary to point out some other spheres of decision-making that affect those circuits in an *indirect* fashion. In the majority of cases involving younger wives who came from better-off households, women found it necessary to overcome their husbands' resistance and get permission to participate in paid production in the home and outside. Irrespective of age, women stated that they decided, in accordance with the urgency of weekly needs, the schedules they would follow for paid and unpaid domestic work so as not to neglect their definition of wifely and maternal duties. They also decided the intensity and volume of the obligations they could demand from their children—if they should be allowed to play after school or must help with housework or industrial homework, if they should attend school exclusively or combine schooling with some type of light paid work. In the case of adolescent children, this decision involved the father also and the teenagers concerned, especially the males. The margins of the decisions affecting the circuit *directly* were much narrower as will be seen in the following description of the allocative patterns.

In all households studied, money enters in the form of wages or other earnings.[7] It leaves the household as cash, to pay for the wide range of household expenditures (and in a few cases small amounts are put aside as long-term savings).[8] We will first explore the patterns of flow and distribution of money between entry and exit

113

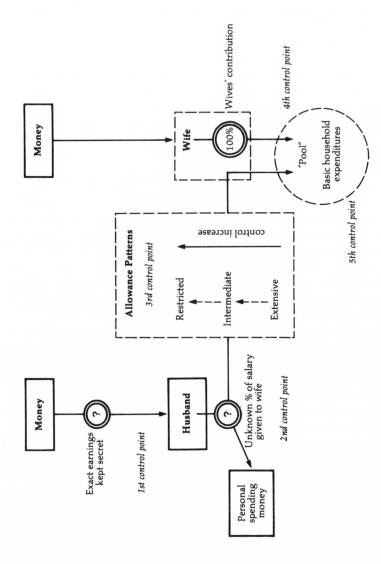

Figure 6.1: *Pool Pattern*

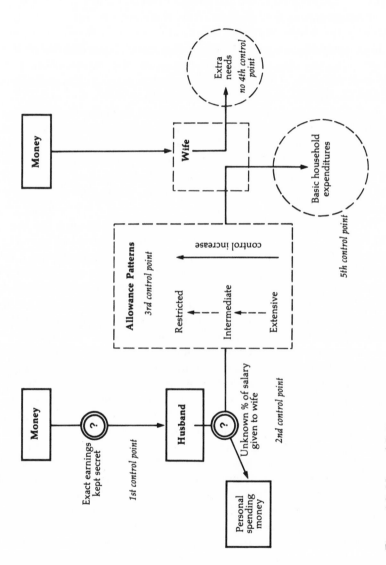

Figure 6.2: *Nonpool Pattern*

points, noting the *main control points* along this flow. We will then link these patterns to the exchanges of unpaid domestic work among members of the household.

Evidence revealed two different allocational patterns. In the *pooling, or common, fund* go a portion of the husband's earnings, plus the earning of the outworker wife. This fund (found in 62% of our sample of 53 households) is used to cover the basic expenditures of the households; in other words, it becomes the basis of household reproduction. This pattern was predominant in lower-income households, where husbands' wages either just reached minimum legal wage, or fell below this line. The pattern was also found where husbands' incomes were higher but their contributions to the common fund did not meet basic household needs as defined by their wives. Half the women in this subgroup also held one or two other jobs besides outwork, the most common combination being with work in washing, ironing, or as a part-time, paid domestic servant (See table 6.1, Groups A + B and C).

The second pattern found is the *housekeeping allowance:* the husband fills the role of main economic provider or breadwinner. He hands over to his wife a portion of his earnings as a housekeeping allowance to cover basic expenditures. The wife in turn uses her earnings to cover expenditures above and beyond the minimum standard of living secured by the allowance. This pattern (38% of the sample of households studied) was found mostly in higher-income household where the main providers earned three or more times the minimum legal wage; but also in a few households (10%) where husbands earned less than three times the minimum wage but more than the minimum. Twenty-five percent of the wives in this category held a job apart from homework, such as selling clothes and household items, or petty trade. A few combined homework with going out to wash, sew, iron, or do paid domestic service (see table 6.1, Group D).

The flow of incoming money in both groups was subject to certain controls exercised by men. In the pooling pattern, the *first control point* was the husbands' ability to withhold or share information on the actual amount of their earnings. Almost half the wives in this group were not sure exactly how much their husbands earned each week. Even when wives did know their husbands' earnings it was usually the weekly wage and not the amounts received as overtime, bonuses, tips or *mordidas*. Wives felt that husbands hid this information to keep the women dependent, and they resented it. Many of them expressed anxiety and helplessness, others rage, when talking

Table 6.1 Distribution of Homeworkers of Groups A+B, C, and D, and Husband's Class Position and Income (%)

Groups	Household Composition and Phase of Family Cycle				Industrial Homework		Husbands' Class Position and Level of Income*													
	Young nuclear	Young extended	Adult nuclear	Adult extended	Only	+ Other paid	Proletariat			Subproletariat				Petty bourgeoisie		Peasant	Retired	Other: Armed Forces		
							(2)	(3)	(4)	(1)	(2)	(3)	(4)	(3)	(4)	(1)	(1)	(2)	(3)	(4)
A+B (N:14)	35.8	21.4	28.6	14.2	21.4	78.6	28.6	28.6	—	28.6	7.1	—	—	—	—	—	7.1	—	—	—
C (N:19)	42.1	26.3	26.3	5.3	68.4	31.6	15.9	15.9	10.5	—	15.9	—	10.5	—	5.2	5.2	—	5.2	10.5	5.2
D (N:20)	70.0	15.0	15.0	—	75.0	25.0	10.0	35.0	25.0	—	—	10.0	5.0	10.0	5.0	—	—	—	—	—

*Incomes: (1) = less than minimum wage; (2) = equal to minimum wage; (3) = up to twice the minimum wage; (4) = more than twice the minimum wage.

about it. Most suspected that their husbands were not pooling all they could to meet collective expenses.

The *second control point* was closely related to the first: the husband's decision as to what portion of his earnings he would keep as personal spending or pocket money. Wives did not object to their hubands' withholding a certain amount as pocket money; on the contrary, they considered it legitimate if the men had to pay for transportation to and from work, meals at noon, and also drinks with *cuates* (pals) after work, a custom considered to be a sign of maleness. In certain cases, pocket money was used to buy clothes, shoes, etc., needed for the husband's work or social life. What wives did mind was the amount held back for pocket money; in fact disagreement about this is the main source of quarrelling and physical abuse among spouses of this group. Despite the conjugal battle 75% of husbands had the final say on the issue—only in 14% of the cases was it a joint decision. Three wives defined it as their decision, meaning that they calculated the minimum amount of housekeeping money they needed, and their husbands agreed without too much resistance. In general, the average amount kept as pocket money came close to 25% of declared earnings.

The *third control point* is the form in which the allowance or contribution is given to the wife: as a lump sum, or in installments. This control point is very important because it exerts a direct influence upon the quality of the marital relationship. We found three main patterns: the first was the *extensive allowance;* that is, the weekly contribution was handed over in full and was a fixed amount. With the wife's contribution, this pool covered all the expenditures of the domestic group: rent, normal food bills, cooking fuel, light, water, school expenses, clothes, etc. The wife still had the responsibility for stretching this fund to cover everything, without requesting further contributions, except in emergencies. The opposite situation was a *restricted allowance* covering only normal food bills, gas for cooking, and daily school expenses. The third pattern was an *intermediate allowance*, which covered these items, plus clothing or rent. Only 40% of the wives in the pooling group did not feel pressed to request funds for expenses not covered by the original allowance. Just under 40% received the intermediate allowance, and about 10% the restricted. The extensive pattern was the one preferred by most wives, despite its numerous shortcomings. In favor of the extensive pattern, wives reported that this meant they did not have to worry so much about husbands' possible noncontribution because the money kept back by husbands, supposedly to cover rent, electricity, or clothing would not in fact be spent on drinking, cards, horse races, or other women. The extensive allowance also saved the wife the repeated humiliation of begging and nagging to secure the promised amount. A wife who is not forced to beg, quarrel, or engage in manipulative behavior—directly or through her children—is relatively less dependent than one who must do such things. On the negative side, and because the extensive allowances were low, wives who had the whole responsibility for making ends meet found that this required a great deal of ingenuity and was a source of profound psychological stress. It was the reported reason behind two attempts at suicide during the course of fieldwork. Wives who received restricted or intermediate allowances did not view this as a form of division of labor, with reponsibilities divided between themselves and their husbands, but instead as a means for keeping them in a state of uncertainty, worry, and dependence until the next rent was paid. It is important to stress that pattern chosen for allowance did not appear to be related to the level of the husband's earnings, but rather to his personal preference.

Wives' contribution to the common fund is a *fourth control point*. In all cases, they pooled their entire earnings, not keeping the equivalent of male pocket money. The decision to pool earnings was declared (often with great pride) to be the wife's own choice in virtually all cases. In actual fact, they have little choice, given that their incomes are very low, and the ideology of maternal altruism (Whitehead, 1981) encourages them to devote their earning to meet collective rather than individual needs. Among older women, with very conflictive conjugal relations and without access to retirement or pension, investing in children's food and education could also introduce a measure of personal interest in women's altruism. This mixture of ideology and rational calculation is not quantifiable, but it should be kept in mind that, irrespective of the underlying rationale (bare needs, ideology, rational calculation, or a combination of all three), even though wives pool their total earnings, their contribution to the common fund is generally lower than that of their husbands. Only in a few cases where husbands earned less than the minimum legal wage did the outworkers' contribution equal of occasionally surpass the mens' share (53% of the weekly pool).

This information indicates how husbands' different and better-paid class position outside the household is translated into a commanding position within the family/household context. The situation also reinforces—among younger wives whose contribution to the fund is the lowest—feelings of insecurity and dependence. Wives talked disparagingly about the level of their contributions to the common fund. Moreover, as there is no wives' equivalent of personal spending money, whatever they spend on themselves must be saved from the housekeeping, thus competing with collective expenditures they have defined as their own. A feeling of guilt and of depriving her children often mars any pleasure a women might have on the rare occasions when she buys something for herself.

We have already suggested that wives' managerial role is fraught with problems and anxiety. This raises the question of whether, or to what extent, a wife's role in handling a very limited fund of money, already largely committed to necessary basics, should be considered a manifestation of control. In our view this semblance of control is illusory. In reality, the wife has no financial autonomy; the pool must cover unavoidable expenditures. Besides, husbands do not withdraw from the scene after delivering their share, but continue to exercise control. This is the *fifth control point*, which has several aspects. First, a man makes sure that *his* money is spent on basic family needs as well as on his own desired level of personal comsumption in food, clothing, etc. No wonder, then, that one of the wives' main incentives to earn a few pesos as outworkers, washerwomen, or maids is associated with a wish to expand their limited sphere of management.

Secondly, in the case of heavy drinkers or alcoholics (the majority of husbands fell within the first category), it is common for them to "borrow" money from the pool to cover drinking expenses, particularly if their pocket money is already gone by the middle of the week. This suggests that wives actually have no control over the disposal of the pool. At most, a woman can budget[9]—that is decide whether she will feed her family with tortillas and beans or a piece of meat, whether she will buy her daughter a dress or her son some underwear. This budgeting nightmare is particularly acute at the end of the month when the rent is collected. When the wife is handed an extensive allowance, it is her responsibility to have put aside money each week to pay the rent at the end of the month. In most households, this goal is seldom attained so the final week of the month is marked by food consumption decreased in quantity and quality and, in some cases, (see note 8) attempts to borrow from relatives or neighbors. Doña Soledad refers to this situation in the following words:

He gives me the gasto [housekeeping allowance] all right, but I must see that everything is fine, that nothing is lacking, good food for him, yes, the best pieces are for him. I have to keep for him the best of what I get, if he wants beef, or whatever. He usually wants beer or sometimes *pulque*. He says: *Vieja* [old woman] is the pulque already here? Or bring me some beer. I'll pay you later! He never does. On Thursday I am without a cent and I have to ask my *comadrita* to complete the week. He collects his money on Saturday and that day I get the gasto, and start returning what I owe. You know, to manage the allowance is a difficult job, prices are going up and we must buy food, no matter what. And if something goes wrong or he gets angry at me, he may even cut off the allowance of that week.

Thirdly, husbands have ultimate veto power on types of spending. All decisions concerning major expenditures, which are usually infrequent, and important in the sense that they set the general life style of the household—buying a piece of land for later settlement, electrical appliances, new furniture—are taken by husbands or in a few cases are a matter of joint decision making.

We now turn to the other pattern: the *housekeeping allowance*. Some features are similar to the ones already mentioned: just over 50% of the wives did not know the exact amount of their husbands' earnings; husbands kept pocket money, wives did not; the allowance was delivered as a lump sum in a third of the sample; for the others it was restricted—in one case it was daily. Wives' reactions were similar to those in the pooling group, the majority preferring an extensive allowance. Wives budget rather than manage different types of expenditures, and they are subject to similar restrictions concerning major expenditures. However, because these are higher-income households, fewer quarrels about strictly money matters were reported.

A fundamental difference is that husbands' and wives' earnings are earmarked for different kinds of consumption. Basic needs—rent, food bills, gas, clothes, schooling—are covered by the housekeeping allowance; so-called extras are met from wives' earnings. In general these expenditures improve the family's standard of living in quality or variety of goods; or they are simply treats—buying fruit or some special food or giving the children Sunday outing money. It is useful to list some of these expenditures; for children: underwear, socks, pants, toys, treats such as cokes, sweets, fruit; transportation to and from school; better-quality shoes or clothes for special occasions such as weddings or fifteenth-birthday parties; for the household: pots, pans, sheets, blankets, curtains, food blenders, sewing machines, kitchen furniture, a typewriter. Wives' money was used also for savings, medical emergencies, family outings on Sunday, taking the children to movies; their own clothes, shoes, or underwear, or for helping poor relatives without having to ask the husbands' permission.

Problems arise largely over husbands' and wives' contrasting definition of what constitutes basic expenditures, or what is the minimum acceptable standard of children's clothes, schooling, outings. Indeed some of the items wives pay for are hardly extras; some allowances afford only a bare level of survival and do not include the extra items of clothing, toys, or treats that can make life more bearable. But it is husbands who decide minimum standards; these are seldom shared by wives. Furthermore, couples often do not agree on the urgency of a given expenditure, but it is the husband who decides not only what is basic but when it is needed. As Doña Chela expresses it:

> I need this money [from homework] to purchase shoes or clothes for the children. He buys them when he feels like it, not at the time they are needed. For example, my daughter Lupita, her shoes are old, she has no dress to wear at her aunt's wedding. I told him Lupita has no shoes, no dress. He thinks they are not necessary. So I will buy them with my work.

The description of distribution patterns makes clear that none of the assumptions regarding the monolithic household/family are valid in our sample *strictu sensu*. Husbands and wives differ in the definition of the basic necessities of the family complex, their consumption priorities, the way in which income should be distributed, and the proportion to be allocated for the common fund, if there is one. We do not find, therefore, the household to be a collective entity adopting decisions on allocative patterns according to a single corporative interest; instead, we find *main* control points, all along the allocative circuits, and it is through these mechanisms that the majority of husbands impose the basic features of the household's survival. Women's control of their earnings has not given them significant control over total income flow because they cannot renegotiate the main control points along that flow.

Wives' subproletarianization—the element that enables them to "complete" the weekly common fund or contribute substantially to cover basic needs, or make up for expenses not recognized by the husbands—remains, therefore, subordinated to overall male control. What must now be examined, by relating circuits of distribution to intrahousehold exchanges of unpaid domestic work, is the cost incurred by wives in pursuing these labor strategies.

Distribution Circuits and Exchanges of Unpaid Domestic Work

In both the pool and the housekeeping allowance groups the industrial homeworker, in her character of wife and mother, habitually carries out all tasks required for the daily and generational reproduction of labor power. The list is long and includes quantifiable and non-quantifiable tasks. Among the former are housecleaning and dishwashing, sewing, mending, washing and ironing, buying and cooking of food, the search for water from a collective source in periods of drought, supervision of children's homework, care of the children and of sick and elderly people, transportation of children and elderly people to the doctor. Within the nonquantifiable enumeration we find sexuality and the provision of affection and the emotional and psychological nurturance of members of the household. We will be dealing here exclusively with exchanges of quantifiable, unpaid, domestic work.

From explanations of the wives, we have distinguished in the Pool Set a continuum of situations—which we call Groups A, B and C—according to two basic axes: the proportion of the contribution made by the woman interviewed to the weekly household fund compared with that of her husband and, possibly, of other household members, and the husband's fulfillment or non-fulfillment of his role as the household's economic provider. A third, nonquantifiable factor, the quality of conjugal interaction will be taken up in the next chapter.

We find, therefore, *within the pool continuum*, the following subcomplexes:

Group A: Wives who contribute a substantial amount of the weekly pool (more than 40%) and whose husbands are regular economic providers (20.8% of the subsample of 53 wives).

Group B: Wives who contribute more than 40% of the weekly pool but whose husbands have almost stopped contributing, do so sporadically, or, in one case and for reasons of sickness, does not provide a housekeeping allowance (5.4%).

Group C: Wives who contribute less than 40% of the weekly pool and whose husbands remain the main economic providers (35.8%).

Those axes articulated the domestic work exchanges among household members, but they operated in a variety of ways according to the phase of the family life-cycle and the kinship composition of the respective households.

Before undertaking this analysis, however, a brief reference to some characteristics of households in Groups A + B, and C seems in order.

As mentioned earlier, households that form the pool continuum have, in general, less access to economic resources than those of Group D (the housekeeping allowance set), but there do exist internal differences that should be pointed out.

As shown in Table 6.1, Groups A + B are made up of the more modest households of the sample: 35.7% of the husbands earn wages less than the legal minimum. Close to 80% of the wives combine industrial homework with other activities within the sub-proletariat, in the personal services and autonomous sectors. These tasks are undertaken in a stable fashion (see n. 16, Chapter 5) and constitute the principal source of income of the women interviewed.

Group C occupies a position equidistant between the poorest extreme (Group A + B) and that of the best relative position (Group D, the housekeeping allowance set). Only one peasant husband earns an income inferior to the legal minimum, and close to 60% of the husbands earn an income of between twice and more than twice the legal minimum. Only 31.6% of the wives have jobs in addition to industrial homework, and these are carried out almost without exception in the home itself. The owner of the hardware store (mentioned in Chapter 5) constitutes an atypical example within this set, given her stability and higher level of income relative to the rest of Group C.

We now turn to the examination of domestic work exchanges in Groups A + B, and C (Pool Continuum) and D (Housekeeping Allowance Set) according to phase in the family life-cycle and kinship composition of the respective households (see Chapter 2 for definitions).[10] In order to simplify the discussion, we shall stress the differences between groups. Findings pertinent to educational level and help received from offspring and other kin and their labor insertion, for instance, are to be taken as similar, unless otherwise indicated.

Table 6.2   *Average Weekly Working Hours by Groups A, B, C, and D*

Phase of Family Cycle	Group A			Group B			Group C			Group D		
	Unpaid Domestic Work	Paid Work	Total	Unpaid Domestic Work	Paid Work	Total	Unpaid Domestic Work	Paid Work	Total	Unpaid Domestic Work	Paid Work	Total
Young nuclear (N = 27)	56	55	111	49	56	105	66	37½	103½	67	25	92
Young extended (N = 11)	49½	51½	101	—	—	—	54	37	91	61	29¾	90¾
Adult nuclear (N = 12)	46	44½	90½	42	34	76	60	27½	87½	58	34	92

NOTE: Extended households in advanced phases have not been analyzed because of the small number of cases in each group.

Households in the Earlier Phases of the Family Cycle

In the nuclear households of the young cycle, one notices the greater number of hours worked per week by wives belonging to Group A (111 hours) and B (105 hours), which represent 231% and 219%, respectively, of the maximum legal workweek (48 hours). The wives who make up Group D work 92 hours, which represents 192% of the legal workweek; Group C also occupies an intermediate position: 103 hours 30 minutes, which is equivalent to 216% of the maximum legal workweek.

When these hours are broken down into the portion dedicated to paid work and that dedicated to housework, the opposite tendency appears. In other words, while the women belonging to Groups A and B reduce housework to 56 and 49 hours respectively (117% and 102% of the legal workweek of 48 hours), the women from Group D dedicate a maximum of 67 hours to housework (140% of the legal workweek). Conversely, the wives from Group A and B concentrate their efforts on paid work (55 hours and 56 hours per week), which represents 115% and 117% respectively of the legal workweek; for their part, the industrial homeworkers from Group D dedicate 25 hours to remunerated work, or 52% of the maximum legal workweek.

In the eyes of the wives from Group A and B (and husbands from Group A), economic need justifies dedicating a maximum number of hours to paid work and consequently a relative neglect of housework. The rhythm of work done by these women was particularly intense—it should be remembered that the majority of them carried on some other remunerated activity in addition to industrial homework—and the daily hours could vary in accordance with the urgency of family need for money; for example, the women might decide to take in more washing, setting aside industrial homework, or she might work intensely at both activities, putting off housework that could be postponed (washing/ironing, housecleaning, sewing and mending, etc.), until Sunday.

In the case of the wives from Group D (Housekeeping Allowance Set), the work stability of the husbands, the higher incomes, and the regularity of the weekly household allowance permitted these women to dedicate their income to "extras." At the same time, they were required (either by their own standards or by husbands to whom a well-kept house was important) to maintain a level of housework and care of household members not observed in the rest of the sample. Only in Group D could we notice stable daily schedules and days and hours dedicated to housecleaning, closet cleaning, shopping, family excursions. The time dedicated to the children, overseeing either their homework or their play, was also given a high priority by the workers in this group. On the other hand, the existence of a more complete domestic infrastructure—larger homes included a separate living room, kitchen and bathroom, and a variety of furniture and utensils—required a greater concentration on housework, in order to take advantage of this same comfort. Remunerated work appeared then as a secondary activity, coming after the fulfillment of the principal obligations of housewife, wife, and mother. It is not surprising that in our sample the highest weekly averages for time spent on housework were registered by this group. At the same time, all of these women stated that they rested on Sundays, meaning that they did a minimum of housework, enjoyed afternoon excursions with husband and children, and watched television this day as well as during the week, etc.

Finally, the internal distribution of schedules in Group C showed a concentration on housework similar to that in Group D (66 hours per week, or 138% of the legal weekly maximum, but approximately 12 hours more than the latter for remunerated work and some 18 hours less than Group A). The wives in Group C, therefore, fulfilled their domestic obligations first, and then dedicated the rest of their time to remunerated work, thus sacrificing hours of relaxation both during the week and on the weekend in order to attain this objective.

The long, total workdays of all the groups were also partially the result of the type and life-cycle of the households considered. They were young, nuclear households where the women interviewed had little help with housework and industrial homework on the part of younger children, in addition to the scanty or nonexistent contribution of the husbands, a common characteristic in all the groups in the sample.

As a first approach to the help received from children and husbands, we have calculated the percentage of husbands and children old enough to help (6 or more years) who actually do help effectively the woman interviewed either with housework or industrial homework. See Tables 6.3a and 6.3b.

It should be noted that the help demanded from children for housework and industrial homework is greater in Group A than in Groups D and C. In Group A, even girls under 6 help, something that does not happen in the other groups. The case of the house-

Table 6.3a   Percentage of Husbands, Daughters, Sons, and Other Relatives over Six Years of Age Who Help in Domestic Work and Homework

| | Group A | | | | | | | | | | Group B | | | | | | | | | |
| | Husbands | | Daughters | | Sons | | Other Female Relatives | | Other Male Relatives | | Husbands | | Daughters | | Sons | | Other Female Relatives | | Other Male Relatives | |
Phase of Family Cycle	D	H	D	H	D	H	D	H	D	H	D	H	D	H	D	H	D	H	D	H
Young nuclear	100	25	100[a]	100	67	67	—	—	—	—	100	0	100	0	67	0	0	100	—	—
Young extended	100	33	0	0	0	50	100	50	—	—	—	—	—	—	—	—	—	—	—	—
Adult nuclear	100	33	100	100	43	71	—	—	—	—	100	0	100	0	100	50	—	—	—	—

D = Domestic work.

H = Homework.

[a]In addition, there were four daughters, under six years of age, who helped in unpaid domestic work and homework.

Table 6.3b Percentage of Husbands, Daughters, Sons, and Other Relatives over Six Years of Age Who Help in Domestic and Homework

Phase of Family Cycle	Group C										Group D									
	Husbands		Daughters		Sons		Other Female Relatives		Other Male Relatives		Husbands		Daughters		Sons		Other Female Relatives		Other Male Relatives	
	D	H	D	H	D	H	D	H	D	H	D	H	D	H	D	H	D	H	D	H
Young nuclear	63	13	42	29	78	62	—	—	—	—	71	14	64	73	20	53	—	—	—	—
Young extended	80	20	33	33	17	17	80	40	50	50	67	0	67	100	0	100	33	33	0	100
Adult nuclear	80	20	92	31	20	40	—	—	—	—	67	33	83	67	20	53	—	—	—	—

D = Domestic work.
H = Homework.

hold from Group B is atypical, since a daily visit by the maternal grandmother substitutes for children's help in carrying out homework. The gender division of help in domestic work and industrial homework should also be underlined: a greater proportion of daughters than sons help; this characteristic is less pronounced, however, than in households from the advanced cycle. The gender differentiation is not only quantitative but is fundamentally qualitative. The daughters help, according to their age, with lighter tasks, such as carrying messages, doing minor shopping, taking out the garbage or; if they are more than 10 years old, they may do all or part of the grocery shopping, clean the house, wash dishes and clothes, iron, take care of younger brothers and sisters bringing them to school or overseeing their play. Whatever their age, sons do only minor tasks, concentrating their activities outside of the nucleus.

The help the female workers can demand in industrial homework depends a great deal on the type of work. There are tasks that mothers consider too dangerous to delegate to small children because of the physical risks, for example, polishing plastic with a scalpel or cutting lace with scissors.

Nevertheless, they require help with simpler tasks, such as wrapping up, but not cutting, the roll of lace; filling cellophane containers with seeds; or completing the less complicated phases of the assembly of pens and toys, as in putting the wooden beads on the wires of an abacus.

What help is given by husbands? Although a high proportion of them help to some degree, particularly in the neediest households (Group A and B), this help is concentrated almost exclusively in activities outside of the home: paying bills, carrying out formal transactions, sometimes making a weekly trip to the central market. Inside the home, they can take care of repairs, and a few supervise their children's homework or play with them. There was no instance of collaboration in housecleaning or food preparation, except in one extreme case of a woman's sickness when no other female relative was available. Husbands' help with industrial homework is also minimal. Occasionally, they might tie up cardboard boxes or pack seeds with the children, or in the case of a husband with a car he might pick up blankets from a factory that his wife could sell to her acquaintances.

Exchanges of incomes and housework and help with industrial homework between spouses and children must be seen in connection with the possible "expulsion" of the minors to the work force, their retention in school, or a combination of both alternatives. The following findings are similar in all groups, whatever the composition of the household and the stage in the family life-cycle. All children of primary or secondary-school age, go to school. The labor-force participation of working-age children (those who are 11 years or more) is low in all groups[11] and underlines the significance of the maternal contribution in lower-income households (Groups A and B and some members of Group C). By extending to the maximum her own total workday, the mother prevents the premature expulsion of her offspring into the workforce. The prolongation of the time spent working and the skills exercised in the administration of the budget, stretching the allowance to the limit, were the underlying mechanisms permitting this high level of school attendance.

In the *extended* households, in the earlier phases of the family cycle, the system of counting on help from resident adult relatives for housework and industrial homework was fundamental in the work strategies of the majority of wives. The effectiveness of this collaboration depended on a series of factors such as: the gender of the relative in question, the reason for her or his being in the home, and if she or he belonged to the husband's or the wife's side of the family. Male relatives, especially those of the husband, hardly helped in any domestic task at all and were considered an additional responsibility in an already hard workweek. The women interviewed, however, could be sure of counting on the help of their mothers, sisters, and aunts living in the home, especially if the latter depended on the income from the nucleur family for their present or future subsistence, for paying for schooling or periods of "climatization" before looking for work in Mexico City.

The reduction in hours spent in housework made possible by female cooperation oscillated between six hours in Group D, six and a half in Group A and 12 in Group C. (See table 6.2). While the number of hours dedicated to paid work did not change greatly, the help received with housework permited the industrial homeworkers longer periods of relaxation during the week and (particularly to women in Groups A and C) also on weekends by reducing the total number of hours worked to 101 and 91 hours, which represents 210% and 190%, respectively, of the legal workweek. The collaboration of female relatives, moreover, means the substitution of young children or adolescents, in the carrying out of domestic responsibilities (see tables 6.3a, 6.3b).

Two examples illustrate the significance of this collaboration for the labor strategies of the women interviewed. In Betty's household, the conflict and tension accompanying the presence of kin and their influence on the quality of the marital relationship are evident. In our first interview, Betty's 17-year-old, single sister, a commercial-school student and helper in housework and industrial homework, lived in the home. In later visits, tired of serving breakfast and dinner to boarders, Betty decided to work again as a domestic by the hour, giving her sister weekly pocket money for taking care of the children. Their association was not lasting, because Betty did not want to accept her sister's lazy boyfriend. The sister moved to her sister-in-law's house and Betty called on her peasant mother-in-law to take care of the children. This collaboration resulted in even more conflicts because the mother-in-law began to spoil Betty's husband, and to criticize her daughter-in-law for being "very ambitious and neglecting her children." In our last interview, Betty had succeeded in getting her mother-in-law to return to her home, placing one of the children in a nursery school and leaving a toddler with her sister-in-law, reducing to a minimum her industrial homework, and dedicating more hours to working as a maid. Although Betty's husband was a factory worker who earned twice the legal minimum wage, his contribution to the household fund was insufficient to carry out other plans that Betty considered important: moving out of that crowded *vecindad*, buying some furniture, and improving the children's diet. Given the fact that the husband was stingy and had to be begged for the household allowance (a situation that Betty found humiliating), to increase the amount of paid work outside the home seemed the only road open to Betty.

In our second example, by contrast, Chepa's 20-year-old sister also lived with her, while working in a sewing workshop and attending a commercial school. Given her multiple tasks, this sister helped only on the weekends. Chepa did not consider that she could ask her sister for more help, because the latter worked in order to help her family in the country. This arrangement, although it did not "free" Chepa, did enable her to help her parents indirectly (she had helped them directly when single, but now was not given enough money by her husband) and to take care of her small children while doing industrial homework.

Help by resident females in unpaid domestic work and industrial homework (see tables 6.3a and 6.3b) is not accompanied, except in one case, by a cash contribution to the existing common fund, despite the fact that half of these female relatives are themselves engaged in paid work.[12] Their incomes are spent on personal expenses, savings to get married and, most commonly, aid to poor parents in the country. A similar pattern is found among male relatives. Although all of them are engaged in paid work, only a minority make a contribution (very low) to the family pool, using most of their salaries for their own expenses or in some cases to help relatives in the country.

Households in the Advanced Phases of the Family Life Cycle

In the *adult nuclear* households,[13] the differences between the average number of hours worked per week by the three groups of women interviewed are reduced. Thus we find in Table 6.2 that complex A completes 90 hours 30 minutes; complex D, 92 hours; and complex C, 87 hours 30 minutes (189%, 192% and 182% respectively of the maximum legal workweek of 48 hours). The only industrial homeworker in Group B completes 76 hours per week (158% of the legal workweek). Group B completes 76 hours per week (158% of the legal workweek).

The wives from Group A (economically needier), continue to be the group that dedicates more hours to remunerated work: 44 hours 30 minutes (93% of the legal workweek), and along with the wives of Group B, the ones who dedicate fewer hours to housework: 46 hours and 42 hours (96% and 88% respectively of the legal maximum workweek). Regardless of the fact that the weekly averages are high, they are also considerably less than those of the nuclear groups of the young cycle, a circumstance that underlines the enormous help that the industrial homeworker receives with her housework, especially on the part of her daughters. See Tables 6.3a and 6.3b.

In these households, with adolescent and/or grown children one notes a very marked gender division in help with housework. The total number of daughters in Groups A and B, 92% of those in Group C, and 83% of those in Group D help their mothers with tasks that demand great responsibility, almost replacing their mothers on some days. The sons either do not help with housework or help with only tasks such as messages and shopping. In the only household without daughters, the adolescent and grown sons helped with housecleaning and shopping but not with washing clothes or preparing meals. Help with industrial homework is more egalitarian on the part of both genders, although daughters tend to predominate once again (see table 6.3a and 6.3b). Help on the part of the husbands follows the same patterns as those found in other groups, except in the case of the military man, who if he feels like it, may return from the base and mop the kitchen floor, wash the refrigerator, or wax or fix things. But in all these cases husbands' help is optional and depends on their mood and good will.

An interesting question is why these wives of Groups A, B, and C, who count on the enormous help of their adolescent or grown-up daughters, do not dedicate more time to paid work. In other words, we observe a strategy of less than maximum effort in paid work, especially in the neediest households of Group A. This indicates that women prefer to reduce slowly the rhythm of work, and relax more, at least on Sundays after lunch, and perhaps at times during the week. Older women with declining health and energy feel they have already worked and contributed enough to the support of their households. Now they want to take advantage of a period of relative economic stability (when husbands do not fail to fullfill their economic obligations as in the past, and/or when a few grown-up children are making a contribution to the pool). [14]

In this manner they hope to regain strength for other periods of intensified effort which may lie ahead. This is the case of Doña Soledad, whose work history we presented in the appendix to Chapter 5. But averages hide individual variations. One example is Doña Goya, from Group A, introduced also in Chapter 5. Mother of 10 children (between 3 and 17 years of age), she has a stable job washing several times a week, and is married to a proletarian husband earning the minimum legal wage. She wants all her children at least to finish high school or junior college. Goya works a total of 111 hours per week (231% of the legal workweek), herself completing 59 hours of housework despite great help she receives from her four oldest daughters, and with all her working-age offspring collaborating on industrial homework (assembly of toys). During the visit to Doña Goya, we could appreciate the authentic "labor army" this wife had organized, when everyone turned to, after the children had finished their schoolwork. With this extra effort on the part of all able members of the household (except her husband), Goya stretched the common fund to support eight children and adolescents—in kindergarten, primary, secondary, and (the eldest daughter) in nursing school.

Conclusions

The "decomposition" of homeworkers' households according to patterns of income allocation and control, and the links between the latter and exchanges of unpaid domestic work uncover the hardships in the implementation of women's work strategies. Simultaneously, we learn how women's control of their earnings is only minimally translated into a bargaining mechanism pertinent to wives' share of unpaid domestic work.

To the external observer the exchanges of incomes and labor described seem obviously asymmetrical as they imply a disproportionate amount of total hours worked by wives. But this finding must be also "decomposed" into its paid and unpaid components to better link it to women's strategies. By increasing the number of hours devoted to paid work, women articulate their definition of family needs and objectives of collective well-being that involved, in particular, their children. In a nonspecified number of cases, specially among older women, collective welfare may also include wives' evaluation of their long-term material interests and security. Also, enlarging the common fund through their work strategies and income allowed women to mitigate husbands' control over their lives and also to increase their own self-esteem.

Conversely, time spent on unpaid domestic work represents women's fulfillment of their duties as mothers and wives, as established by the working-class marriage contract although certain chores involved in their mothering experience and managerial domain were not experienced solely as duties but also as rights and part of their legitimate gender sphere. This uneasy equilibrium between goals, duties, and rights is not static; women redefine them according to past history and current experience of conjugal dynamics.

What needs to be stressed is that within the different contexts of pool and housekeeping allowance groups, women's capacity to maneuver the duty component of their total workload is very limited. In fact, women's bargaining capacity is reduced to deciding whether to concentrate on paid or unpaid work (in young nuclear households) or to diminish their own share of housework by having elder daughters or other female relatives substitute for them (in adult, nuclear and young, extended households respectively). They can mobilize claims to other women's labor. In no case, however, have women been able significantly to diminish their own contribution by having husbands (or other male relatives) undertake a share of domestic work.

How are women's labor strategies related to society's processes of class formation and reproduction? In the first place, these strategies facilitate husbands' own proletarianization. Concomitantly, income derived from women's subproletarianization in industrial homework and other paid activities, as well as their fundamental contribution in domestic work and the socialization of their children are essential elements in the reproduction of a working class fragmented along gender lines. As has been argued by many authors, the salary of the proletarian husbands is insufficient to cover the family's maintenance and reproduction, which is not guaranteed by capital, but depends upon women's total workload.

Likewise, the study of distribution circuits and the definition of household needs and priorities provides additional light on the mechanisms of working-class reproduction made possible by women's labor strategies and sacrifices.

Since men with pocket money can contribute in different ways to their own personal consumption and also to the support of other households or casas chicas (a room/house partially shared with a concubine) it is not possible to identify a single household strategy for the reproduction of the working class. Each household constitutes the locus of the strategies of the spouses, converging in one and the same arena and involving a different commitment for its continuation. Men's strategies involved collective and individual components; the women's, closely linked to the present and future situation of children, tended towards an overall, collective character. In fact, proletarian husbands, because of their own class insertion—which guarantees protected wages and social security coverage—can afford to be more individualistic than wives, in particular older and less educated ones, who, because of their own work history and current labor insertion, know that almost certainly they will not join the ranks of the proletariat. Correspondingly, they are more compelled to develop collective strategies because they are dependent on husbands' present and future good will, and also on their children's eventual support. The quality and viability of class reproduction at the household level appears in this way to be intimately connected to women's strategies and forms of subordination as a gender.

Seven

The Marriage Contract
Renegotiation and Consciousness

This chapter will develop further the links between wives' restricted control of intrahousehold patterns of money flow and allocation and the renegotiation of gender relations within the household. Our aim here is to understand the spheres, attainments, and limits of wives' struggles within this domain. Why do women comply with seemingly asymmetrical exchanges of income and unpaid domestic work? How are these material exchanges related to more intimate areas of conjugal dynamics (sexuality, control of wives' fertility, companionship, nurturance, feelings of affection and rejection) and to women's consciousness of gender oppression and subordination? And how are these "private" family episodes linked to processes of class and gender construction that transcend the inmediacy of today's household?

In order to answer these questions, we will argue that it is necessary to examine the normative expectations regulating legitimate or "proper" interaction and exchanges between husbands and wives— the working class marriage contract; its insertion within the larger framework of wives' consciousness as "interpretation of the world"; as well as the control mechanisms used by both partners when ideology fails and compliance must be secured at whatever cost.

The Working Class Marriage Contract

No single, static, working-class marriage contract exists;[1] instead marriage involves continuous renegotiation of the terms of interaction and exchange between spouses. In our sample, these processes are associated with several features: the level of husbands' contribution to the pool; the quality of their behavior towards their wives;

the importance of wives' contribution to the common fund and their evaluation of the marital situation and possible alternatives; and wives' general life-experience (whether young, recently married, or older and more sceptical).

Most couples at the beginning of their union had differing expectations of what married life should be like. Hence the conflicts and violence characterizing the daily routines of most of the families interviewed. When ideological constraints are no longer effective, there is usually resort to economic and coercive mechanisms in an effort to resist or impose a refashioned definition of family interaction. Advances, withdrawals, realignment of forces—usually with the collaboration of daughters or sons—were common features of the marital struggle.

The expectations of conjugal roles commonly held by women comprised several dimensions. In the first place, husbands should provide a housekeeping allowance large enough to support the family. Given that earnings are generally low, the housekeeping allowance should at least cover most basic expenditures without encroaching on the males' right to some personal spending money. Half the women stated that men should help in some domestic chores, although they admitted that this expectation was seldom fulfilled. Great emphasis was placed on the quality or nature of husbands' behavior. Wives expect a modicum of "respect," by which they meant not to be physically or verbally abused and not to be humiliated by open unfaithfulness. They expect also some delicacy of treatment (*delicadeza de trato*) or sensitivity to their feelings, particularly regarding sexuality, and recognition of their contribution as wives and mothers to the well-being of the household. They also expected to have some control over their fertility (number of children desired) and use of contraceptives either by themselves (in the case of older wives) or in consultation with their husbands (the younger wives). A few women, in particular young and recently married ones, also mentioned that they expected companionship, affection and love. In exchange, wives should provide unpaid domestic service, child care and sexual exclusivity. As far as paid work is concerned, most women in the pool group said that life for them has always meant work and will probably always mean working for a living. They *had* to work if they wanted to secure a basic standard of living or education for their children. They also *wanted* to work to secure a minimum degree of autonomy and control over their lives. Wives in the non-pool group also defended their *right to work* for many of the same reasons including the need for autonomy and self-esteem. Only three women said that their rightful domain was exclusively domestic and resented having to undertake paid employment.

It is important to stress that all wives thought that their behavior—in the domestic and public spheres—should not transgress the limits imposed by the "respect" owed to their "masters" (their señores) respect being defined as obedience and deference, although the exact definition and limits of respect varied according to each individual's marital experience.

The elements mentioned as constituents of wives' duties under the marriage contract: unpaid domestic work; child bearing and rearing; and sexuality and in particular, their articulation, may be differently defined and enacted according to women's conception of "proper" wifedom-motherhood and gender-related worlds and values. These also define their rights under the contract and form part of wives' conciousness as comprising "visions" or "interpretations of the world." At this point, a digression on our conceptualization of consciousness seems necessary for the analysis to be developed in the remainder of this chapter.

On Consciousness

Discussions of women's consciousness—a concept seldom if ever defined—usually conflate two of the possible connotations of the term.[2] The first one, which we will call consciousness as comprising "interpretations" or "visions" of the world, refers to a set of symbols in terms of which the human agent approaches and makes sense of nonsocial and social reality as well as herself/himself. These interpretations of the world may include a mixture of bits of explanations based on folklore, and/or common sense, scientific knowledge, religion, empirical observations and the subject's own present and past experience; they are expressed in her/his definition of norms, values, and role expectations, all of which make up the codes that provide meanings to her/his inner and external worlds.

Theorization of consciousness as "interpretation of the world" and the empirical study of processes of construction of class, gender, ethnic and racial significations, their interconnections, sources and variations are still undeveloped. All the more so if one rejects the notion that working-class women's and men's consciousness is a simple mystification of a dominant class ideology or, conversely, the isolated and homogeneous outcome of working people's own experience, impervious to the influence of other social strata. However, the precise nature of the links between a society's dominant value system and ideology—starting by a simple question: is there a dominant ideology?—and consciousness as "world views" of subordinated classes (and within these, their internal differentiations according to gender, race, ethnicity) remains a matter for research and debate.[3]

The second connotation of consciousness is awareness, or "paying attention." As such, consciousness is a relational concept that always makes reference to something—to be conscious of class exploitation, of gender subordination or ethnic/racial oppression, of self or others—and calls upon the capacity to perceive an object within a context, to "being aware of its place in a larger frame of reference" (Etzioni, 1968). By means of this consciousness, the interconnections among societal details are perceivable as, for instance, the relation between wife-beating and generalized male domination within a sexist society, whether capitalist or socialist.

Although consciousness as vision and consciousness as awareness are usually related, it is important to differentiate between them. No individual is explicitly aware of all longitudinal and lateral interconnections she/he knows about, and the extent and topics of attention vary greatly during the course of a life span. On the other hand, given the awareness of a particular interconnection, it is possible to deepen consciousness, and here the role of information and theory (as new sources of signification) becomes important. But under what conditions does consciousness of self, race oppression, gender subordination, class exploitation develop? When human subjects are simultaneously constructed members of gender, class, racial, and ethnic categories, it is logical to hypothetize that consciousness along these lines must be intimately related. For example, is it possible that what is commonly defined as class consciousness and its different levels (Lenin, 1973; Mann, 1973) is, in fact, only the generalization of the experience of the adult, male, white, First-World industrial proletariat, which is taken as a measuring rod for ascertaining the presence or absence of a universal class consciousness?[4]

It remains, therefore, a legitimate matter of inquiry to examine the links and feedback mechanisms between those areas of consciousness as "awareness of," and the factors that may influence their depth and scope. For example, although it is commonplace to refer to the existence of a dialectical relationship between praxis and consciousness, we have only perfunctory knowledge of the dynamics of the determination. Within feminist practice, consciousness-raising groups have proved effective as a means of socializing individual experiences of gender oppression. In line with the radical feminist theory from which it emerges, however, the conceptualization of gender subordination and consciousness is frequently carried out in universal terms, irrespective of class, race, and the ethnicity within which gender is differentially constructed and experienced. In our view, this theoretical and empirical lacuna is another manifestation of dualism in feminist thinking and one of the most important challenges this theory must eventually overcome.

In this preliminary approximation to women's consciousness of gender subordination, we have followed several lines of argument. In the first place, we have tried to establish to what extent homeworkers' perception of their situation as working mothers-wives expresses awareness of gender subordination and long-run gender interests as defined in Chapter 1. These are taken as benchmarks against which women's perceptions are compared and explained. Secondly, and in line with the conceptualization, we did not treat consciousness as a unitary phenomenon that a person either has or has not, but as a many-faceted process that may involve one, some, various, or all dimensions in which gender domination is commonly exerted (wifedom, motherhood, work roles, reproduction, etc.) Thirdly, we assumed that for each of these dimensions levels of awareness may be ascertained. Does the woman perceive herself as being *individually* oppressed, and on what grounds? If she does, to what extent does she perceive that she is not alone but that other women share her predicament? And to what extent, if it exists, is this socialized experience of individual oppression understood in structural terms, as an expression of gender subordination, institutionally defined, and in contradiction with long-term gender interests?

Finally, since we have examined women's proletarianization as a process of simultaneous creation, re-creation and possible questioning of class and gender relations, we expected that consciousness along both lines may be closely intertwined. The nature and scope of our data do not allow us to examine levels of class consciousness and its gender specific dimensions. Instead we have paid special attention to class elements in our exploration of wives' "interpretation of the world" and levels of awareness.

As these may be influenced by many and different social and individual factors, apart from class, their study becomes a very complicated exercise.[5]

Let us return to the constituent elements of the working-class marriage contract and explore wives' conceptions of "proper" motherhood and wifedom as these relate to the legitimacy of undertaking paid work. As we shall see, their elaboration is congruent with their view of themselves as *working* wives and mothers and with other aspects of their consciousness as "interpretations of the world" concerning relations between the genders, inside and outside the family domain.

In general terms, women conceived their role in society as essentially that of wife and mother. This should not be interpreted as the simple expression of a dominant ideology. For a number of reasons women rescued the personally rewarding elements of their enactment of motherhood, and justified the continuation of their overall unhappy married life. Women have thus negotiated their interpretation of wifedom/motherhood in the light of their experience as working-class women and their individual work trajectories and family histories.[6] This reconciliation, which rejects the definition of wife and mother as a full-time job and re-evaluates a remunerated working role within the definition of "proper" motherhood, and wifedom is not without tensions. Among the women with a post-matrimonial work history prior to industrial homework (as seen in Chapter 5, this included women who worked outside the home in factories, hospitals, etc.), the paid work of the wife/mother, either in or out of the home was vindicated as necessary and legitimate— simply what one would expect from a working-class woman worried about the well being of her children and home. For many of these women, especially those who had at one point or another headed the household, paid work was a positive sign that differentiated them from weak women afraid of the external world. Doña Gudelia expressed herself as follows on the subject:

> I think that if a wife works outside the home, it is because the need is great or because she doesn't have a husband, or he's sick, or because she has to struggle for the well being of her children. If a woman works, it is because she wants to get ahead and buy things for her children and help her husband. And so neighbors and relatives won't talk. This is why I think it's all right, because those women don't give up so easily, not like other women who haven't got a cent and don't make up their minds to go out and work out of pure laziness in my opinion.

Among the women with no postmatrimonial occupational history prior to industrial homework, remunerated work on the part of the wives-mothers is also vindicated. But in this case the limits are much narrower since it is the legitimacy of work inside the home that is in question in the case of either industrial homework or some equivalent task, in order to reduce to a minimum the tension between the roles of working wife and mother. This we call a restricted definition of proper motherhood. The reality of these women (who were a majority of the non-pool group) regarding their own class history, present class position, and the level of income of their husbands, has an obvious influence on the interpretation of their paid work as mothers and the limits of its legitimacy. In direct contrast, with respect to their relationship with their husbands, the women defended their right to work as a way to forge a space that they control.

This close relationship at the ideological level between patterns of women's class insertion and gender construction is also present in wives' conceptualization and awareness in the sphere of paid work.

We have seen in Chapter 5 that women's postmarriage subproletarianization in the homework, autonomous, and personal services sectors reflected the influence of gender, It also allowed fulfillment of the restricted definition of "proper" motherhood sustained by the women of the housekeeping allowance set. Simultaneously, as women's consciousness does not dissociate their work roles from those of wife and mother, but, on the contrary, seeks to reconcile all of these in some way, the degree of work dissatisfaction and job consciousness (that may be considered a level of class consiousness) is played down by that reconciliation. This ideological feedback in turn influences the attitudes of the women with respect to an eventual insertion in other proletarianization processes outside the home and the weighing of possible courses of action to try in the attempt to better their collective situation as homeworkers. In fact, all the women are job conscious, that is, they show awareness of the problems all homeworkers share because of the specific employment setting (low wages, intermittent work supply, lack of fringe benefits, etc.) Moreover, 81% of them thought their wages were unfair, and 72% that it is better to work in a factory than to be a homeworker because salaries are higher and job security and benefits greater. In spite of this realization, the women immediately point out the positive elements in homework, derived from their present definition of proper motherhood. In the first place, this evaluation is reflected in their attitude when faced with the possibility of a concrete job offer in a factory—60% said they would not accept it if offered. Secondly, with regard to the channels for action to affirm their rights as workers, 23% of the group of women who believed that the wages paid them were unjust, thought individual action could be attempted (try to convince the supplier to raise her wages), while only 5% favored collective action (uniting the women in the area to ask for improvements). The overwhelming majority answered that nothing could be done or that they didn't know what to do. By the same token, the majority of the 53% of the industrial homeworkers who spoke in favor of unions thought they wouldn't be of use in their particular field.

Evaluating possibilities for collective action, the women recognized the objective, organizational difficulties involved (dispersion, clandestinity, easy replacement by other mothers with small children in case of protest). Besides, the majority felt that their interest as mothers was at stake in case of an eventual mobilization. It was preferable to be satisfied with the current wages than to be at risk through an action that could deprive them of their meager earnings and leave them with no possibility of working *in the home*. It is evident that there exists a complex inter-relationshsip between job consciousness and possible other levels of class consciousness and struggle on the one hand, and consciousness as vision of appropriate gender roles and women's experience of the same on the other, This needs further exploration.[7]

Wives' perception of "proper" wifedom/motherhood is congruent with other aspects of their "interpretation" concerning appropriate relations between the genders. As far as formal, legal rights were concerned, women thought that they should have the same rights as men for education, work, equal payment for equal work. In other areas of the public world, however, the women's vision showed only a limited renegotiation of predominant value systems concerning "respectable" womanhood. For instance, the great majority accepted a double standard in morality and sexual life, entertainment, having a good time, outings, the right to have male and female friends.[8] As an illustration, when commenting on women's right to go out or have a good time, they mentioned that it was proper for women to enjoy themselves in a morally pure way (*divertirse sanamente*); that is, not in the same way as men enjoy themselves because men have more rights in this sphere. The limits of what constitutes divertirse sanamente for wives are given by the definition of "respect" due to husbands: it is all right to talk to other women but not to men; go to the park, not alone or with other women, but accompanied by children; visit relatives and attend religious affairs. Two wives mentioned going to the movies (with their children). Even within these quite narrow limits, most women found it impossible to get their husbands' permission to enjoy themselves.

This description of wives' current definition of their marriage contract may be summarized by saying that it consecrates a number of "legitimate" reciprocities which do not erase the gender division of labor—in or out of the household. On the contrary, wives distinguish between complementary spheres that women and men are supposed to inhabit. Their conception of fair or symmetrical exchanges between spouses did not contemplate therefore the elimination of those spheres or equal sharing within dimensions of marital interaction (for instance, in parenting and domestic chores), but centered on husbands' not transgressing the limits of "respect" due to wives.

Though the research did not focus on husbands' expectations of marital roles, the main difference from women's expectations would appear to lie in the area of emotional interaction and "respect." Men expect and usually get respect as obedience and deference, but generally they do not feel obliged to offer it in return by attending to wives' emotional and psychological demands: whether by recognizing and appreciating women's roles as housewives and mothers; by offering companionship or affection; or by abstaining from verbal violence and contemptuous behavior. Men expect and benefit from the double standard. They believe that the place of women is in the home, but they usually justify their wives' paid employment (after initial opposition) on the grounds of economic necessity. Given that definitions of "respect" due to husbands and wives are at least partially contradictory, this is a shady area in which struggles for fairness (justo trato del esposo) may easily focus and find their boundaries.

Renegotiation of the Terms of Conjugal Interaction

We have seen how the marriage contract is subject to continuous renegotiation between husbands and wives. What needs to be explored further is the degree to which womens' access to an independent income empowers them in the bargaining process and its limits. We will thus look at the distributional patterns and other exchanges as one "moment" in the unfolding of conjugal interaction.

Pooling Group

Before starting the analysis of subgroups within the pooling group, a caveat is in order regarding husbands' attitudes toward their wives' paid work. Forty percent of husbands in the sample—mainly higher-income workers of Group C—opposed their wives' decision to look for a job, particularly one outside the home, because they felt their wives would not be able to take care of the house, the children and the husband properly. Husbands also feared that once women were allowed to work—especially outside the home— "they lose respect for their husbands" and the husbands themselves lose face or are criticized by (male) relatives and friends for a breach of the marriage contract. Husbands alone should support the household; women should concentrate on housework.

Becoming an industrial homeworker solved most of these problems: the worker is invisible, earnings are low so that men very seldom lose the role of main bread-winner. Moreover, wives are always at home, ready to attend to their husbands' wishes. Nonetheless, three women reported that they had started outwork without their husbands' permission. Given that the men had broken the toys or the boxes their wives were assembling, these women were unsure whether they could continue working in the face of so much opposition. Husbands' initial or actual opposition thus has to be kept in mind when trying to understand womens' perception of their situation.

We will start our analysis with group A, and then point out the main differences in Groups B, C and D (housekeeping allowance set).

Group A: *Wives who contribute a substantial amount of the weekly pool (more than 40% and whose husbands are steady economic providers— 20.8%).*
Wives in this category are crucial economic providers, contributing more than 40% of the common fund. As women in other groups, they had to pool their earnings because husbands' contributions alone were insufficient. Despite women's important contribution, they were unable to force their husbands to tell them the level of their earnings, or to influence the amount of pocket money men withhold or modify substantially the narrow confines of their own budgeting activities. Control of their earnings (as seen in Chapter 6) could not be translated into a more significant control of total cash flow, as wives could not bargain the main control points. We also remember, from Chapter 6, the very long schedules of paid and unpaid domestic work completed by wives of this set. Nevertheless, women's crucial contribution to the common fund was not an effec-

tive bargaining mechanism concerning their load of unpaid domestic work.

In other potential areas of autonomy, decisions are more likely to be taken by older wives, or jointly with regard to work outside the home and going out to visit relatives or friends (wives decided in 33% of the cases). Decisions concerning child-rearing are almost exclusively wives' domain, but disciplining of children/adolescents (particularly the latter) is mainly in the husbands' sphere (45% of cases; joint decision, 30%). Decision-making on children's future work or schooling tend to be shared or fall within wives' domain. In the area of biological reproduction, half the women decided on number of children and use of contraceptives (40% joint decision). Finally, the area of sexual relations shows wives' bargaining power at its lowest. Although only one elderly woman said that it is a wife's duty to engage in sexual intercourse with her husband under any circumstances and the remaining women thought that both partners should agree as to if and when to engage in sexual relations, when asked about actual behavior, 70% of the wives—irrespective of age—reported that husbands decide. The reasons given for compliance against their will include: husbands' physical coercion or threat of violence; prevention of quarrelling; to prevent husbands' accusations of their wives having extra-marital sex; and not to give husbands an excuse to sleep with another woman.

The picture that emerges is one of limited and slow renegotiation, in the form of joint decision-making, in areas that use to be exclusively male. The pressure of economic necessity, coupled with loss of actual control over wives' whereabouts—when she goes out to wash, iron, perform paid domestic work—contribute to this effect. Wives' behavior, however, still falls largely within the range of "respect" owed and avowedly paid to economically reliable husbands, whether in the private or public spheres, and beyond the mere fulfillment of household or wifely chores that were taken for granted.

Wives defined "respect" as obedience to their husbands wishes or commands, and not doing anything without permission, such as going out, or visiting relatives; and not engaging in any behavior he disapproves of (like talking to neighbors). Respect also implied being ready to get up in the middle of the night and feed him if he happened to come home hungry; serve him and his friends (usually meaning spending the allowance to buy drinks); wait for him until he comes home; speak to him with deference, never resorting to foul language; never answer back in a loud tone; be ready to respond to his whims—"go and pay the bills," "go and borrow from Mrs. X. . . . "

Some violations at these limits were reported by wives—particularly older women—in all groups in three main areas. First women admitted engaging in loud complaining and generally quarrelsome behavior if husbands interfered with their legitimate spheres: child care and housekeeping, including the amount of the housekeeping allowance. Second, heavy drinking, gambling and involvement with other women elicited similar reactions. Third, with regard to visiting parents (mothers in particular), relatives, *comadres*, and girl friends, husbands' prohibitions were considered unacceptable. In such cases respect was reinterpreted to mean not disobeying the husband in public, and not engaging in forbidden behavior before his very eyes.

In the case of women of Group A, and in contrast with other groups, there has been a change in wives' definition of the boundaries of "respect." Most women report that now they have the right to answer back, not to accept his directives submissively, and to make their views known as long as this is not done publicly. One third of the women in this group reported that they no longer consult husbands about visits to parents or relatives. Doña Betty's feelings are typical of this group:

> Now that I get my own money, I feel better, less short of money, because now I know how much money I have for the week. Before I used to ask him for everything [he gave her a daily allowance]. I obey and respect him, but I feel I also have some rights . . . before he used to shout at me if he thought I was spending too much on the children, or did not give him the food he wanted. Now I tell him: "with the small salary you earn and you go and spend it on drinking with your friends. Look at me, I am also earning, and I do not buy anything for myself, but all I get I put in the house." It is not fair. Once or twice he slapped me in the face, he said I had shouted at him ["le había alzado la voz"]. I felt I was right. Mind you, it is not that I feel proud, or that I think that I am better than he is, but I feel I have the right to tell him: "Look, why do you do this or that, like drinking with your cuates, playing cards? I am helping him, so somehow I have the right to expect a different behavior ["exigirle una conducta distinta"].

What are the factors that account for the stretching of the limits of respect and simultaneously allow only the slightest of bargaining within the overall marriage contract?

Let us explore the configuration of symbolic, economic, and coercive control mechanisms involved in the contract's enactment, beginning with women's perception of their situation as working mothers and wives. A necessary starting point is an examination of their definition of paid work and its parameters. The tasks themselves were unanimously thought boring, repetitive, and tiresome, but all women interviewed stressed the significance of paid work in their lives for a number of reasons. First there was the economic rationale: the way to enlarge the common fund and ensure minimum decision-making about how to budget ("sentirme más independiente con el gasto, menos nerviosa"). ["to feel more independent with the 'gasto,' less nervous"]. With the exception of two women, the rest also mentioned a second reason: a means of diminishing or at least checking husbands' control in this area ("no tener que darle explicaciones de que hago con el dinero, poder gastarlo sin que haga preguntas" ["not to have to explain what I do with the money, to be able to spend it without being questioned"]). Third, paid work was a way of preserving a measure of self-respect: not having to beg him for money or be humiliated by his derogatory remarks when he was reminded that the housekeeping allowance was too small. Finally, women felt useful contributing money (and not just unpaid, devalued housework) to the survival of the family.

Within this broader context, let us consider in more detail how both satisfied and unsatisfied wives elaborate on their experience as mother and wives. All of them share a common definition of "proper" motherhood. As we have seen, women do not hold a conception of appropriate motherhood that precludes in principle the performance of paid work outside the home (particularly among wives in the pool group), or inside the home (mainly among wives of the nonpool set), although at this stage of their lives they would prefer the latter.

Homework has facilitated a restricted definition of "proper" motherhood that reconciles mothering with paid work inside the home, thus avoiding criticism. They are not leaving their children with strangers, they are not abandoning them for "selfish reasons" like going out to work. Mothers of this set, who most often combined homework with a number of paid activities outside the home and whose total work schedule was among the heaviest in the sample, did, however, feel individually oppressed, weighed down by a combination of adverse economic and family circumstances that did not allow them to give to their children the attention and care they thought they deserved. It is not surprising, therefore, that they did not seem aware of the subordinating features associated with an "exclusive motherhood syndrome," particularly if we consider the objective features of their insertion into the ranks of the urban sub-proletariat.

For these women, indeed for all the mothers of our sample, motherhood, even if frustrating much of the time, full of stress because of pressing economic urgencies and lack of available time to devote to their children, also represented an emotionally fulfilling, rewarding experience, whereas their occupational alternatives did not. Thus women could feel individually oppressed by their mothering experience, while unaware of being subordinated due to a definition of exclusive motherhood that, except for short periods, few of them had a chance to fulfill. As a consequence, they would not seek to renegotiate the marriage contract along this dimension.

On the conjugal side the picture is more complex and heterogeneous. Affection given and received from husbands was mentioned by two women who found other conjugal exchanges also symmetrical. They mentioned as their reasons for working, economic problems and the need to feel useful by helping to support the household. So far, their marital experience had coincided with the expectations they held before they married; previous consciousness as "interpretations" of the world and definition of "respect" were congruent with actual life, explaining why they were not conscious of being oppressed by prevailing forms of conjugal dynamics. The rest of the women of this group, on the contrary, have started questioning some aspects of marital interaction. These women rate their marriage as fair, more or less, "OK," or pretty bad, or they give a conditional answer; all right on the economic side ("mi gasto no me falta"). But they find husbands wanting in other areas. Some complain about verbal or physical violence (marido violento, grosero y discutidor), or heavy drinkers, who demand sexual services women are forced to provide in disgust, or husbands who demand a high standard of domestic attention, irrespective of wives' total workload.

These women are conscious of being oppressed at an individual level, along different dimensions, but *the boundaries of awareness and aspirations to renegotiate the contract are restricted to the normative expectations held.* In contrast to other groups, however, in Group A the recognition of wives' fundamental contribution to the pool has prompted some redefinition of the old limits of "respect," and the women have managed to impose some restructuring of interaction to coincide more closely with those limits, but their fundamental world view remains unchallenged.

Given that women of this subgroup feel individually oppressed by their husbands, are they aware that other women are similarly oppressed? Is consciousness of a common predicament as wives accompanied by awareness of common gender interest? And what gender interests are shared? Women know that other women of their class, their own mothers, comadres, relatives and girlfriends are also oppresssed along the same dimensions. They also view men, in general, as a pretty bad lot. In Doña Goya's words:

> Yes they are *machistas* in the sense that they believe they have the right to command and that we women are worth nothing [las mujeres no valemos nada]. The majority are very domineering, they like women to be the object of their whims [que nos sometamos a sus caprichos], to whatever they want. Besides, they are jealous and they do not allow us to work in peace. And if he happens to turn into a *desobligado* you will have to support him instead of having him supporting you.

Consciousness of a common gender interest seems to exist only insofar as women they know also experience non-fulfillment of the marriage contract by their own husbands. This awareness is mostly accompanied by explanations of other women's misfortunes as suffering derived from an individual bad man: that comadre or friend has had bad luck. Each woman interviewed compares herself with other women who have experienced a similar or worse fate than she has and concludes that she could have fared still worse and that her situation is not so bad. After all, basic support is certainly not lacking from husbands in this group, and, as they often remarked, they had not married the worst of the kind!

To summarize the discussion so far, we have seen that a combination of factors sustains the limited renegotiation of interaction and the new boundaries of overt display of "respect." A fundamental element is the partial at least, fulfillment of wives' expectations concerning husbands' obligations under the marriage contract. Furthermore, women have known that their earnings were insufficient and too unstable to support a home and preferred to put up with an unhappy or unsatisfactory marriage rather than risk a definitive separation. Most of them have also felt resentful of and oppressed by the nature of conjugal exchanges but have remained in the home because they judged it was the best life alternative. Threats of withdrawal of economic support, fears ("How am I going to manage with the children?"), threats of or actual physical and verbal violence in some cases have also become effective mechanisms to secure compliance and the new dynamics of marital exchanges. This combination of immediate factors and wives' own history helps explain—in all the groups of our sample—why working women's recognition of long-run gender interests and their awareness of subordination are only partial. We have seen women who claimed formal equality before the law, the right to work, education, and at least shared control of their fertility. A handful of them questioned the double standard in morality, sexuality, entertainment, but none questioned the prevailing household and societal gender division of labor. Therefore, a demand for unqualified equality with men, presently understood as abolition of the gender division, could not be appealing in their eyes. They felt that for women of their class, education, and skills, removal of the gender division would be translated into a work situation that was intrinsically explóitative and alienating (as it was for the men of their class), while they would risk being deprived of their current share of motherhood/household management. It should be remembered here that paid work was not undertaken as a source of professional satisfaction (except perhaps in the case of the beautician in the sample), but as a necessary step to carry out renegotiating strategies. In contrast, motherhood and, to a lesser degree, some household chores, were deemed personally rewarding, particularly if women were able to perform them at their own rhythm.

Similarly, the goal of attaining complete financial and personal autonomy from men seemed to these women unrealistic and in conflict with their perceived access to socioeconomic resources through a man. Their experience told them that life was more bearable if they could count on male economic and social protection for themselves and their children, and a father figure to discipline their male offspring. As seen in Chapter 5, the majority of women started married life looking for economic and social protection and a measure of affection. When the latter element proved unattainable, they settled for a predominantly instrumental orientation towards their situation. Within this context, complete and overt control over biological reproduction may be seen as imperiling women's ability to use their procreative capacity as a bargaining mechanism. They want to control, but not openly. Thus, although their definition of the marriage contract may appear to the observer from another class as the epitome of gender subordination, most working-class women thought that it was better to marry than to fend for themselves.

In brief, and for all the women interviewed, class and gender interplay in the concrete reality of everyday life in a way that qualifies the relevance of some of the universal long-run gender interests. These are either not recognized or admitted, even to themselves, and are not acted upon, if they seem, in women's eyes, to endanger or conflict with their few pleasurable life experiences or their current precarious strategies for survival that include living with a partner as a basic component.

Group B: *Wives who contribute more than 40% of the weekly pool, but whose husbands have almost stopped contributing, do so sporadically, or, for reason of sickness, do not provide a housekeeping allowance (5.4%).*
Although this subgroup is extremely small it is worth discussing because the three wives have openly "lost respect" for their husbands, in words, action, and thought. They report going out without permission; they do not wash, iron, or cook for their husbands as they used to; they manage, rather than budget the common fund; they get jobs against their husbands' will; they resort to foul language if they feel like it; and even strike back when husbands try to beat them.

Doña Dontila, for example, is a woman who for 25 years had endured a very unhappy marriage and whose husband is now sick and too weak to abuse her physically any longer. Her newly acquired freedom includes the pleasure of smoking in his presence (before she had to hide in another room); buying anything she wants (within her limited budget) without admitting his interferences; and refusing to provide him with pocket money (which incidentally is given to her husband by his daughter from a former marriage). If one considers that Doña Dontila's married life is a long history of emotional and physical violence, that her earnings as a seamstress used to be "expropriated" by her husband, and that she was never given an allowance to budget but had to ask for every household expense and give back the change, it is understandable that her present reaction takes the form of "revenge" for past humiliations and sorrows.

The most important single factor to account for these changes in conjugal style is husbands' desobligacion; that is their failure to provide a housekeeping allowance, sometimes for weeks on end, sometimes reducing the amount to an insignificant sum. A combination of factors has given rise to a new pattern of marital interaction:

wives' crucial contribution to the common fund and their realization of this fact; loss of husbands' role as breadwinners, and husbands' lack of respect for wives' feelings, displayed through violence, abusive language, and open unfaithfulness.

These couples represent the pinnacle of an egalitarian life style in our sample and the limitations must be noted. Wives have assumed what may be considered a dominant position in housekeeping/financial matters and reportedly no longer engage in sexual intercourse against their will. They are aware that with some assistance from kin they can support the household by themselves. However, they continue living in marriages they define as bad, very unhappy, or disastrous, and justify this in terms of common rationales—the need of a man to discipline the sons; social protection; hope of the man's eventual return to more orderly habits; religious convictions. Doña Dontila had suffered from her husband's strictness and defined this grief as a test from Heaven rather than oppression; the other two women had stretched to the limit their traditional conjugal roles, but had not gone beyond them. Their conception of working-women's motherhood is similar to that of Group A. Their definition of a good husband or wife, has not been challenged. The more egalitarian pattern of exchanges has been achieved primarily as a result of husbands' default in the economic sphere. Consequently, Group B women do not question gender roles per se, but only their nonperformance.

Group C: *Wives who contribute less than 40% of the weekly pool, and whose husbands remain the main economic providers (35.8%).*
Economic necessity prompted wives in this category to contribute to the common fund, and they were very conscious that their low earnings and job instability prevented them from assuming a dominant or even important domestic financial role. As is the case with other groups, the struggle over the amount of husbands' pocket money, and form of delivery of allowance does not seem to have been greatly affected by the women's contribution. Husbands' decision-making power was also high in the sphere of wives' mobility. Men decided whether wives' should work outside the home (husband's decision in 50% of the cases; joint decision in 22%); whether wives may visit relatives/friends (husband's decision 50%, joint decision 34%). Husbands were also responsible for disciplining children/adolescents (husband's decision 75%; joint decision 20%). Joint decisions were more common concerning wives' biological reproductive capacity—whether to have any more children (joint 67%, wives' de-

cision 20%), and whether wives should use contraceptives (53% joint, 40% wives)—and the childrens' future—whether they should remain at school or start working (82% joint, 18% wives). Decisions over childrearing pertained to wives in 80% of the cases; 20% were joint decisions. Concerning sexual relations, although 87% of the wives thought that both partners should agree as to if and when to engage in sexual intercourse, husbands still decided in 80% of the cases.

This picture of women's relative powerlessness coincides with their definition of strict "respect" owed to husbands previously defined as reliable breadwinners. Among women with no postmarriage labor trajectory prior to homework, their initiation as industrial homeworkers does not seem to have changed significantly the overt patterns of conjugal interaction and old limits of respect, as they themselves acknowledged when asked to compare their situation before and after starting homework. Doña Chepa's comments are typical of this group: "Yes, you see, everything is exactly the same, I have not overlooked one thing [no me he desentendido de nada], I hurry up. When he arrives from work, everything is ready, there is food, the house is clean, all is as before."

In contrast, among older women with postmarriage labor trajectories prior to homework, 'respect' may mean they defer to their husbands to a greater degree now, when their contribution to the fund is low, than they usually did when they vere virtual heads of households. Doña Soledad is a case in point. Soledad's bargaining power seemed to be at its lowest point at the time the interviews took place. At that time she had to use her children to make her husband deliver his contribution to the pool (he was particularly fond of their youngest daughter who was in charge of initiating Soledad's strategy to have him "deliver the goods"). Now that she earns little money, Soledad knows that she has to command less, shout less (mandar y gritar menos, ser paciente), although this strategy does not seem to play down her previous awareness of gender oppression.

The continuation of present-day marriage dynamics is ensured by the same combination of factors detailed for Group A. Women talked extensively on the topic of motherhood, emphasizing the significance it played in their lives and economic stress that made it oppressive at times, but they were not aware of being subordinated in this sphere. Consequently, this dimension was not open for further conjugal renegotiation.

With regard to wifedom, a third of the women of Group C (all of them, except one, being young wives in the earlier phases of the family cycle) accept the limits of normative expectation concerning the good husbands role—el esposo bueno y obligado—and pay due respect to the steady economic provider who treats them well, who is not an open philanderer or a heavy drinker, who does not insult or physically abuse them. These women rated their marriage "good" and three of them actually said they loved their husbands and were loved in return. In the same fashion as satisfied wives of Group A (p. 148), expectation of marriage and experience coincide, and women are not conscious of gender oppression in this realm. Not surprisingly these women's reasons for undertaking paid work emphasized the importance of contributing to the common fund and the well-being of the family.

The rest of the women of this group were already aware of some dimensions of conjugal oppression prior to their search for paid jobs, in much the same ways as women of Group A and for similar reasons (violence, heavy drinking, imposed sexuality). Although women expect to be at least partially supported, they resent being constantly reminded of this fact, and treated as if they were no more than garbage (me trata como si fuera una basura), denigrated by husbands who were still the main providers, or having their household chores and wifely attention unrecognized or devalued. These wives rate their marriages fair or pretty bad, although stressing it is acceptable, albeit limited, on the economic side.

This high level of individual awareness of conjugal oppression (that they thought they shared with other distressed wives) is not accompanied by consciousness of all long-run gender interests.

The same points made for Group A are applicable here. Women's small contribution to the pool has given them some confidence (in the case of the younger wives) or increased their sense of self-worth (in the case of older women who had, at times, been temporary heads of the households), but economic dependence on husbands' support is the crucial factor in marriage survival. Besides, potential or actual resort to physical/emotional coercion was an effective mechanism to keep "uppity" wives in their place and teach them, if needed, a lesson in marital "respect."

This interplay of symbolic, economic, and coercive control mechanisms in daily life is illustrated in the following excerpts from our interview with Doña Adelina, an older woman, who on many occasions has supported her present household and a previous one.

Well, as my mother used to say, it's better to have to say "what will he [the husband] do" than "what will I do" since, in my opinion, it's preferable to be married, or to live in free union if you can't get married, than to be alone.

Q: *Why do you believe that women are better off with a husband?*

A: In the first place, for the respect that one gets—yes, because remember what they say about the fallen tree that everyone gets wood from. People think that you already fool around if you are alone, even though they know that you do honorable work. But people don't say that; they say "God only knows where she's from and where she's going—who knows who's waiting for her "because, since the tongue has no bone, people can say anything they want. For my part, being respected is the most important thing to me; above everything else, respect is important. Another thing is that a responsible husband is a big help, because, let's say that even if he doesn't give me money at a particular time, because he hasn't got it or for whatever reason, at least one can say "I'm going to borrow some money because I know that on such and such a day my husband gets paid, and on that day I'm going to pay the debt." Of course one can work, too, and solve one's problems, but some days one is sick and doesn't get paid, and then you wonder where the money will come from to feed your children. If you are living with someone, with a husband, he will worry about you and may take you to the doctor or may give you money to go if he can't go with you. So then one can say "I have someone to help me". . . .

Q: *And the love, the affection that a husband can give, isn't that important to you?*

A: Well, as far as needing a husband for that . . . (implying sexual relations), I can tell you that the less of that I have from this husband, the better. The fact is that I don't like it very much. How can I tell you? Luckily he's never been disgusting or forced me and doesn't go around feeling me all the time, and doesn't do things when the children are around. I must say he's been good in everything. But as far as I'm concerned, I'd love it if he'd say: "Let's do it every two weeks, here's the money to run the house, and I'm going to the barracks. . . ."

Q: *And wouldn't you miss him?*

A: No, because he'd be bringing me what I need most—money for my children.

Group D: *The housekeeping allowance group (38%).*
Women in this group looked for a paid job in order to purchase items that they and their husbands defined as extras; to have autonomous control over their own earnings; to avoid begging their husbands for each and every item they felt was needed for the household; and to prevent further humiliation and loss of self-esteem. Husbands in this group strongly resisted their wives' desire to work. Getting permission was a protracted process as these higher-income earners did not easily accept their wives' right to work, for fear of losing face in the eyes of family or friends or losing control over their wives' activities and their own proud self-image and esteem as sole breadwinners. Husbands had to be reassured that customary housekeeping standards would not be neglected, that wives would continue serving them with old time devotion and respect. For these husbands, industrial homework, rather than outside factory work, offered fewer risks.

Not surprisingly, young wives in this group face special problems in trying to establish a new style of family interaction. This distributional pattern acts as a powerful material and ideological mechanism to reproduce gender asymmetries within the household. As the breadwinner's role has not been affected but rather strengthened by the pattern of money allocation, wives are not justified in male eyes, or in their own, if they engage in disrespectful behavior. Wives are still supported: thus they must refrain from showing off their earnings, lest this display could humiliate or demean their husbands' status. When ideological pressures prove insufficient, wives' compliance is ensured through more direct means: withdrawal of support or violence.

As far as decision-making is concerned, these households were similar to the third pooling group (Group C) in patterns of money allocation and other spheres of potentially autonomous decision-making. One exception concerns the amount of the housekeeping allowance. Wives of the nonpool group report a higher percentage of their own or joint decision-making in this area, which could be atributed to husbands' much higher incomes (58% husbands' decision; 26% joint decision). This is exemplified by Sra. Rosa:

> I obey him as usual. My husband has always been the head of this house. I think this is good. But I could command more [mandar mas] and I do not want to; it is a form of showing him respect. My income is not important, it is additional money to manage; he gives me what is needed for the house. My money would show more if

wages were higher . . . but all the same I feel fine having it. I buy things I want. I do not have to beg him. I do not feel worried if I know that I do not need to touch his allowance. If I work, I can buy things in installments and I can pay them. If I do not work, I cannot buy those things without his permission, because I would not know how to pay them. I feel less worried, more secure [más segura], but I do not feel superior to him, because I owe him respect.

While the conjugal interaction here also resembles that of Group C, the wives' perception of their situation is somewhat different, and the distributional scheme appears to have exerted considerable influence upon some dimensions of conjugal awareness among younger wives. Women have gained in autonomy and self-respect, but enhanced self-esteem has not led to comparable self-confidence (excluding a third of the women who had, at various points, been actual heads of household). How is this process related to individual awareness of conjugal oppression? At first sight this is the most satisfied group of the sample, with half the women rating their marriages as good. Doña Ramona's words are typical of what we heard from this subset:

My marriage is fine, especially because he has always been good to me. I have not had problems, he does not beat me, or give me a bad life. Yes, he is the husband I wanted to have, because he does not drink, is "obligado" and never, never leaves me without an allowance [gasto].

However, of these ten women, only three gave a picture of their marriage situation that coincided with the previous definition of normative expectations. The remaining seven seemed to play down the elements of respect due to wives and emphasized husbands' role as providers. These women, together with six who rated their marriage as more or less "OK," or could not give a clear answer, appear to avoid admitting, not only to the researcher, but to themselves, the obvious lack of fit between expectations and husbands' actual behavior. These women—the best provided for in our whole sample—have been indoctrinated with the view that a reliable and good provider is, by definition, a good husband, although they have incorporated other attitudes and behavior traits in their overall conception. Since husbands were living up to such an important area of prescribed marital norms, the marriage had to be good, evidence to the contrary notwithstanding. In the course of our conversations, that uneasy reconciliation was at times shattered. Women referred to their lack of alternatives and feared that if they were to separate from their husbands, their children would be deprived of possibilities of education, even though they themselves could survive in a hostile environment. In all these cases, the distributional patterns conform to and reproduce society's (and women's own, albeit at times hesitant) definition of women's situation, acting as a powerful obstacle to further awareness. The fear of being deserted by their husbands was particularly acute among those younger women who had only worked as homeworkers after marriage and whose husbands belong to the nonmanual proletariat (engineer, bookkeeper, supervisor of a shop and a factory). These women with high school or technical education (two of whom had worked when single in nonmanual/skilled occupations: secretary, beautician) now regretted their loss of past skills, and their dependence; they were taking or had taken tranquilizers to calm their "nervous condition." They tried to compensate for the disparity between their own and their husbands' class position and income by excelling in the role of "perfect housekeeper."

Finally, the four remaining women in this category, who rated their marriages as bad, except in economic terms, were fully aware of being oppressed at an individual level. Husbands' shortcomings were so blatant and routine that they could not be hidden or rationalized by the veil of ideology. Moreover, these women resented their husbands' presence around the house (one openly admitted hating him and hoping he would leave and never come back). But they would not consider separation, in the foreseeable future at least, because they could see no economic alternatives to their present predicament. Individual awareness of oppression in this group, as in all others, has not led to consciousness of all long-run gender interests, goals, or action. Similarly, a configuration of current ideological, economic, and coercive mechanisms interplay to bolster the dynamics of prevailing marital exchanges.

Conclusions

The preceding discussion has pointed out that no simple link exists between wives' control of an independent income, the renegotiation of gender relations, and women's awareness of gender subordination within the household. Patterns of marital interaction and dimensions of consciousness appear to be dialectically mediated by the allocational processes described.

With regard to the renegotiation of conjugal dynamics, we have seen that within the common fund group, when wives contribution is small and husbands are steady providers, the prevailing form of interaction is not significantly affected; wives' decision-making power is low, and respect due to husbands strictly defined and pursued (Group C). When wives' contribution is crucial to household survival and husbands are regular providers, women have succeeded in renegotiating some of the terms of marital exchanges through redefining the range and limits of "respect" they feel obliged to pay husbands and demanding new rights of "respect" due them in return (Group A). Those wives who are obliged to support the household because of husbands' *desobligación*, have the highest degree of decision-making power in the sample, and may even be considered to hold a dominant position in financial and housekeeping affairs (Group B). Conjugal interaction in the housekeeping allowance group (D) resembles that of the first pooling group (C) with a similar pattern of strict, outward respect paid to husbands and low decision-making power for wives.

It should be stressed that even the smallest areas of control conquered by women are manifestations of power, not of authority understood as legitimate power and accepted as such by husbands. Besides, these areas of control were not substantial if we consider wives' present definition of the marriage contract. This fact leads us once more to the historical processes of class and gender construction that limit women's access to and control of resources that would allow them a more encompassing renegotiation of prevailing exchanges. As described, women did not perceive it was in their interest to abolish the sexual division of labor implied by those exchanges, but only to alter the dimensions they judged oppressive or asymmetrical according to their current definition of conjugal "respect." Within this framework, we found that neither the economic resources coming from subproletarianization nor the other resources available to women, such as those relating to affection and the expression of feelings—companionship, sexuality, emotional support—nor the services women can supply such as housework, procreation, and child care, are in fact effective means of empowerment in the domestic domain. A key factor seems to be the degree of need felt for these resources or services and the alternative avenues of access available to men and women. As long as husbands maintain their economic predominance, they have a wider potential for access to other women from whom they can receive the kind of attention they now require from their wives. The irreplaceable, individual factor—affection, companionship, or the understanding of a given woman—seems to be appreciated by only a minority of husbands. Companionship, understanding, and emotional closeness are sought by husbands in their buddies (cuates). Although the love or affection that a wife may provide is a valid resource for her when reciprocated, very few women considered themselves loved by their husbands. Not love only, but also procreation, physical attraction, and sexuality are perishable resources whose effectiveness decreases with time and whose limitations the women in our sample fully recognized.

Given the need for economic resources experienced by the women and their children, the difficulty in obtaining them through an independent income, the vital nature of the household allowance supplied by the husband, and the women's perceived need for the husbands' social protection, the existence and reproduction of prevailing patterns of conjugal exchange acquire a logic of their own. But, however small the changes in interaction and limits of "respect" that women have accomplished may appear to the observer, these changes do not look insignificant to the women themselves. In all cases, paid work appears to have bolstered women's self-esteem, and this may be conducive and/or necessary to any attempt to change their situation in the future. Besides, changes in the definition of respect due to husbands and wives or expectations and dimensions of awareness cannot automatically lead to a new life-style. Husbands resist any encroachment into their ancient prerogatives. In this regard, a capitalist/sexist society places at their disposal a whole array of individual and social-control mechanisms—economic, coercive, ideological—including the manipulation of wives' fears and insecurities derived from the reality of their dependent position and often from the internalization of a subordinate image of themselves. Women then counteract with the weapons of the oppressed: with attempts at seduction and adulation; with tears; with the need to create a sense of guilt through selfless devotion to home and husbands; with manipulation of significant others; with pretence of frigidity or with expression of open contempt.

Thus, family interaction is fraught with friction. Seventy-five percent of the women reported frequent discussions and quarrels over shortage of money; budget administration; children's discipline; husbands' irresponsibility—drinking, unfaithfulness, and jealousy. These conflicts lead easily to violence. Not surprisingly, the majority of women thought their marriages were a failure and half of them had separated at some point in their married life. They were forced to return by their need of economic and social protection, or in a few cases by need of company and affection—seldom, if ever, fulfilled.

The empirical findings of this chapter, in particular with regard to women's consciousness as "interpretations" of the world, raise some important questions for feminist theory and practice concerning how adequately to conceptualize gender subordination and gender interests from the perspective of working-class women in the Third World, questions which can not be answered within the scope of this research. The identification of long-run gender interests undertaken in Chapter 1, and deduced from the theoretical stance adopted in this study, cannot include the simultaneous consideration of the remaining relations of domination in which women may actually be involved. As a consequence, we find discrepancies between some of these long-run gender interests (for instance: the abolition of the gender division of labor, personal autonomy from men, etc.) and women's recognition when these interests are seen as endangering their life-rewarding experiences and their current avenues for economic and social survival. This lack of congruence between working-class women's concrete gender and class reality and the conceptualization of gender interests formulated at a more abstract level of analysis posits a fundamental challenge to feminist theory and decision-making, a subject to be taken up in our concluding chapter.

Eight
Development as If Women Mattered

In the light of findings and conclusions of our study, it is time to return to some of the questions raised in Chapter 1. At the general level, our research uncovers the connections between the seemingly unrelated processes of capital accumulation, the dynamics of a national and even international division of labor and patterns of household interaction based upon gender subordination in daily life. It seems to us that the contributions of our analysis can be summarized along several dimensions:

1. Our case study of homework and subcontracting of maquila production presents a vertical picture of the industrial productive structure of Mexico City today. The picture is parallel to similar processes taking place in other countries as part of current restructuring of the national and international economy. It is a process that responds to a cheap-labor strategy in order to lower costs of production. In this case, however, production is specifically oriented toward the domestic market and therefore very different from the maquiladora system of export-oriented production typical of such areas as the US/Mexican border. This picture allows us to show, on the one hand, the continuum formed by these firms and, on the other, the market segmentation associated with different levels of subcontracting. It allows us also to show the articulation between the regulated and the underground sectors of the economy and to point out the shortcomings and inadequacies of the literature that postulates a clear-cut separation between the formal and the informal sectors.

Homework is located at the lower end of this hierarchical structure and very much at the heart of the illegal economy. We have found it to be a highly exploitative form of production, carried out mostly by women, and taking advantage of gender-related differentiation within the household. It is a form of capitalist production at the household level that represents a disguised form of subproletarianization. It is also part of women's work strategies allowing them (mainly wives/mothers) to contribute to the family budget and renegotiate gender relations within the household.

2. Our study deals also with some key issues in class and gender formation. It contributes to the understanding of the making and re-creation of the urban working class in a Third World country such as Mexico. Thus, we have shown how these processes are linked to patterns of gender differentiation according to phases in the family life-cycle, and how male and female insertion in the work force is not autonomous but mediated by household/family reciprocities that allow men to consolidate their position both in class and gender terms. We have also explored the specificity of female proletarianization. By focusing on milestones in women's lives as part of their family, class, and gender history, we found conditioning elements whose interplay progressively shapes women's long-term employment patterns.

Additionally, these historical milestones, by limiting wives' access to socioeconomic and "symbolic" resources, also affect homeworkers' current capacity to forge spaces of control over their lives. In fact, we did not find that women's control over their incomes empowered them significantly in the bargaining of gender relations within the home. By decomposing the household unit, we showed the asymmetrical nature of household exchanges (income, unpaid domestic work, personalized attention, sexuality) that underlie women's labor strategies. At the same time, this analysis pointed out the complexity of the links between women's control of their earnings and the reinforcement or undermining of male domination within the household.

Finally, the analysis of the definition and enactment of the working-class marriage contract, and of forms of women's conciousness, allowed us to uncover two fundamental mechanisms of husbands' control over their wives. Husbands' predominance, though, was found to be based, not on ideological mechanisms alone, but significantly on privileged access to income and coercive means of control. The interplay of class and gender relations that confronts the relations of wives and husbands within the household thus effectively sets limits to women's struggles.

3. Throughout the book, we have emphasized that the processes of creation and re-creation of class and gender relations take place simultaneously and involve both material and ideological dimensions. Our effort has been to distinguish between them analytically while pointing out their concrete articulation and the mechanisms by

which this articulation takes place. Our objective was to avoid the analytical dualism that derives from the conceptualization of class and gender relations as part of two semiautonomous systems.

Let us illustrate with three examples from different chapters. First, we have shown that a close connection exists between the constantly changing productive and labor market structures and the dynamics of the seemingly private sphere of the household. In particular, we have seen how a process of decentralization of production through levels of subcontracting that shift production to the domestic domain—as in the case of homework—intersects with existing articulations of class, gender, and generational relations within the household. In other words, what appears to be isolated phenomena within the home (women's work strategies) are connected with global processes whose center of gravity is at the higher levels of the subcontracting pyramid. Second, we have shown how a hierarchical productive structure makes use of socially constructed gender traits to place women at specific tasks and job clusters. That is, gender takes a material expression, while gender and class are formed simultaneously at the workplace. In this process, ideological and material aspects converge in the creation and re-creation of class and gender inequalities. For instance, lower wages for women might be related to a specific division of labor but also to an ideological "justification" based on the view that women are secondary workers or supplementary income earners.

Third, the concentration of women in homework is in part the result of conditioning factors that include ideological elements—social definitions of "proper" wifedom and motherhood and their own renegotiating strategies—and material elements such as the household division of labor and husbands' own class insertion and primary contribution to the household. At the same time this concentration is also the outcome of a historical process that includes the various milestones in women's lives. Each of these milestones involves also ideological and material dimensions and was found to have long lasting influence on women's subsequent occupational histories.

This demonstrates the need to emphasize, as stated in Chapter 1, the role played by ideology in analyzing economic reality while simultaneously pointing out the material basis of ideological processes. Much too often, in theory as well as in development practice, the dialectics between the two are forgotten—with a tendency to reduce the complexity of change to its economic or ideological dimensions alone.

4. Why are we stressing the need to overcome analytical dualisms and what are the political implications of this stand? If class

and gender dimensions are viewed as an integral and integrated part of reality, it is difficult—if not impossible—to deal with one without the other. The implication is that any development scheme ' or policy, government program, plan or revolutionary change directed at (for example) poverty, employment policies, or inequality in general cannot separate the issue of gender inequality from other concerns and relegate it to a secondary place. Also implied is that dealing with gender inequality only (e.g., by sponsoring unqualified, long-run gender interests without taking into consideration the connections with class differences) is bound to have limited results. As pointed out in Chapter 3, any policy aimed at eliminating the wage gap between men and women is likely to have limited results if a continuous restructuring of the labor process creates new labor hierarchies and places women at the lower end. Similarly, a program aimed at eradicating poverty among female-headed households in an urban area requires, on the one hand, measures that strengthen women as a group (for example, setting up an organization that would allow them to socialize their seemingly individual problems and raise their consciousness with regard to their subordinate condition in society). Such a program also requires dealing with the class roots of this poverty, through such measures as a redistribution of resources and income and other types of policies such as training and educational programs.·

In this sense, issues such as "feminist equity" that have been raised by some feminists dealing with women and development (Black and Cottrell, 1981) need to be scrutinized. This question of equity has been raised in response to the failure of development (in theory and practice) in dealing adequately with the "continuing subordination of the female half of humanity. : . . Development with feminist equity would . . . be more than integration of women into development by recognizing their roles as resources and recipients and their claims to equal benefits. That would entail equity, and it is the least that can be asked. *Feminist equity* would entail a rethinking of the processes and priorities for change" (pp. 268–69).

Although we can agree with this statement, feminist equity in this case would seem to deal only with gender-based inequalities, at the same time disregarding inequalities based on class. In our view, a "rethinking of the processes and priorities for change" is incomplete if it disregards women's (and men's) class-related problems—such as sanitation, health, water provision, housing, transportation, electricity and other neighborhood services, schooling and nutrition, and even hunger—in a way that the connections between gender and class issues are made clear. These survival needs commonly color women's perception of gender-related issues, priorities, and programs. For example, the urgency of hunger and malnutrition may qualify women's response to a campaign against male violence and sexual harassment, even when both problems could presumably be tackled simultaneously. This rethinking also amounts to asking what precisely is our vision of development and what implications does it have for the concrete issues raised in this study—a subject to which we will return.

5. What type of policy recommendations or strategies, if any, can be derived from our study? This is a difficult question, given the constraints set up by the economic, social, and political reality dealt with and the need to distinguish between what is possible in the short run and what could be achieved if long-term changes were assumed. For example, what can be recommended to deal with the highly exploitative situation that we encountered regarding homework?

One possibility would be the creation of some type of collective organization to improve the working conditions of home workers and to secure a legal minimum salary and fringe benefits as well as to deal with their contact with jobbers and firms. As pointed out in Chapter 4, the main problem with this approach is that it may do away with this type of employment. To the extent that the differential costs between home and factory work would be eliminated, the incentive would be removed for firms to shift production outside of the workshop or factory. In addition (even if this were not a problem) the isolation, dispersion, and clandestinity inherent in homework, and women's knowledge of the existence of a large reserve of wives/mothers ready to take their place, make collective organization extremely difficult.

Yet the women homeworkers interviewed that had an opinion on trade unions (only 40%) were not against the principle of unionization. They were afraid, however, of the practical consequences of any attempt to organize. A number of reasons for that fear were voiced, particularly that of losing the possibility of a much-needed source of income. To illustrate, in one of the areas visited there had been an attempt to organize a group of homeworkers to demand higher wages from the jobber. In retaliation, and to teach the "rebellious" neighborhood a lesson, part of the homework was moved to another area of Mexico City. As a result, the group of organizers had to face the anger of other coworkers who blamed them for having deprived them of their work.

Even if there were attempts to organize a trade union, it would be difficult for homeworkers to meet the strict regulations set up by Mexican law, which would imply significant costs and require organizational and legal skills hardly available to the women we encountered. In addition, the success of this type of organization depends upon the possibility of establishing a significant degree of control over the labor supply. This would be quite impossible in a situation such as that in Mexico City where the supply of would-be homeworkers seems unlimited. Finally, the unstable character of homework, as shown in Chapter 4, would make it difficult for a union to survive or justify its existence.

For seamstresses who own the machines and tools used in production, a possibility may exist to set up some form of cooperative organization among themselves. This would, however, require surfacing their work from underground to the regulated economy. Among other things, this would imply an increase in labor costs at least to the minimum wage. This, too, could wipe out the jobber's incentive to subcontract. In addition, as in the case of the trade unions, the formal organization of cooperatives would also require costs and skills, which could hardly be met by the women themselves. A cooperative form of production, however, might be able to compensate for the higher costs with an increase in productivity and/or product quality. It is here that outside help from government or other institutions could be useful not only to provide training and management skills and financial help but also to organize collective services to meet women's domestic needs (child care and health services for example).[1]

Despite the exploitative nature of homework and the difficulties of improving the situation, we do not conclude that, from the perspective of women themselves, their engagement in homework is totally negative. According to the homeworkers, their wages, no matter how low, can be used as a lever to secure a minimum space of autonomous control; as a mechanism to pursue goals of household well-being; and to ameliorate the damage to self-image caused by economic dependency on their husbands. However, from the perspective of long-term changes and development objectives, it is difficult to be optimistic about the possibilities offered by this type of paid work.

In Search of a Redefinition of Development

To conclude on a more general note, we want to emphasize that the analysis in these chapters contains an implicit concept of development that has been voiced progressively by women during the past decade. This concept derives from a holistic vision with several dimensions. One dimension derives from recognizing that the traditional emphasis given to economic growth per se ignores noneconomic objectives that are essential for full development of human beings and human potential. A noneconomistic approach to development would encompass the many dimensions of human development (educational, psychological, sexual, involving also community ties and human relations in addition to economic factors).[2] Economic growth is a necessary but not sufficient condition for the maximization of this potential, as indicated by the disappointing results of decades of growth that have benefited only a small proportion of the world's population, failed to successfully achieve self-sustaining development for many countries, or have even created new conditions for impoverishment and hunger.

Second, it is a corollary that dealing with these aspects of development requires focusing on redistribution of resources and the eradication of roots of oppression and discrimination within countries as well as between the center and the peripheral countries.

Third, a holistic approach derives from the search for societies that are more humane and just and denounces the evils that can so easily be observed in today's world: extremely high and unjustifiable levels of military expenditures in the face of hunger and other forms of human misery; violence of all forms; misuse of technological advancements; degradation of ecological systems; energy waste and other problems too numerous to mention. All of this is parallel to unprecedented levels of accumulation of wealth and resources on a world scale and to growing inequalities between rich and poor countries.

Fourth, for women in particular, a holistic approach requires inclusion of the area of reproduction as a fundamental component of human activity and part of the development process. This implies the eradication of the asymmetric division of labor in domestic work and child rearing and the implementation of policies that will ensure women's own control of their sexuality and reproductive capacity.

Among women, this holistic approach has been gradually underlined by those concered with development issues during the United Nations Decade for Women.[3] But who listens to women and to those with a similar vision? Although the Decade conferences attracted increasing attention within the international community, they were often treated as "women's events" and not given enough serious consideration.[4] In addition, a holistic vision of change is still regarded in many development circles and government agencies as naive and utopian at best and radical and divisive at worst. Yet, more than any other vision, it is likely to represent the needs and aspirations of a great majority of the world's population.

How can such a vision materialize and acquire legitimacy and strength? To begin with, such a perspective can be realized only through a democratic process that would express goals and objectives originated from the bottom up; that is, a form of decision-making that is inherent to feminism. This perspective also requires policies and actions that, as part of the rethinking of development, are effective means for channeling aspirations and programs set up at the grass-roots level. An important dimension of this rethinking, of direct relevance for our study, is the "subjectification" rather than the "objectification" of women, that is, the inclusion of women's needs, *as expressed by women themselves*, in any program for change.

The gap is overwhelming between this vision and strategy and the reality that we observe. In many countries of the Third World, the direction of change is backward rather than progressive—as reflected by stagnant economies, problems of foreign debt and economic dependency, and the impoverishment of a large proportion of the population.[5] In capitalist countries, the inherent inequality in the distribution and control of resources (derived from the concentration of the means of production in the hands of a relatively small number of people and institutions) places many limits on the empowerment of large sectors of society. Hence, the implementation of a holistic approach to development would require fundamental changes in the economic foundation of society. In particular, from a women's perspective, this necessary step should include also specifically defined gender objectives, without which the achievement of equality between men and women is not guaranteed.[6]

To return to the instance of our study, this vision leads to long-term changes and strategies beyond the short-term recommendations mentioned earlier. These would include a network of interdependent objectives such as changes in ownership and control of the means of production; improvement of the educational background of women and upgrading of their skills; designing of employment strategies; changes in socialization processes affecting the formation of gender traits; equal sharing by men and women in child care and domestic work or the setting up of more socialized facilities for day care and other domestic services; and improved services for birth control and family planning. This is not an exhaustive list but an illustration of concrete goals whose realization will depend on the political, economic, and social change taking place in Mexican society.

Notes

1. We use "recompostition" to indicate how class and gender can take new forms with continuous changes in the labor market and in gender relations. See Elson and Pearson (1981).

2. Among books published, see, for example, Youssef (1974), Safa and Nash (1976), Wellesley Editorial Committee (1977), Buvinic, Youssef, and Von Elm (1978), Beck and Keddie (1978), Bukh (1979), Rogers (1979), Black and Cottrell (1981), Young, Wolkowitz, and McCullagh (1981), Nelson (1981), León (1982), Benería (1982), Nash and Fernández-Kelly (1983), Buvinic et al. (1984), Charlton (1984), Bunster and Chaney (1985), Heyzer (1985).

3. It is impossible to include a complete list of the contributions to the literature; references included here should be taken as illustrations only.

4. See the literature on basic needs (ILO, 1976) and some of the documents written for the Nairobi Conference at the end of the UN Decade for Women (DAWN, 1985).

5. An example is the domestic labor debate as an effort to conceptualize the nature of domestic work as household production and as instrumental for the reproduction of the labor power and the functioning of the economic system. For a summary on the literature on the subject, see Himmelweit and Mohun (1977). For a feminist critique, see Molyneux (1979).

For a more recent example, Vogel (1983) represents an important effort to analyze systematically the deficiencies of traditional Marxism for understanding women's subordination and to incorporate the contribution of new feminist theory into Marxist analysis. In the process, Vogel expands Marxist categories to include reproduction and its significance to understand women's condition. Missing in her analysis, however, are the ideological aspects of the social construction of gender, which she tends to subsume into "the material," despite the fact that, in her case, the material includes the spheres of reproduction and (as in traditional Marxism) production.

6. There is no analytical consensus on the distinction between Marxist and socialist feminism. The terms tend to be used interchangeably. See Barrett (1978) and Jaggar (1983) for an illustration of different uses.

7. This is not to say that sex and gender are not dialectically related. We agree with Jaggar (1983: 110) that "a historical and dialectical conception of human biology sees human nature and the forms of human social organization as determined not by our biology alone, but rather by a complex interplay between our forms of social organization, including our type of technological development, between our biological constitution and the physical environment we inhabit."

8. See Chetwynd and Hartnett (1978) for definition of a "sex- role system" that includes some of the factors mentioned in our definition but excludes differentiations by class and race and emphasizes cultural aspects. On the ranking of male and female traits, see Gilligan (1982).

9. Giddens (1981) defines domination as "structured asymmetries in access to different resources" but does not apply it to gender domination per se, as we do here.

10. See Molyneux (1985) for a similar conceptualization of "strategic gender interests".

11. See Singer (1981) and Portes (1984) to illustrate the first approach for the case of Brasil and Latin America respectively. Poulantzas (1973 and 1975) and Wright (1978) include economic as well as political and ideological "locations" within the total class structure in their examination of advanced capitalist society. A cultural historical analysis is provided by E. P. Thompson (1966) and B. and J. Ehrenreich (1979) for England and the United States respectively.

Given the voluminous literature on the subject of class from a Marxist perspective, it is beyond the scope of this book to engage in the polemics of class definition. We have mentioned only some sources that we consider good illustrations of different approaches. Besides, it should not be assumed that authors who share a common approach necessarily agree on empirical indicators or formal criteria nor on the number of these criteria (compare for example Singer and Portes). In fact, there exists considerable theoretical and political heterogeneity within the Marxist perspective on class, and even contradictory notions held by some authors as shown in the interesting collection of articles edited by P. Walker (1979). See in particular Walker's Introduction and the contribution by B. and J. Ehrenreich. On Marx's connotations of class, see Ollman (1979).

12. As earlier mentioned, the relationship between women's role in reproduction and its influence on women's productive activities has been analyzed from a variety of perspectives. In addition, on the subject of women's relationship to class, see Garnsey, (1978), West (1978), Tilly and Scott (1978), Benenson (1983), Petchesky (1983).

13. Economic ownership of the means of production means the control over investment and productive resources. Possession refers to control over the organization of the productive process and the labor process. By modes

of remuneration Portes (1984) refers to the different ways social classes receive their means of consumption, ways which range from profits to regular salaries, protected and casual wages, and direct subsistence production.

14. See Cockburn (1981) for an elaboration of the view that class and gender formation must be viewed as historical processes taking place simultaneously.

Chapter 2

1. Data in several tables from the World Bank's *World Development Report*, (1983).

2. The inflation rate during this period, as measured by the consumer price index, reached a peak of 28.9% in 1977 (World Bank, 1981).

3. For example, during the 1970–74 period, U.S. investments in Mexico represented 78.6% of total foreign investment, followed by 16.7% of Western European investment (Banco de México, 1979).

4. At the 1981–82 exchange rate of 23 Mexican pesos to US$1.00. These figures reflect the earnings reported by the women interviewed and do not coincide with the amount pooled by household members, which is lower because not all members, (especially male) contributed their total earnings to the household pool. In fact, some members (including some wives, young men and women, and relatives) did not contribute to the pool at all (see Chapter 6 for more detail).

5. On this distinction, see Klein (1983).

6. In one case of a textile firm with 1200 workers, the questionnaire was withdrawn after completion by the engineer who granted the interview, on grounds that some of the information provided had to be double-checked; yet despite promises, the questionnaire was never recovered. This firm, which was giving homework to an asylum and a prison, was the only one of that size found subcontracting directly to the homeworkers.

7. This issue in fact exploded in September 1985 when the earthquake that destroyed parts of Mexico City buried hundreds of garment workers in workshops concentrated in the downtown area. The scandal created by the priority that employers gave to rescuing equipment and raw materials before workers, resulting in the death of many, eventually gave rise to the new independent garment union "Diecinueve de Septiembre," an unprecedented institution in Mexico, in the fall of 1985.

8. For example, we encountered garment workshops that were sending work to the cities of Puebla and Guadalajara, and to smaller towns. In fact, one of the consequences of the creation of the garment union Diecinueve de Septiembre is the intensification of this trend.

Chapter 3

1. For example, a large multinational of 3,000 workers had a list of 300 permanent and 1,500 occasional subcontractors producing parts for a variety

of electrical appliances. It should be noted that this is not the case for all industries. Watanabe (1983) reports, for example, that the automobile industry tends to rely on a very small number of subcontractors.

2. Note that figure 3.2 does not include homework. If it did, the base of the pyramid would widen. It should be noted also that the pyramid is inverted if, instead of measuring the number of firms, we measure total employment at each level.

3. In Italy, the decentralization of production that has taken place since the early 1970s has been the result of subcontracting or expulsion of some production, but also of the subdivision of large integrated plants into small, specialized production units, and the development of a dense, small-firm economy in certain regions (Goddard, 1981; Murray, 1983; Garofoli, 1983).

4. Jenkins (1984) has criticized the use of the Babbage principle to explain the new international division of labor on the grounds that it places too much emphasis on a cheap-labor strategy and neglects the role of technological change in increasing labor productivity and influencing labor costs. Our point here is that the emphasis on cheap labor does not exclude the possibility that capital uses other strategies to lower costs of production.

5. This situation gives firms a great degree of flexibility, at the same time minimizing labor problems. Murray (1983) also gives an example of an Italian firm that shifted from putting out 10% of its production in 1969 to 46% in 1972. When production fell rapidly in 1974–75, work sent out resulted in a loss of 550 jobs but internal employment remained stable.

6. Personal communication with an economist who had worked in both branches.

7. For an elaboration of these points, see Benería (1984).

8. See, for example, the June 1981 newsletter *Panorama Económico*, published by Bancomer, one of the largest Mexican banks.

9. In the firm mentioned earlier with 30–60 as an oscillating number of workers, women represented 80% of the work force; the average age of workers was 20. According to the firm's manager, "young women are ideal for short-term employment because they actually like to stop working, say for a week, so that they can visit their parents in the countryside, go shopping, or help in the home."

10. The high proportion of women employed in the US/Mexican border industries is a well-documented fact (Fernández-Kelly, 1983; Bustamante, 1983). It was often mentioned by firm representatives as an example of the new acceptability of women workers.

11. This is not to say that old prejudices have totally disappeared. Husbands' opposition to their wives' work outside the household was found to be one of the reasons for women's concentration in homework (see Chapters 4, 6, and 7). On the part of employers, four firms in our sample—ranging from small to very large—had a deliberate policy of not employing women. As one manager explained, "they create a new set of problems: relations with male workers—tensions or too much friendship between

them—and even pregnancies." These, however, were exceptions that reflected traditional attitudes rather than the newer trends.

12. Similarly, along the U.S./Mexican border, assembly plants have begun to employ men in a clear shift from previous practices. This has been attributed to a rising labor demand but also to a deliberate policy to employ men because, according to the president of the Association of the Border Assembly Plants, the area had become a "matriarchy." The policy objective is to increase the proportion of male workers to 60% by the end of the decade (Meislin, 1984). Although this objective may prove to be difficult to reach, it illustrates the imposition of ideology on labor-market trends.

13. A good proportion of the literature on the informal sector has taken this position; see Chapter 4 for a discussion of the significance of these arguments with regards to homework.

14. As Doeringer (1984: 122), for example, has put it, small businesses have a "wide range of generic strengths" such as "the ability to expand productive capacity almost at will; the flexibility of production that comes out of the small business sector; the ability to operate on various kinds of short-term credits, informal credit systems; the ability to get raw materials and secondhand parts—on very short notice."

15. Some economists have argued that women's low wages are due to their preference for specific jobs, which results in a large supply relative to demand and therefore in low wages (Killingsworth, 1984). As a result they argue against the implementation of comparable-worth principles on the basis that it goes against market forces. This blaming-the-victim argument assumes that women's supply is autonomous and based on a set of "preferences" rather than on their perception of employers' demands for female labor. Yet, as our analysis indicates, there are reasons to believe that the weight of women's allocation to jobs falls on employers' decisions, i.e., on the demand rather than the supply side. In addition, this argument assumes that wages are *solely* determined by demand and supply variables, an assumption that can hardly be sustained given the different critiques of the neoclassical model of wage determination (Lester, 1942; Thurow, 1965; Doeringer, 1967; Blau and Jusenius, 1976; Treimann and Hartmann, 1981)

16. In particular, see Stone (1973), Marglin (1974), Gordon, Edwards, and Reich (1982), Bowles, Gordon, and Weisskopf (1984), Naples (forthcoming).

Chapter 4

1. We found a few cases also in which the jobber managed a very small-scale production unit as a family enterprise; although workshops are often operated as a family business, they rely mostly on wage labor.

2. These figures are based on an exchange rate of 23 Mexican pesos for US$1.00, which was the official rate at the time data was collected.

3. It must be pointed out that our estimates of hours worked are subject to error because of difficulties in computing accurately, first, the number of

hours dedicated to homework and, second, the hours of help provided by family members. Interviews were carried out with these difficulties in mind: our estimates are based on figures arrived at after the scrutiny allowed by repetitive questioning during the interviews. (See also n. 10, chap. 6.)

4. This percentage is likely to be overestimated because of the difficulty of gathering complete information about earnings from all household members; women interviewed did not always know the exact incomes of husbands and sons and daughters interviewed did not have the information about their parents.

5. As explained in Chapter 3, the word "maquila" in Mexico is used to represent very precisely the fragmentation process of modern production through which specific tasks can easily be separated out in time and space. The concept refers to vertical subcontracting; i.e., to production carried out under contract from another producer who provides raw materials and gives specific instructions about what is expected.

6. In some cases, the purchase is normally done after an initial period in which the machines are loaned by the jobber; it implies a family decision in order to allocate pooled income to that purpose; payments are made through installments. In other instances, women generate their own savings to acquire their own machine(s).

7. Alonso distinguishes four categories of garment workers: a) those who work alone (unipersonal workshops) or b) with other family members (multipersonal workshops); c) seamstresses that hire young women, and d) the head seamstress as a fulltime manager of the workshop. In the latter case, the number and diversity of sewing machines are greater, and the young women tend to be placed in a separate room in a way that it resembles "a small clothing factory" (p. 28).

8. This has implications for labor-supply theory. It has been pointed out that conventional labor-supply theory based on individual decisions about allocation of working time does not apply to situations where there is income-pooling within the household (García et al., 1982). In this case, it is argued, the domestic unit rather than the individual should be the analytical base. Although this model is more adequate to describe the empirical reality of the urban poor, it does not take into consideration the fact that the implicit family dynamics do not affect each family member equally. For women, it often means a subordination of individual choices either to male family members or to the ideology of domesticity. From a feminist perspective, the model is insufficient because it does not capture the specificity of gender relations—an important objective in pointing toward avenues for change.

Chapter 5

1. We are indebted to Harold Benenson (1983) for his notion of "transitional stages in women's lives" and their influence upon women's future location in the class structure. However, we have reinterpreted that insight

according to the theoretical and conceptual framework developed in Chapter 1.

2. This conceptualization of the subproletariat draws upon Singer (1981) and Portes (1983). The sectors we distinguish within this class are our own, since most authors do not differentiate between the personal services, homework, and autonomous sectors. In our view, this distinction is important because in the first two, women predominate (which cannot be said of the autonomous sector), and we are interested in knowing how many of the women interviewed (and in which stages of their work history) worked in one or another of these sectors. For the same reason, tables 5.3 and 5.5 draw, within the general-waged subproletariat, a distinction between women who work in any private enterprise (except in the garment industry) and women who sew in workshops, and table 5.6 distinguishes between women engaged in any autonomous activity and those sewing at home.

3. According to García, Muñoz, and Oliveira (1982), big enterprises in Mexico City hire workers on a contractual (permanent) basis, as well as casual laborers. The latter may have a better chance of eventually becoming permanent within a given firm than those who do not have previous experience in the same enterprise or field. This seems to have been the case for most proletarian husbands in our sample, and for the few women who were also made permanent.

4. If the focus of the investigation lies in the "cultural" aspects of class, and the woman interviewed lives, during her period of origin, in a household group with a different cultural milieu from that which she would have had living with the person who supported her economically, it could be argued that her class of origin is that of the head of the household in which she lived, disregarding a strict economic criterion. This is a frequent situation when women come from households which are broken or were never effectively constituted (daughters of single mothers), and they are raised by relatives in rural areas with a "peasant culture," but their main economic support comes from the mother's income and derives from the latter's domestic or casual work in the city. One-third of the women with a subproletariat in personal services' origin were raised by their maternal grandmothers and a few from other sectors by sisters, aunts, and godmothers.

5. It is also possible that the woman interviewed had her own class position when she was eleven, if she had started paid work at an early age. In the case of peasants' daughters, the majority had participated in some kind of farm activity when they were six or seven. Some also accompanied their parents within the same area or travelled to more distant places, and participated in harvesting tasks, as unpaid members of a working family group. The same may be said of daughters of agricultural day laborers. As previously mentioned, other women were intermittently employed as domestics in town, when their wages were needed for household reproduction. However, and according to work histories, in the period considered as "of origin," the women interviewed were economically dependent on another person or family group.

6. For Mexico City, this relationship was confirmed by García, Muñoz, and Oliveira (1982).

7. The role of the mother of the woman interviewed appears to have been fundamental in the decision regarding the form and quality of organization of domestic work, which of her daughters would work outside the home or stay in school, how the domestic/labor relationship would be articulated, especially concerning the care of younger brothers and sisters. This sphere of female decision continues in the present home of the industrial home workers (see Chapter 6).

We also want to point out that the picture here is different from Benenson's (1983) findings for the U.S., where early pregnancy or teenage marriage usually means stopping formal education and precludes the possibility of securing job skills and experience as single women. Within our sample, the decisions concern whether to have the young woman continue in school, work for wages on a more or less regular basis, or substitute for mothers at home. Marriage or first cohabitation does not stop education as much as does a hard and disappointing work history when single.

8. Undoubtedly, formal education involves not only class but also gender elements (and possible ethnic/racial ones); but this question goes beyond the limits of our research.

9. At the time of our fieldwork, only 15 percent of the women interviewed were living in consensual unions; in half of the cases, however, civil or religious marriage had followed consensual unions, months or years after the relationship had been established.

10. The "style" of premarriage household interaction previously mentioned can contribute to a more rapid "expulsion" from the household of origin of the female workers who were not satisfied with their jobs when single or who had less possibility of future occupational advance because of a low educational level.

11. Both the proletariat and the subproletariat are far from homogeneous and there exists a lively debate concerning their different sectors. Of particular importance is the one concerning the character of the professional, technical, managerial, and administrative sectors. These nonmanual wage earners make up a "new petite bourgeoisie," according to Poulantzas (1973, 1975); they belong to a "professional-managerial class," according to Ehrenreich and Ehrenreich (1979); and to the "professional-technical class" (Portes, 1984); or occupy "contradictory locations within class relations'" (Wright, 1978). Wives could not describe with precision whether husbands had, or had not, control over the labor power of others, a basic criterion for that class's membership. We consider that the four husbands were subordinate white-collar employees, a nonmanual fraction of the proletariat, and we have registered them as such.

12. Fifteen female workers did not interrupt their paid labor activity at the time of marriage or impending motherhood, but the majority of these women did change the type of work done, preferring activities in the auto-

nomous and personal services sectors, or some kind of industrial homework. Forty percent of these women live in consensual union, suggesting that women in this kind of relationship feel less secure and give more importance to an independent income.

13. We would have liked to compare high and low fertility women within the sample to see to what extent reproduction divides women within the same class (Petchesky, 1983), but this was not possible because our sample includes women belonging to different stages of the family cycle and, in general, we are dealing with high-fertility women. We do consider the divisive influence of reproduction from another perspective, by comparing different class insertions of the same women, at different stages of the same cycle.

14. Although they start their postnuptial career with industrial homework, five of these women later enter another field of remunerated activity (as domestics paid by the hour, an occasional factory worker and an autonomous worker) and temporarily stop doing industrial homework during emergencies or when a marked decline in the availability of industrial homework occurs. Once this situation is overcome, they return and they were doing industrial homework at the time of this study, either exclusively or combined with some other activity (see table 5.6).

15. It should be noted that these are total incomes, while in Chapter 4 we refer to incomes derived exclusively from industrial homework for the total sample of 140 women. In the cases in which the incomes equal or exceed the minimum, the women work more than the 48 hours per week required for the legal minimum.

16. Although it is true that all industrial homework is unstable, in some areas a relative stability does exist; for example, in sewing, lace, sweets and toys, in the sense that although the weekly or monthly supply might vary or be interrupted, the supply continues all year. In considering the total number of years spent in industrial homework, this type of continuity, all types of industrial homework, and the time per annum worked (even when interrupted by periods of nonremunerated activity), were taken into account. For these reasons, and because we are referring only to the wives and not to the total number of women in the sample, these data cannot be compared to those analyzed in Chapter 4.

17. Within the general-waged subproletariat, the periods of time spent as workers in shops and restaurants varies from two to nine months. In the personal services and autonomous activities, it was not possible to register all the entrances and exits from the labor market, because the women themselves did not remember them. In personal services we could register blocks or periods of "ins and outs" corresponding to a definite stage in the life or family cycle of the homeworker: some of them were as long as three, four, and even eight years, with interruptions of weeks or months. An atypical case is that the oldest industrial homeworker (64 years old) who washed clothes for 22 years before beginning industrial homework. Among autonomous workers the periods were shorter, depending on the commercial

success of the activity undertaken; in general, the activity was initiated for a few months, then abandoned and then undertaken again, or alternated with some other autonomous activity. An exception is the beautician who went from house to house and who in 14 years of marriage never entirely abandoned the profession she held when single.

18. Since the sample includes couples in different phases of the life-cycle, the same evolution cannot be expected for those who have been married for only a few years as for those who have married for 20 or more years when the husband is either retired or close to retirement. We are dealing, therefore, with only a single "moment" in the work trajectory of the husbands. In two cases in the sample, this "moment" corresponds to the work history of the second partner.

Chapter 6

1. These chapters are based on interviews with 53 wives, as explained in Chapter 2.

2. Interest in household analysis has been a worldwide and multidisciplinary tendency. In the field of household economics, which also operates with a model of the household as a unit of consumption and production, see Becker (1981) and Schultz (1974). For a critique of these positions, see Dwyer (1983).

3. Not all studies ignore the existence of intrahousehold conflicts, García, Muñoz, and Oliveira (1982) being a case in point. However, if these conflicts are not understood as an expression of underlying relations of domination, the notion of role complementarity cannot be overcome.

4. See B. Thorne and M. Yalom (1982) for a collection of articles bearing on this subject, and the studies cited by Dwyer (1983).

5. To illustrate the variety of possibilities for household "decomposition," we can mention: "production, reproduction, sexuality and socialization structure" (Mitchell, 1971); a sex-gender system (Rubin, 1975); social relations of production, reproduction, and consumption (Rapp, 1982).

6. Allocative patterns change historically and cannot be generalized for the whole working class or the whole conjugal life of the couples interviewed. Studies on income allocation within working-class households include Hunt (1978) for the U.S., Pahl (1982) for Britain, and Zuluar (1982) for Brazil.

7. Although this study centers upon flows of direct wages, the indirect wages of proletarian husbands, represented by social security coverage for him and his family, should be kept in mind. Together with access to public services, knowledge, and information about the location of the latter, informal networks of reciprocal exchanges of goods and services (see n. 8), these direct and indirect wages are part of the social economic resources that family members exchange in daily interaction.

8. In a single household a set amount from the common fund was saved to pay off a loan to finish building the house. In the remaining cases, savings varied according to whether they were made by wives or husbands.

There were two types of savings among women: 1) short-term money left over from the common fund or weekly household allowance, which was generally used to pay monthly expenses, rent, or some other payment that would fall due in the next few days; to make installment payments on clothes, or to pay back loans made the week before; and 2) "long-term" or savings proper, taken from the common fund or allowance, or from the portion of the wives' earnings within the housekeeping allowance set, whose purpose is to meet emergencies, to make special purchases (furniture, curtains, household utensils, Sweet Sixteen Birthday parties [which in Mexico are held when girls turn 15 years old]) and in the case of a seamstress, savings for the purchase of the machines necessary to set up a workshop. Twenty-seven percent of the wives belonging to the Common Fund Group and 45 percent of the Housekeeping Allowance Set made Type 2 savings.

The majority of wives in the Pool Group saved by means of a method called *tanda:* A group of neighborhood women committed themselves to paying a small, weekly sum for a certain number of weeks or months, in accordance with the total commitment made. One of the women administers the fund, and each week one of the group, according to a prearranged order, receives the sum total of the contributions.

With respect to the husbands' savings, the information given us by the wives was incomplete, since the majority of them were not sure if the husband did in fact save a weekly or monthly sum, how much it was, and what use it would be put to. With this caveat in mind we find that among the husbands of the Pool Group, 21 percent have a savings account in the Credit Union of the factory they work in, and three have a *tanda* arrangement with their fellow workers. Thirty percent of the husbands belonging to the Housekeeping Allowance Set also saved.

Finally, we would like to point out that the population interviewed does not usually have recourse to the informal reciprocal exchanges (of goods and services) among equals that is common among the so-called marginal neighborhoods. The exception is found among a minority of the households in which the breadwinner earns less than the legal minimum, or among husbands who do not fulfill their financial obligation to their families. In these cases the woman interviewed received help from relatives to buy clothes, shoes, and schoolbooks, or received secondhand items directly. Also, four wives belonging to the Pool Group constantly had recourse to loans from relatives or neighbors in order to stretch the weekly allowance. These short-term debts were usually repaid when the next allowance was collected.

9. Pahl (1982) makes the distinction between "control" and "budgeting" which we find useful, although we have not used these terms in the same fashion.

10. Although in Chapter 2 we do characterize various types of extended households, as well as all households, according to whether they belong to the earlier or advanced phases of the family life-style, we cannot maintain this distinction in our analysis of 53 households that make up the subsam-

ple, because the number of cases in some cells is too small. Therefore, we have summarized the categories by distinguishing four general headings: nuclear from the earlier phases, extended from the earlier phases; nuclear from the advanced phases, and extended from the advanced phases of the family cycle.

In addition, we would like to stress that calculating the schedules of hours for the industrial homeworkers was one of the most difficult tasks in our investigation (along with the determination of the distribution circuits), given the nature of industrial homework and of the other remunerated tasks undertaken by the women (erratic, unstable, etc.). The industrial homework can begin, be interrupted, continue, according to what the industrial homeworker decides; be carried on at the same time as other tasks, such as the supervision of homework and play of the children, or at different phases in the preparation of food. A medical emergency: for example, taking the children to see a doctor at Social Security or to be vaccinated, would postpone the industrial homework until later. The reverse is also true: an urgent order from the intermediary can postpone the washing (it will get done another day) and reduce to a minimum the housework done that day, causing it to accumulate for the weekend. The more or less regular supply of industrial homework, and the need of the woman interviewed to accept more (or the same amount) of industrial homework, combine with the factors already mentioned to make approximate the averages for the arduous, total working days put in by the women interviewed.

11. Only three children work; two sons attend high school. The daughter who works has already finished high school and now helps in a pharmacy. The three of them keep part of their earnings to buy school supplies or for their own expenses and give the rest to their mothers as a contribution to the Common Fund.

Needless to say, all labor insertions of children from *young* nuclear or extended households place them in the ranks of the mushrooming subproletariat of Mexico City.

12. With the exception of two women, the rest of the female and male live-in kin belong to the waged or autonomous subproletariat of Mexico City.

13. We shall only refer to nuclear households in the advanced phases of the family cycle since our sample includes only three extended households at this stage and they correspond to different pool groups (A, B, and C), which precludes any generalizations.

14. Only one daughter and one son held permanent positions. With regard to adult children's allocation of their incomes, the situation was heterogeneous. The daughter who was a secretary was one of the main contributors to the common fund in one of the households where the breadwinner's income was less than the legal minimum; the other daughters used their earnings for personal and school expenses. The son with a permanent job is the main contributor to the common fund in his household; the sons who belong to the family that is paying off their house also regularly contribute half their earnings; the sons of another household do this sometimes; a

teenager who loads and unloads in the market also contributes (when he gets work); and one last son, a construction worker, does not contribute and, according to the woman, saves his money for "his vices" (he smokes marijuana).

The contribution made by grown children does not follow, therefore, any single model; it depends instead on the extent of the economic need in the household in question and the woman's skill in convincing the "reluctant" children of the need for this help. In the case of engaged sons, who might be interested in saving for their own future household, loyalty to the household where he lives and obligation to his mother compete with the claims of his future wife.

Chapter 7

1. We are not referring to the legal obligation involved in the formal marriage contract, but to women's explanations when asked about normative and behavioral aspects of their unions.

2. Our conceptualization of consciousness does not pretend to exhaust the variety of standpoints on this controversial subject. Compare, for example, Giddens (1964) with Etzioni (1968), and, from a feminist perspective, Rowbotham (1979).

3. This important topic is developed by Abercrombie and Turner (1980), although from a strictly (male) Marxist perspective.

4. Goldberg (1983) makes a similar point in her study of women officeworkers.

5. Our data mainly refer to "discursive" consciousness (Giddens, 1984), but do not allow us to explore in detail what he calls "practical" consciousness; that is, "What actors know (believe) about social conditions, including especially the conditions of their own action, but cannot express discursively" (p. 375). We agree with Giddens, however, in that "it is often in the manner in which activities are carried on, for example, that actors in circumstances of marked social inferiority make manifest their awareness of their oppression." We tried to fill this lacuna to the extent that participant observation of homeworkers' lives was possible through anthropological fieldwork.

6. Our findings are in agreement with Eisenstein's (1983) concerning working women's consciousness in the U.S. from 1890 to World War I.

7. Although we do not have systematic data on women's "world views" concerning social differences, from in-depth conversations with a number of them, we may distinguish: first, a dichotomic interpretation (the poor and the rich) usually provided by the poorest of the women interviewed; second, a trichotomic view (the poor, the middle sector, and the rich) or a more sophisticated vision of five echelons (the very rich, the common rich, the middle sector, the poor, which included the women interviewed, and the very poor, which included casual laborers without access to means of subsistence). Some of their explanations of the origins of these

differences rested on a secular interpretation of the world: "rich people are rich because they exploit the poor," others were based on religion ("God made them rich") or on fate; they could also be mixed. What we want to stress here is that women perceived a class difference between themselves and the patronas they served as maids, or the wives of owners of factories or restaurants where they worked, irrespective of the vocabulary used to express this difference. They knew they did not belong to the same social category as the middle-sector women they worked for. This should remind us that to expect from working women an awareness of common gender interests with women not from their own class may mean to extrapolate unduly hegemonic, middle-class, feminist concepts to working women's own perspective and experience.

There is considerable literature on the topic of class consciousness within the tradition of (male) Marxism. Mann (1973) and Reich (1972) provide a good, albeit androcentric, introduction to the subject. For a criticism of the main trends within orthodox and New Left Marxism, see Roldán (1978).

8. A few did not justify the double standard, but would not copy men's behavior—have lovers, have friends of the other sex, drink—because they felt that what is good or bad should be accepted by both partners, and men's violations of these limits did not legitimate women's misbehavior. Finally, three women said that they did not see anything wrong in men and women having the same right to enjoy themselves, but they personally would not engage in similar activities because their reputation would suffer (*se desprestigiarian*). These women show a disjunction between consciousness and action attributable to their very realistic interpretation of the likely negative consequences of their engaging in "improper" wife behavior, an outcome which they were not ready to face.

Chapter 8

1. A cooperative form of production can allow for a significant degree of flexibility in work organization that could be very useful for the women of our study. To illustrate, a woman-run cooperative among the Mondragón complex of cooperatives in Spain has totally flexible work schedules that allow women to choose the number of working hours worked as well as to make their own schedules.

2. This has, of course, been said before by a variety of authors. For example, the basic needs approach to development also included concerns beyond the conventional economic-development objectives (ILO, 1977).

3. For an excellent summary of these concerns, see DAWN (1985). The road towards this more inclusive vision of development has been protracted because of the different problems facing women in industrialized and Third-World countries. Given the extreme problems of poverty, hunger, economic crisis, and maldistribution of resources facing the Third World, it is not surprising that women from these countries tended at first to em-

phasize class rather than gender issues. This was typified by their clash in the first Decade meeting in Mexico City in 1975, with women from the more industrialized Western countries, particularly from the United States, who placed more emphasis on gender issues. Many Third World women, however, have gradually articulated class and gender in their politics—a shift that was visible in the second and third Decade conferences in Copenhagen (1980) and Nairobi (1985) and particularly in the Nongovernmental Organizations (NGO's) meetings. A similar though not simultaneous path was followed by feminists in most Western European countries who gradually incorporated gender issues into their class politics, particularly during the 1970s. At the same time, an increasing number of women from the United States were sensitized to class and Third-World issues. As a result, we have witnessed a tendency towards convergence on the part of women from different countries and regions, which, although still not representing a majority, offers a promising avenue toward international cooperation within a holistic vision.

4. It was not uncommon, for instance, for newspapers to relegate articles about the United Nations Decade conferences to women's pages with fashions, cooking, and other "feminine" topics.

5. For example, from 1960 to 1982, average annual growth rates for some African countries like Chad, Uganda, Niger, and Ghana were negative (World Bank, 1984). In Latin American countries like Argentina, Bolivia, Chile, and Peru, economies have either retrogressed or stagnated. Peru's per capita income, for instance, was no higher in 1985 than in 1965. For many of these countries, as well as for others in the Third World, accumulated foreign debt has reached such proportions that it is difficult to foresee the possibility of its repayment. As a Latin-American economist put it, this implies a level of dependency on the more developed industrialized countries "next to which colonialism was a child's play." For the poor strata of the population, this situation is also exacerbating problems of hunger, malnutrition, and social reproduction that will affect the human development of future generations.

6. As has often been pointed out by feminists writing on socialist countries, change in these societies in terms of eradicating gender inequalities has been uneven and insufficient, but positive (Croll, 1979; Molyneux, 1981, Tadesse, 1982). The reasons for this are manifold and beyond the scope of our work; for an interesting analysis on the subject, see Molyneux (1985).

Bibliography

Abercrombie, Nicholas and Brian S. Turner. 1980. *The Dominant Ideology Thesis*, London: George Allen and Unwin.

Allen, Sheila. 1981. "Invisible Threads," IDS Bulletin: 41–47.

Alonso, José A. 1979. "The Domestic Seamstresses of Netzahualcoyotl. A Case Study of Feminine Overexploitation in a Marginal Urban Area," Ph.D. diss., New York University.

———. 1981. "The Domestic Clothing Workers in the Mexican Metropolis and Their Relations to Dependent Capitalism." In Nash and Fernández Kelly, eds.: 161–72.

Anker, Richard, Mayra Buvinic, and Nadia Youssef, eds. 1983. *Women's Role and Population Trends in the Third World*. Geneva: International Labor Office.

Arizpe, Lourdes. 1975. "Women in the Informal Sector: The Case of Mexico City." Wellesley Editorial Committee: 25–37.

Avelar, Sonia María de. 1977. "Notas teóricas y metodológicas para el estudio del trabajo industrial a domicilio en México." *Revista Mexicana de Sociología*, 34 (October–December).

Banarjee, Nirmala. 1981. "The Weakest Link," in IDS Bulletin: 36–40.

Banco de México. 1979. *Información Económica. Sector Externo*. Monthly bulletin. August.

Bancomer. 1981. *Panorama Económico*, June.

Barrett, Michele. 1980. *Women's Oppression Today*. London: Verso Editions.

Beck, Lois, and Nikki Keddie, eds. 1978. *Women in the Muslim World*. Cambridge: Harvard University Press.

Becker, Gary S. 1981. *A Treatise on the Family*. Cambridge: Harvard University Press.

Benenson, Harold. Forthcoming. "Wives Outside the Occupational System." In Helena Z. Lopata, *Research in the Interweave of Social Roles*, Vol. 4. Westport, Conn.: JAI Press.

Benería, Lourdes. 1983. "Rural Development, International Markets and Labor Appropriation by Sex. A Case Study of l'Oulja Region, Morocco."

Study prepared for the Program on Rural Women, International Labor Office, Geneva.

——, 1984: "Gender, Skill and the Dynamics of Women's Employment." Paper prepared for the conference on Gender in the Work Place, sponsored jointly by the Brookings Institution and the Committee on the Status of Women in the Economic Profession. Washington, D.C., November.

——, ed. 1982. *Women and Development; the Sexual Division of Labor in Rural Societies.* New York: Praeger.

Benería, Lourdes, and Gita Sen, 1981. "Accumulation, Reproduction and Women's Role in Economic Development: Boserup Revisited." *Signs* 7, no. 2: 279–98. Winter

——. 1982. "Class and Gender Inequalities and Women's Role in Economic Development." *Feminist Studies* 8, no 1 (Spring): 157–76.

Bilac, Elisabete Doria. 1978. *Familias de Trabalhadores, Estrategias de Sobrevivencia. A Organizaçao da Vida Familiar em uma Cidade Paulista.* Sao Paulo: Ediciones Símbolo.

Black, Naomi, and Ann Baker Cottrell, eds. 1981. *Women and World Change: Equity Issues in Development.* Beverly Hills: Sage Publications.

Blau, Francine D. 1975. "Sex Segregation of Workers by Enterprise in Clerical Occupations." In Edwards et al. eds.: 257–79.

Blau, Francine D., and Carol L. Jusenius. 1975. "Economists' Approaches to Sex Segregation in the Labor Market: An Appraisal." In M. Blaxall and B. Reagan, eds., *Women and the Work Place.* Chicago: University of Chicago Press: 181–200.

Boserup. Ester. 1970. *Woman's Role in Economic Development.* London: George Allen and Unwin.

Bowles, Samuel, David M. Gordon, and Thomas E. Weisskopf. 1984. *Beyond the Waste Land.* Garden City: Anchor Press/Doubleday.

Braverman, Harry. 1974. *Labor and Monopoly Capital.* New York: Monthly Review Press.

Brenner, Johanna, and María Ramas. 1984. "Rethinking Women's Oppression." *New Left Review* 144 (March-April): 33–71.

Brighton Labor Process Group. 1977. "The Capitalist Labor Process." *Capital and Class* (Spring): 3–26.

Bromley, Ray, and Chris Gerry, eds. 1979. *Casual Work and Poverty.* London: John Wiley & Sons.

Bukh, Jette. 1979. *The Village Woman in Ghana.* Uppsala; Scandinavian Institute of African Studies.

Bunster, Ximena, and Elsa Chaney. 1985. *Sellers and Servants: Women Working in Lima.* New York: Praeger.

Burch, Thomas, Luis F. Lira, and Valdecir Lopez, eds. 1965. *La familia como unidad de estudio demográfico.* San José: Centro Latinoamericano de Demografía.

Bustamante, Jorge A. 1983. "*Maquiladoras:* A New Face of International Capitalism on Mexico's Northern Frontier." In Nash and Fernández-Kelly, eds.: 224–56.

Buvinic, Mayra. 1984. "Projects for Women in the Third World: Explaining Their Misbehavior." International Center for Research on Women, Washington, D.C.

Buvinic, Mayra, Margaret Lycette, and William Paul McGreevey, eds. 1983. *Women and Poverty in the Third World*. Baltimore: Johns Hopkins University Press.

Buvinic, Mayra, Nadia Youssef, and Barbara Von Elm. 1978. "Women-headed Households: The Ignored Factor in Development." International Center for Research on Women. Mimeographed.

Castro, Mary García. 1982. "'Mary and Eve's' Social Reproduction in the 'Big Apple': Colombian Voices." Occasional Paper No. 35, New York University: Center for Latin American and Caribbean Studies.

Chaney, Elsa M. 1985. "Women's Components in Integrated Rural Development Projects." Paper prepared for the panel "Las Intervenciones del Estado en el Sector Agrario y sus Efectos Sobre la Mujer Rural en Perspectiva Comparativa." Forty-fifth International Congress of Americanists. Bogotá. July.

Charlton, Sue Ellen M. 1984. *Women in Third World Development*. Boulder, Colo.: Westview Press.

Chetwynd, Jane, and Oonagh Hartnett, eds. 1978. *The Sex Role System: Psychological and Sociological Perspectives*, London: Routledge & Kegan Paul.

Cockburn, Cynthia. 1981. "The Material of Male Power." *Feminist Review* 9 (Autumn): 41–58.

Cohen, Regina. 1983. "Socialización Diferenciada. Un Estudio de Caso Sobre Educación Informal Impartida por Mujeres Trabajadoras Populares del Distrito Federal y Area Metropolitana." Licenciatura thesis, Universidad Nacional Autónoma de México.

Connolly, Priscilla. 1982. "Crítica del 'Sector Informal' como Concepto Aplicado con Referencia a la Estructura Ocupacional de la Ciudad de México," Paper prepared for the Symposium on Informal and Peripheral Economies in Sociological Theory, Tenth World Congress of Sociology, Mexico City.

Cordera, Rolando, and Carlos Tello, 1981. *México: La Disputa por la Nación. Perspectiva y Opciones del Desarrollo*. México: Siglo Veintiuno Editores.

Croll, Elizabeth J. 1979. "Socialist Development Experience: Women in Rural Production and Reproduction in the Soviet Union, China, Cuba, and Tanzania." Discussion paper, Institute of Development Studies, University of Sussex.

Davies, Rob. 1979. "Informal Sector or Subordinate Mode of Production? A Model." In Bromley and Gerry: 87–104.

DAWN (Development Alternative with Women in a New Era). 1985: *Development, Crisis, and Alternative Visions: Third World Women's Perspectives* (written by Gita Sen, with Karen Grown). New Delhi: Institute of Social Studies Trust.

Deere, Carmen Diana, and Magdalena León de Leal. 1982. "Peasant Production, Proletarianization, and the Sexual Division of Labor in the Andes." In Benería, ed.: 65–94.

Doeringer, Peter B. 1967. "Determinants of the Structure of the Industrial Type Labor Markets." *Industrial and Labor Relations Review* 20, no. 2 (January): 206–20.

———. 1984. "Comments" on Conference on Gender in the Work Place, The Brookings Institution, Washington, D. C., November.

Dwyer, Daisy H. 1983. "Women and Income in the Third World: Implications for Policy." The Population Council: Working Paper No. 18, June.

Edwards, Richard D. 1973. "Social Relations of Production at the Point of Production. *The Insurgent Sociologist* 8, no. 2 and 3 (Fall): 109–25.

Edwards, Richard C., Michael Reich, and David M. Godon. 1973. *Labor Market Segmentation*, Lexington, Mass.: D. C. Heath.

Ehrenreich, Barbara, and John Ehrenreich. 1979: "The Professional-Managerial Class," In Walker, ed.

Eisenstein, Sarah. 1983. *Give Us Bread But Give Us Roses: Working Women's Consciousness in the United States, 1890 to the First World War.* Boston: Routledge & Kegan Paul.

Eisenstein, Zillah, ed. 1979. *Capitalist Patriarchy and the Case for Socialist Feminism*. New York: Monthly Review Press.

Elger, Toni. 1979. "Valorization and 'Diskilling': A Critique of Braverman." *Capital and Class* 7, (Spring): 58–99.

Elson, Diane, and Ruth Pearson. 1981. "The Subordination of Women and the Internationalization of Factory Production." In Kate Young, Carol Wolkowitz, and Roslyn McCullagh, eds.: 144–66.

Etzioni, Amitai. 1968. *The Active Society.* New York: The Free Press.

Evans, Peter. 1979. *Dependent Development: The Alliance of Multinational, State, and Local Capital in Brazil.* Princeton, N. J.: Princeton University Press.

Felton, Nadine. 1986. "The Socionomic Origins of the Lowell, Mass., Mill Women, 1800-1860. Paper presented at the Conference on Women and Work: Past, Present and Future. Rutgers University, May.

Ferber, Marianne A., and Joe L. Spaeth. 1984. "Work Characteristics and the Male-Female Earnings Gap." *American Economic Review* 74, no. 2 (May): 260–64.

Ferguson, Ann, and Nancy Folbre. 1981. "The Unhappy Marriage of Patriarchy and Capitalism." In Sargent, ed: 313–38.

Fernández-Kelly, M. Patricia. 1983. "Mexican Border Industrialization, Female Labor-Force Participation, and Migration." In Nash and Fernández-Kelly, eds.: 205–23.

———. Forthcoming. "Advanced Technology, Regional Development, and Hispanic Women's Employment in Southern California." In Richard Gordon, ed., *Micro-Electronics in Transition.* San Francisco: Westview Press.

Fröbel, F., J. Heinrichs, and O. Kreye. 1980. *The New International Division of Labor*, Cambridge University Press.

Galbraith, John K. 1973. *Economics and the Public Purpose*. Boston: Houghton Mifflin.

García, Brígida, Humberto Muñoz, and Orlandina de Oliveira. 1979. *Migración, Familia y Fuerza de Trabajo en la Ciudad de México*. Cuadernos del CES, No. 26. Mexico City: Centro de Estudios Sociológicos, El Colegio de México.

———. 1982. *Hogares y Trabajadores en la Ciudad de Mexico*, Mexico City: El Colegio de México.

Garnsey, Elizabeth. 1978. "Women's Work and Theories of Class Stratification." *Sociology* 12: 223–43.

Garofoli, Gioacchino. 1978. *Ristrutturazione industriale e territorio*. Milan: Franco Angeli Editore.

———. 1983. "Sviluppo Regionale e Ristrutturazione Industriale: Il Modello Italiano Degli Anni '70." Paper presented at the symposium on "Reflexiones en torno a la economía los paises mediterráneos desarrollados." Sitges, Spain, September.

Garza, Gustavo. 1976. "Estructura y dinámica económica de la ciudad de México." Master's thesis, El Colegio de México: Centro de Estudios Económicos y Demográficos.

Giddens, Anthony. 1981. *A Contemporary Critique of Historical Materialism*. London: Macmillan.

———. 1984. *The Constitution of Society*. Cambridge: Polity Press.

Gilligan, Carol. 1982. *In a Different Voice*. Cambridge: Harvard University Press.

Goddard, Victoria. 1981. "The Leather Trade in the Bassi of Naples." IDS Bulletin: 3035.

Goldani, Ana M. 1977. "Impacto de los inmigrantes sobre la estructura y el crecimiento del area metropolitana." In H. Muñoz, O. Oliveira, and C. Stern, eds., *Migraciones y desigualdad social en la ciudad de México*. Instituto de Investigaciones Sociales (Universidad Nacional Autónoma de México) and El Colegio de México: 129–37.

Goldberg, Roberta. 1983. *Organizing Women Office Workers: Dissatisfaction, Consciousness, and Action*. New York: Praeger.

Gordon, David M., Richard C. Edwards, and Michael Reich. 1982. *Segmented Work, Divided Workers*, Cambridge: Cambridge University Press.

Gutmann, Peter. 1977. "The Subterranean Economy." *Financial Analyst Journal* (November-December): 24–34.

Hartmann, Heidi. 1976. "Capitalism, Patriarchy, and Job Segregation by Sex." In M. Blaxall and B. Reagan, eds., *Women and the Work Place*. Chicago: University of Chicago Press: 137–70.

———. 1981. "The Unhappy Marriage of Marxism and Feminism: Towards a More Progressive Union." In L. Sargent, ed.: 1–41.

Heyzer, Noeleen. 1982. "From Rural Subsistence to an Industrial Peripheral Work Force: an Examination of Female Malaysian Migrants and Capital Accumulation in Singapore," In Benería, ed.: 179–202.

————. 1985. *Missing Women: Development Planning in Asia and the Pacific.* Kuala Lumpur: Asian and Pacific Development Center.

Himmelweit, Susan, and Simon Mohun. 1977. "Domestic Labor and Capital," *Cambridge Journal of Economics* 1, (March): 15–31.

Hooks, Bell. 1984. *Feminist Theory: From Margin to Center.* Boston: South End Press.

Hunt, P. 1978. "Cash Transactions and Household Tasks." *Keel Sociological Review* 26, no. 3.

IDS Bulletin, 1981. "Women and the Informal Sector" 12, no. 3 (July).

ILO (International Labor Office). 1972. *Employment, Incomes, and Equality: Strategy for Increasing Productive Employment in Kenya.* Geneva.

————. 1976. *Poverty and Landlessness in Rural Asia.* Geneva.

————. 1977. *The Basic Needs Approach to Development.* Geneva.

————. 1978. "Condiciones de Trabajo. Formación Profesional y Empleo de la Mujer." Report prepared for the Eleventh Conference of American State Members of the ILO.

Jaggar, Alison M. 1983. *Feminist Politics and Human Nature.* Totowa, N.J.: Rowman and Littlefield.

Jenkins, Rhys. 1984. "Divisions over the International Division of Labor." *Capital and Class* 22, (Spring): 28–57.

Kerlinger, Fred N. 1973. *Foundations of Behavioral Research.* New York: Holt, Rinehart and Winston.

Killingsworth, Mark R. 1984. "The Economics of Comparable Worth: Analytical, Empirical and Policy Questions." In H. Hartmann, ed., *New Directions for Comparable Worth.* Washington: National Academic Press.

Klein, Renate Duelli. 1983. "How to Do What We Want to Do: Thoughts about Feminist Methodology." In G. Bowles and R. D. Klein, eds., *Theories of Women's Studies.* Boston: Routledge & Kegan Paul: 88–104.

Leff, Gloria. 1974. "Algunas características de las empleadas domésticas y su ubicación en el mercado de trabajo de la ciudad de México." Licenciatura thesis, Universidad Nacional Autónoma de Mexico.

————. 1976. "Las Migraciones femeninas a la ciudad de México." Research report, El Colegio de México, Centro de Estudios Sociológicos.

Lenin, V., 1970: "What Is to Be Done?" In *Collected Works*, vol. 5. Moscow: Progress Publishers.

León, Magdalena ed. 1982. *Debate sobre la Mujer en America Latina y el Caribe.* Volumes 1-3. Bogotá: ACEP.

Lester, Richard A. 1942. "Shortcomings of Marginal Analysis for Wage-Employment Problems." *American Economic Review* 36 (March).

Lomnitz, Larissa. 1978. "Mechanisms of Articulation between Shantytown Settlers and the Urban System." *Urban Anthropology* 2: 185–205.

Longhurst, Richard. 1982. "Resource Allocation and the Sexual Division of Labor: A Case Study of a Moslem Hausa Village in Northern Nigeria." In Benería, ed.: 95–118.

López, Hugo, Marta Luz, and Oliva Sierra. 1982. "El Empleo en el Sector

Informal: el Caso de Colombia." Manuscript, Center for Economic Research, University of Antioquía.

MacEwan, Arthur. 1985. "The Current Crisis in Latin America." *Monthly Review* 36, no. 9 (February: 1–18).

Mann, Michael. 1973. *Consciousness and Action Among the Western Working Class.* London: Macmillan.

Marglin, Stephen A. 1974. "What Do Bosses Do? The Origins and Functions of Hierarchy in Capitalist Production." *Review of Radical Political Economics* 6 (Summer): 60–112.

Margulis, Mario. 1980. "Reproducción Social de la Vida y Reproducción del Capital." *Nueva Antropología,* Año IV, nos. 13–14, (May): 47–64.

———. 1982. "Reproducción de la unidad doméstica, fuerza de trabajo y relaciones de producción." Paper prepared for the seminar on "Grupos domésticos, familia y sociedad," El Colegio de México, July.

Marx, Karl. 1967. *Capital.* Vol. 1. New York: International Publishers.

Meade, Teresa. 1978. "The Transition to Capitalism in Brazil: Notes on a Third Road." *Latin American Perspectives* 5, no. 3 (Summer): 7–26.

Medrano, Diana. 1981. "Desarrollo y Explotación de la Mujer: Efectos de la Proletarización Femenina en la Agroindustria de Flores en la Sabana de Bogotá." In M. León, ed: 43–55.

Meislin, Richard. 1984. "Mexican Border Plants Beginning to Hire Men." *The New York Times,* March 19.

Mercado, Alfonso. 1980. "La transferencia de tecnología dentro y fuera de empresas transnacionales en la industria de fibras poliester: las experiencias internacional y mexicana." *Iztapalapa* 1, no. 2 (January–June): 181–93.

Mies, Maria. 1982. *The Lace Makers of Narsapur: Indian Housewives Produce for the World Market.* London: Zed Press.

Minian, Isaac. 1981. *Progreso técnico e internacionalización del proceso productivo: el caso de la industria maquiladora de tipo eléctrico.* Mexico City: CIDE.

Mitchell, Juliet. 1971. *Woman's Estate.* New York: Vintage Books.

Molyneux, Maxine. 1979. "Beyond the Domestic Labor Debate." *New Left Review* 116, (July–August).

———. 1981. "Women in Socialist Societies: Problems of Theory and Practice." In Young, Wolkowitz, and McCullagh, eds.: 167–202.

———. 1985. "Mobilization without Emancipation? Women's Interest, the State, and Revolution in Nicaragua." *Feminist Studies* 11, no. 2 (Summer): 227–54.

Moser, Caroline, and Kate Young. 1981. "Women of the Working Poor." *IDS Bulletin:* 54–62.

Muñoz, Humberto, Orlandina de Oliveira, and Claudio Stern. 1971. "Categorías de emigrantes y nativos y algunas de sus características socioeconómicas: comparación entre las ciudades de Monterrey y México." In *Migración y desigualdad social en la ciudad de México.* Instituto de Investigaciones Sociales (Universidad Nacional Autónoma de México) and Colegio de México: 61–73.

Murray, Fergus. 1983. "The Decentralization of Production—The Decline of the Mass-Collective Worker? *Capital and Class* 19 (Spring): 74–99.

Naples, Michele. Forthcoming. "The Unravelling of the Post-War Truce between Unionized Workers and Capital and the Productivity Crisis in Mining and Manufacturing." *Review of Radical Political Economics*.

Nash, June, and Patricia Fernández-Kelly, eds. 1983. *Women, Men, and the International Division of Labor*. Albany: State University of New York Press.

Nelson, Nici, ed. 1981. *African Women in the Development Process*. London: Frank Cass.

Netting, Robert McC. 1984. *Households*. Berkeley: University of California Press.

O'Connor, David C. Forthcoming. "Women Workers and the Changing International Division of Labor in Microelectronics." In Lourdes Benería and Catharine Stimpson, eds., *Women and Structural Transformation in the United States*. New Brunswick: Rutgers University Press.

Ollman, Bertill. 1979. *Social and Sexual Revolution: Essays on Marx and Reich*. Boston: South End Press.

Oppong, Christine. 1978. "Household Economics, Demographic Decision-making: Introductory Statement." IUSSP Conference Proceedings, Helsinki, September.

Pahl, Jane. 1982. "The Allocation of Money and the Structuring of Inequality within Marriage." Canterbury: Health Services Research Unit, University of Kent.

Peek, Peter. 1978. "Family Composition and Married Female Employment." In G. Standing and G. Sheehan, eds., *Labor Force Participation in Low-income Countries*. Geneva: International Labor Office.

Pessar, Patricia. 1982. "Kinship Relations of Production in the Migration Process: The Case of Dominican Emigration to the United States." New York University Research Program in Inter-American Affairs, Occasional Paper No. 32.

Petchesky, Rosalind P. 1983. "Reproduction and Class Divisions Among Women." In Amy Swerdlow and Hanna Lessinger eds., *Class, Race, and Sex. The Dynamics of Control*. Boston: G. K. Hall.

Phillips, Anne, and Barbara Taylor. 1980. "Sex and Skill: Notes Towards a Feminist Economics." *Feminist Review* 6.

Phillips, Lynne, 1985. "Relaciones de Género, Desarrollo Rural y el Estado Ecuatoriano," Paper prepared for the panel on "Las Intervenciones del Estado en el Sector Agrario y sus Efectos sobre la Mujer Rural en Perspectiva Comparativa," International Congress of Americanists, Bogotá.

Portes, Alejandro. 1983. "The Informal Sector: Definition, Controversy, and Relation to National Development." *Review* 7 no. 1 (Summer): 151–74.

———. 1984. "Latin American Class Structures: Their Composition and Change During the Last Decades." Occasional Paper No. 3, School of Advanced International Studies. Baltimore: Johns Hopkins University.

Portes, Alejandro and Lauren Benton. 1984: "Industrial Development and Labor Absorption: A Re-interpretation." Paper prepared for seminar on "Urban Informal Sector in the Center and Periphery." Baltimore: Johns Hopkins University, June.

Poulantzas, Nicos. 1973. "On Social Classes." *New Left Review 78.*

————. 1975. *Classes in Contemporary Capitalism.* London: New Left Books.

Rapp, Rayna. 1982. "Family and Class in Contemporary America: Notes Towards an Understanding of Ideology." In Thorne and Yalom, eds.

Reich, Wilhelm. 1972. *SEX-POL Essays, 1929–34,* ed. L. Baxandall. New York: Random House-Vintage.

Reiter, Rayna, ed. 1975. *Towards an Anthropology of Women.* New York: Monthly Review Press.

Rogers, Barbara. 1979. *The Domestication of Women: Discrimination in Developing Societies.* New York: St Martin's Press.

Roldán, Martha. 1978. *Sindicatos y Protesta Social en la Argentina: 1969–74. Un Estudio de Caso: el Sindicato de Luz y Fuerza de Córdoba.* Amsterdam: CEDLA.

————. 1982. "Subordinación Genérica y Proletarización Rural: un Estudio de Caso en el Noroeste Mexicano." In M. León, ed., 2: 75–101.

————. 1984. "Industrial Homework, Reproduction of Working Class Families, and Gender Subordination." In N. Redclift and E. Mingione, eds., *Beyond Employment: Household, Gender, and Subsistence.* Oxford: Basil Blackwell.

————. Forthcoming. "Domestic Outwork, Patterns of Money Allocation, and Women's Consciousness." In C. Moser and K. Young, eds., *Women, Work, and Consciousness.*

Rubbo, Anna, 1975: "The Spread of Capitalism in Rural Colombia: Effects on Poor Women," in Reiter, ed.: 333–54.

Rubin, Gayle. 1975. "The Traffic in Women. Notes on the Political Economy of Sex." in Reiter, ed.: 157–210.

Safa, Helen, I. 1981. "Runaway Shops and Female Employment: The Search for Cheap Labor." *Signs 7,* no. 2 (Winter): 418–33.

Safa, Helen I., and June Nash, eds. 1976. *Sex and Class in Latin America.* New York: Praeger.

Sargent, Lydia, ed. 1981. *Women and Revolution.* Boston: South End Press.

Sassen-Koob, Saskia. 1982. "Exporting Capital and Importing Labor: The Role of the Caribbean Migration to New York City." New York University,Center for Latin American and Caribbean Studies, Occasional Paper No. 28.

Schmink, Marianne. 1982. "Women in the Urban Economy in Latin America." Working Paper No. 1, The Population Council, June.

Schultz, Theodore W. 1974. *The Economics of the Family: Marriage, Children, and Human Capital,* Chicago: University of Chicago Press.

Scott, Allison MacEwen. 1979. "Who Are the Self-employed? In Bromley and Gerry, eds.: 105–228.

Sen, Gita. 1980. "The Sexual Division of Labor and the Working Class Family: Towards a Conceptual Synthesis of Class Relations and the Subordination of Women." *Review of Radical Political Economics* 12: 76–86.

Silva de Rojas, Alicia Eugenia. 1982. "De Mujer Campesina a Obrera Florista." In. M. León, ed.

Singer, Hans W. 1970 "Dualism Revisited: A New Approach to the Problems of the Dual Society in the Developing Countries." *Journal of Development Studies* 7: 60–75.

Singer, Paulo. 1977. *Economia política do travalho*. Sao Paolo: Editora Hucitec.

———. 1981. *Dominaçao e desigualdade. Estrutura de classes e repartiçâo da renda no Brasil*. Rio de Janeiro: Paz e Terra.

Sokoloff, Natalie J. 1980. *Between Money and Love: The Dialectics of Women's Home and Market Work*. New York, Praeger.

Soria, Victor M. 1980. "Estructura y comportamiento de la industria farmacéutica en Mexico. El papel de las empresas transnacionales." *Iztapalapa* 1, no. 2, (January–June): 111–41.

Spindel, Cheywa R. 1982. "Capital, Familia y Mujer: La Evolución de la Producción Rural de Base Familiar. Un Caso en Brasil." In M. León, ed.

Spindel, Cheywa, J. Jaquette, and M. Cordini, eds. 1984. *A mulher rural e mudanças no processo de produçâo agrícola*. Estudos sobre a America Latina. Brasilia: IICA (Instituto Interamericano de Cooperação para a agricultura).

SSP (Secretaria de Programación y Presupuesto)/UCECA (Unidad Coordinadora del Empleo, Capacitación y Adiestramiento). 1976. *La Ocupación Informal en Areas Urbanas*. México D.F. December.

Standing, Guy. 1978. *Labor Force Participation and Development*. Geneva: International Labor Office.

Stevenson, Mary. 1973. "Women's Wages and Job Segregation." In Edwards et al, eds.: 254–56.

Stolcke, Verena. 1981. "The 'Unholy' Family: Labor Systems and Family Structure—the Case of Sao Paulo Coffee Plantations." Paper presented at the Conferencia sobre Aspectos Teóricos del Parentesco en America Latina, Ixtapan de la Sol, Mexico.

———. 1983. Position paper for the workshop on "Social Inequality and Gender Hierarchy in Latin America." Social Science Research Council, Mexico City, October.

Stone, Katherine. 1973. "The Origins of Job Structures in the Steel Industry." In *Labor Market Segmentation*, ed. Richard Edwards, Michael Reich, and David Gordon. D.C. Heath.

Tadesse, Zenebeworke. 1982. "The Impact of Land Reform on Women: The Case of Ethiopia." In Benería, ed.: 203–22.

Tanzi, Vito, ed. 1982. *The Underground Economy in the United States and Abroad*. Lexington, Mass.: Lexington Books.

Thompson, Edward P. 1966. *The Making of the English Working Class*. New York: Vintage Books.

Thorne, Barrie, and M. Yalom, eds. 1982. *Rethinking the Family: Some Feminist Questions.* New York: Longman.

Thurow, Lester C. 1965. *Generating Inequality.* New York: Basic Books.

Tilly, Louise A., and Joan W. Scott. 1978. *Women, Work, and Family.* New York: Holt, Rinehart and Winston.

Tinker, Irene. 1985. "Street Foods as Income and Food for the Poor." Paper presented at the Society for International Development Conference, Washington, D.C., May.

Treimann, Donald J., and Heidi Hartmann. 1981. *Women, Work, and Wages.* Washington, D.C.: National Academy of Sciences.

Vogel, Lise. 1983. *Marxism and the Oppression of Women: Toward a Unitary Theory.* New Brunswick: Rutgers University Press.

Wainerman, Catalina H., and Zulma Recchini de Lates. 1981. *El Trabajo Femenino en el Banquillo de los Acusados. La Medición Censal en America Latina.* México: Terranova.

Walker, Pat, ed. 1979. *Between Labor and Capital.* Boston: South End Press.

Watanabe, Susumu, ed. 1983. *Technology, Marketing, and Industrialization: Linkages between Large and Small Enterprises.* Delhi: Macmillan.

Wellesley Editorial Committee. 1977. *Women and National Development: The Complexities of Change.* Chicago: University of Chicago Press.

West, Jackie. 1978. "Women, Sex, and Class." In A. Kuhn and A. M. Wolpe, eds., *Feminism and Materialism.* London: Routledge & Kegan Paul: 223–39.

Whitehead, Anne. 1981. "'I'm hungry, mum': The Politics of Domestic Budgeting." In Young, Wolkowitz, and McCullagh, eds.: 88–111.

Wilson, Fiona. 1985. "Gender and Class in an Andean Town." Project Paper A.85.2, Center for Development Research, Copenhagen.

World Bank. 1981, 1983, and 1984. *World Development Report.* New York: Oxford University Press.

Wright, Eric Olin. 1978. *Class, Crisis, and the State.* London: New Left Review Editions.

Young, Iris. 1981. "Beyond the Unhappy Marriage: A Critique of the Dual Systems Theory." In Sargent, ed.: 43–69.

Young, Kate. 1982. "The Creation of Relative Surplus Population: A Case Study from Mexico." In Benería, ed.: 149–78.

———. 1983. "Not the Church, not the State." In K. Young, ed., *Serving Two Masters.* London: Routledge & Kegan Paul.

Young, Kate, Carol Wolkowitz, and Roslyn McCullagh, eds. 1981. *Of Marriage and the Market. Women's Subordination in International Perspective.* London: CSE Press.

Youssef, Nadia H. 1974. *Women and Work in Developing Societies,* Westport, Conn.: Greenwood Press.

Zuluar, Alba. 1982. "As Mulheres e a Direçao do Consumo Doméstico." In A. Almeida et al., *Colcha de Retalhos; studos sobre a familias no Brasil,* Sao Paulo: Editora Brasiliense.

Index

201